An Introduction to Comparative Philosophy

An Introduction to Comparative Philosophy

A Travel Guide to Philosophical Space

Walter Benesch
Professor of Philosophy
University of Alaska
Fairbanks

palgrave

First published in hardcover 1997

First published in paperback 2001 by
PALGRAVE
Houndmills, Basingstoke, Hampshire RG21 6XS and
175 Fifth Avenue, New York, N.Y. 10010
Companies and representatives throughout the world

PALGRAVE is the new global academic imprint of St. Martin's Press LLC Scholarly and Reference Division and Palgrave Publishers Ltd (formerly Macmillan Press Ltd).

ISBN 0–333–67832–X hardback (*outside North America*)
ISBN 0–312–16546–3 hardback (*in North America*)
ISBN 0–333–93068–1 paperback (*worldwide*)

This book is printed on paper suitable for recycling and made from fully managed and sustained forest sources.

A catalogue record for this book is available from the British Library.

The Library of Congress has cataloged the hardcover edition as follows:
Benesch, Walter, 1933–
An introduction to comparative philosophy : a travel guide to philosophical space / Walter Benesch.
p. cm.
Includes bibliographical references (p.) and index.
ISBN 0–312–16546–3 (cloth)
1. Philosophy, Comparative. I. Title.
B799. B46 1997
100—dc20

96–34793
CIP

10 9 8 7 6 5 4 3 2 1
10 09 08 07 06 05 04 03 02 01

Printed and bound in Great Britain by
Antony Rowe Ltd, Chippenham, Wiltshire

This *Introduction to Comparative Philosophy* is dedicated to Renate Benesch whose understanding and support have made it possible.

Contents

Acknowledgements

An Introduction to Comparative Philosophy has been long in preparation and many individuals have assisted in its creation. Of critical importance over the years, have been the philosophical discussions with my friend and colleague, Professor Rudolph Krejci whose knowledge of the history and philosophy of science have helped me clarify my own ideas. I want to thank Professor Chung-ying Cheng at the University of Hawaii and editor of the *Journal of Chinese Philosophy* for the encouragement he has given me and for permission to reprint portions of my articles that have appeared in the *Journal.* I also want to acknowledge the gracious permission of Dr B. Srinivasa Murthy to use here a portion of my chapter in the forthcoming *East–West Encounters in Philosophy and Religion* which he is editing for Long Beach Publications. To the International Society for the Comparative Study of Civilizations, I am also indebted for it was in the Society's *Journal* that the outline appeared for what has become *An Introduction to Comparative Philosophy*. To the artist, Sandy Jamieson I am most obliged for his rendition of the three-legged chicken.

To all those students who have encountered 'rough drafts' of the 'guide' as a text in courses in 'comparative philosophy' and 'comparative logics' – your questions and criticisms have been invaluable and I have learned much from you.

To Laura Lee Potrikus, I want to express my sincerest appreciation for the many hours spent typing, proof-reading, transferring between 'incompatible word processing programs', and generally making the manuscript technically possible. Finally, I wish to thank Helen Harrell for proof-reading sections of the text and for her suggestions on improving its clarity.

Prologue

The answer to the question 'What is a human being?' is the possibility of posing the question itself. Beyond this, it is unanswerable. This is the Great Paradox of being human. It is our beginning.

But we do answer the unanswerable question. We answer it daily in our public and private lives in art, religion, science, philosophy, politics... We institutionalize and memorialize and monumentalize our answers. Some of them trivialize us, others terrorize us, many dehumanize us. This is the little paradox of being human. It is our end.

Between beginning and end, we wander within a world that also wanders within us. It is for travel in this world that this travel guide to philosophical space is intended.

Introduction: Philosophical Space

'The chicken has three legs'[1]

In its simplest sense, space for the ancients, East or West, was where things happened, the uncontained container of events. For some Indian schools it was the non-human source of touch and position. For Hindu and Greek atomists alike, space was the emptiness which atoms required for their motion. Euclid held that it possessed three dimensions and that geometry was its science. One of the earliest definitions of matter was that it occupied space, and for the Eleatic philosopher, Zeno, spatial extension was the line between *something* and *nothing*. If something did not occupy space it was nothing. All of these ideas of place, position, sequence, dimension can also be applied as analogies to thinking as well, for any idea occupies a position in a train or sequence of ideas, has origins and ends. Understanding what a word means is to locate it in the thought contexts which it symbolizes. The analogies that can be made between our thinking of *space* and the space of our *thinking* provide the basis for what I am calling *philosophical space* and is the beginning of this guide ...

Philosophical space is a metaphor for meaning. If one associates meaning with the human brain, then physically, philosophical space rests between the ears and behind the face. It is within a world of mental constructs that we relate thoughts, objects and symbols and turn them into literature, music, architecture, religion, science. Answers to questions regarding the meaning of life and the nature of the world in which we live reflect any culture's *philosophical space* where words and thoughts and things interrelate.

This travel guide to philosophical space in the broadest sense is a comparative introduction to philosophy and philosophizing as these are aspects of the human condition everywhere. It focuses in a more specific sense upon the concern for meaning and the corresponding development of thinking methodologies in certain Greco-European, Indian, and Chinese philosophical systems. The text introduces these Eastern and Western traditions in two unique ways:

Firstly: It addresses philosophical space as four different but related dimensions of human thought and experience: (1) the significance and nature of the *objects* of experience and their interrelationships about which we think; (2) the significance and nature of the thinking *subject* in whose awareness objects mean what they mean; (3) the significance and nature of the *situations* in which thinking subjects encounter both their own awareness and the objects of which they are aware; (4) the nature and significance of these subject, object and situational elements as *aspects and perspectives* within a human/nature continuum. These are the sources of the object, subject, situational, and aspect/perspective dimensions of philosophical space. They are introduced and explained using texts from various Eastern and Western philosophies.

Secondly: The guide is more than a compilation of information on various Eastern and Western views, for in each dimension, once it has been explained and explored, one or more of the thinking and reasoning techniques that have been developed within it, will be presented so that readers can incorporate these techniques into their own thinking processes. The travel guide is both an introduction to comparative philosophy and to comparative *philosophizing*. The reader will encounter the object logics of the West, the subject logics of the Indian Jains, the situational logics of the Buddhists and Nyaya, and the aspective/perspective logics of the Taoists, Confucians and Mohists.

The *three-legged chicken* referred to at the beginning of this introduction is the assertion of a Chinese philosopher of the fourth century BCE, that 'A chicken has three legs.' I originally encountered this wonder chicken in a context which labeled the statement a *paradox* and my problem was trying to figure out in what sense it might be so? A paradox is a sentence that seems to have two meanings which are apparently inconsistent with one another; however, there would be nothing paradoxical about three legged-chickens if the sentence's author had been hallucinating or had actually seen such birds. That which finally clarified for me what might have been intended was a second paradox from the same era and list: 'The wheel does not touch the ground.' A wheel does and does not touch the ground for wheel is a concept of a whole that consists of different parts with different functions. In one sense, only a part of a part, that is, a part of the rim but not the entire wheel, touches the ground. The *wheel* in this paradox is a mixture of concepts and things and it combines a wheel's *parts* into the wheel *idea*, while at the same time stressing the particular physical aspect which actually contacts the road. The whole is not the aspect nor the aspect the whole – nor are they separable.

And so with the three-legged chicken, it too is a mix of conception and perception. In order for one to perceive that a chicken has two legs, one must bring the concept of leg as chicken part and function to the actual experience of an actual chicken. This conceptual leg would be the third leg which would enable one to recognize the other two. These legs taken together would equal three. No third leg, no two legs and no two legs, no third leg!

Paradoxes, like people, have both parents and offspring. This is certainly true of the three-legged chicken. In a sense the chicken was born in history when the human intellect first asked in philosophical space, 'Which came first, the chicken or the egg?' and realized that there were at least three possible answers to this question!

The first answer assumes the chicken. This is the Aristotelian and creationist position that any actual entity is the fulfillment of a potential which is determined and defined by a prior actual entity. Where there is no prior actual chicken there can be no potential chicken in an egg which can generate another actual chicken.[2] Potentiality is stabilized and universalized by way of actuality – acorns come from and produce oak trees. Eggs come from and produce chickens. The world began with actual, first creatures.

The second answer assumes the egg. This reflects a contemporary perspective in biology and genetics. S.F. Butler wrote in 1924 that a hen is an egg's way of making another egg.[3] According to this view, any living organism is a collection of genetic material seeking to propagate itself via an encounter with another such collection. The genetic stuff of the herd bull, the tribal chieftain, and the Nobel prize winner has a better chance of successfully completing more such encounters than does the defeated opponent, the single warrior, or the humdrum man on the street whose DNA will never make it to a sperm bank for the gifted and talented. This is a genetic drama in which the actual geneticist or philosopher, or hens and females in general, play at best a supporting role. As Richard Dawkins humorously notes, we are all survival machines for the same kind of replicator – molecules called DNA – but there are many different ways of making a living in the world, and the replicators have built a vast range of machines to exploit them.[4]

The third answer assumes the question itself must come first for its very asking presupposes sets of temporal, spatial, and linguistic interpretations, distinctions and contexts – none of which is either a chicken or an egg. The thinking about thinking that produces this third answer to the chicken/egg question is the origin of the three-legged chicken, for it places questions prior to answers and mental puzzles prior to solutions. And it creates thereby an awareness of the philosophical space wherein questions and answers and statements about the nature of ourselves and our environments hatch and grow feathers. In philosophical space, one realizes that any question posed about *something* is posed from a *point of view*, in a *situation*, and reflects some aspect of experience as well as a perspective upon that aspect. All of these dimensions together determine the possibilities of acceptable answers.

I didn't realize at the time that this was the beginning of a voyage into philosophical space that would traverse many mixtures of wholes and parts every bit as strange as that of the three-legged chicken. The account of this journey has become this traveller's guide to philosophical space.

My own experiences of philosophical space probably began in the second grade in a two-teacher rural school in Southern Colorado where a regular teacher was in charge of the single classroom grades one to four, and where a part-time music instructor appeared once a week to lead group singing and rhythm band. When we used certain words within hearing of the former, she would exorcize them by scrubbing the wicked words out with a bar of soap rubbed firmly across our clenched teeth. The music teacher treated these same words with an adhesive 'X' placed over the mouth thereby taping the wicked words in. Incidentally, we were still expected to hum the songs that those with untaped mouths were singing. We didn't understand what these forbidden terms meant apart from the reactions they elicited from adults. For us, they represented an exciting, dangerous and potentially soapy or sticky source of attention and challenge to authority. I suspect the memory of these experiences remains with me still because even as a child I was puzzled by the radically different approaches to certain words. Such puzzling provides the parameters of *philosophical space* and I believe it occurs many times in many ways to all of us as children and adults. I also believe that mastering travel in *philosophical space* is as important as learning to walk in physical space for it is in the contexts of *philosophical space* that we give significance to our life-long voyages in the physical world.

I may ask 'What time is it?' and look at my watch for the answer. In philosophical space I ask 'Time, what is it?' and looking at my watch doesn't help much with an answer. I may even discover that there are several answers, some of which differ from one another just as radically as the soap and tape approaches. The difference between 'What time is it?' and 'Time, what is it?' although they use the same words, is clearly more than an arrangement of letters and terms. If I think about the relationship between the two questions, or wonder whether the first can be answered without answering the second, I am embarking upon a journey into philosophical space. The traveller's guide is a map for this journey.

How does one approach such a map and take such a trip? I would offer both a suggestion and an apology. First the suggestion: As you read, pause as often as possible and ask yourself what you think about what you have read. 'What could be meant by that?' 'If I were to accept this, where would it take me?' And compare, compare, compare! Compare the aperient analogy of the Greek Skeptic, Sextus Empiricus, with the fish trap of the Chinese Taoist sage, Chuang Tzu, with the clay pot of the Buddhist philosopher, Nāgārjuna. Many comparisons have certainly been included, but make your own. If you can, write copious notes to yourself in the margins and question there too the author's interpretations!

Now for the apology: This is a book written for the general reader interested in the processes of comparative philosophy East/West. I realize that between and among the individuals and events included in it, there are long lists of others that might have been mentioned but weren't. My concern has not been the writing of a comprehensive history of philosophy, but rather producing an introduction and guide to *philosophizing* as a living process. On this basis, materials were selected as representative illustrations of different aspects and historical phases of philosophizing within the four dimensions of what I call philosophical space. It is not written especially for the scholar, who may well criticize its lack of sufficient Greek, Latin, and Sanskrit citations. There are some terms but they are employed either as a sort of shorthand for ideas that have been explained, or because they have become common terms in English as well, for example *Karma*, *Ātman*, *Tao*, *ataraxia*, and so forth. So, to scholars – my apologies. For you I have attempted to adequately trace my steps and identify my sources in footnotes and bibliography.

1 Worlds within Worlds

In his short story, *The Damned Thing*, the nineteenth-century American writer Ambrose Bierce describes the encounter of two beings from different planes of reality. In the tale, a lone hunter and his dog are scouting a mountain meadow one morning when what the hunter assumes to be a breeze flattens a path in the grass ahead of them at the edge of the woods. The dog cowers, whines and refuses to move. The hunter sees nothing except the crushed grass receeding in the distance. This phenomenon of the depressed grass repeats itself a number of times in the weeks that follow and each time it occurs closer to the man and dog. And every time the dog is terrified and cowers at his master's feet. Gradually the man realizes that the dog is able to sense a presence from a plane that is beyond his own five senses which detect only the movement of the grass. The story reaches its climax when the paths of the hunter and this *damned thing* coincide.[1]

As in Bierce's story, our lives are lived in a mixture of conflicting, overlapping and interrelated planes and spaces. Firstly, there is the external, physical world where we set one foot before the other, drive across continents, or journey to the moon. From this world, our senses present us with an array of impressions of a vast and seemingly independent framework of objects and events. This is *physical space*.

Secondly, we live in a mental world of interpretations of our experiences of the physical world. This is *mental space* where space itself exists as a concept and where our sensations are sifted and sorted into the theories, categories, and names which we use to recognize and explain what we encounter in our physical environments.

Thirdly, we live in what I will call *introspective* or *philosophical space* where we evaluate our interpretations, establish priorities between and among our concepts, and struggle with the decision as to whether we should spend our national budgets on moon travel or on relieving world hunger. In philosophical space we turn our mental processes upon themselves to try and understand what we think and why we think it. It is in philosophical space that we examine the assumptions that we use to live in physical and mental space.

The Greek word *phil* means love or affinity for, and the word *sophia* means wisdom. Thus I call this spatial dimension wisdom space. In mental space we define the objects and events we encounter in physical space, but in *wisdom space* we consider the possibilities and problems of defining as a mental process and ask ourselves what it means to define. We try to explain what an explanation is or isn't and may wonder whether *evolution* is a description of events or an explanation of them? In mental space we apply concepts of *true* and *false* to our statements about the sensed world, but in wisdom space we try to define *true* and *false* as concepts and may suspect that no definition of *truth* is either true or false. Wisdom space is the world of self-awareness where we look *inside* and perhaps even change our assumptions in the light of insights gained in this introspective process.

These three spaces, physical, mental, and philosophical, are inseparably interrelated in our experiences of ourselves and our environments, and as a result we frequently confuse them. A classical example of such confusion is implicit in Zeno of Elea's fifth century BCE view of motion. According to Zeno's interpretation of spatial reality and motion, one can never *really* leave any room in which one finds oneself because before one can reach the door one must get half the way there and before one can arrive at this halfway point, one must get half the way to halfway ad infinitum. This paradox, which I will call a *Zenogon* in honor of Zeno, arises when we mistake the one dimensional and infinitely divisible lines of classical geometry, for apparent and physical lines that we draw which no matter how fine will have length, thickness, and height. These latter are not infinitely divisible. Zeno's resolution of the dilemma was to deny the possibility of motion itself.

Physical, mental and philosophical space do share a number of common characteristics. One of the most important of these characteristics is that of *positional relationship*. For example, when one asks where an object is located in physical space, there are many *places* included and excluded by any answer, for example 'in the left-hand corner of the right side of the room', 'in New York', 'in the Empire State Building', 'not on the sixteenth floor'. Any answer corresponds to the positional reference of the question and the questioner.

When one asks what a statement means, that is , tries to locate its meaning in mental space, a series of positional relationships are also involved. Here the positional references are not to places but to concepts, definitions and sequences of ideas. Every statement has both antecedents and consequents and can be a premiss in one line of reasoning and a conclusion in another. Finally, one cannot prove a statement true until there is agreement in philosophical space upon the meanings of the terms used as well as upon a definition of *proof* and *true*. Knowledge in all three spaces is knowledge of relationships. To know is to relate. This relating is expressed in Indo-European languages when one connects subjects to predicates, nouns to adjectives to verbs to adverbs. In Chinese calligraphy one encounters the relationships of radicals and strokes to one another and to the meanings of characters as wholes.

Although these three sorts of space are similar in the sense that implicit in each is some form of positional relationship, they differ from one another in important ways as well, and their differences when ignored can, as in the case of our Zenogons, lead to unfortunate misunderstandings. Our experiences of objects and events in physical space is of specific and immediate aspects like color, form, texture, volume, weight and so on. And the more precisely we analyze an aspect of what in mental space we consider an object or event, the less we actually perceive of the total in physical space. For example, precisely observed, a wheel does not touch the road, rather only a fraction of a rim does so from moment to moment. We do not see or touch a forest, or a tree or even a branch. Rather we are aware of particular color splotches and particular surface textures. In mental space, however, where these partial and particular impressions are interpreted, they are converted into ever greater wholes. The splotches become the leaves, the tree, the forest. These wholes form our concepts of leaf, tree, nature, time, matter, and so on, and these in turn are the general conceptual frameworks within which we make and relate specific observations.

In philosophical space we develop concepts about these ideas, including concepts as to the rules for the conversion of conception and perception discussed above. This process from sense experience to concept, to concept of concept, progresses from awareness of sense impressions to interpretations of these impressions to awareness of the assumptions one makes which influence one's interpretations. Different schools of science and different religions make different assumptions about the nature of human beings or the gods or the world of things and these assumptions provide different interpretations of experience. In philosophical space we are concerned with these assumptions and the interpretations they make possible.

LOST IN PHYSICAL AND MENTAL SPACE

People in all cultures express their individual impressions and thoughts in the common language of the culture. As we listen to one another, we may mistake language sounds and signs for the things they name. Or we may believe that because we recognize the words someone has used, we have understood what they intended.

On my first visit to London years ago, I found myself rushing one evening to keep a date with a friend in a small tea place near a large park. Since I was afraid I would be late and she might leave, I cut across the lawns and through the shrubbery of the park. Detouring around bushes, ponds and flower beds I was soon lost. Although I could hear traffic humming in the distance, the noise seemed to come from all directions. Then, I noticed a large tree with a sign on its trunk. When I approached it, I found a poster proclaiming:

BIRD NESTING STRICTLY PROHIBITED
By order of the Department of Parks.

Even in my despair at not finding a marker or an exit arrow, I was still capable of wondering (1) what sort of birds the park might harbor who could read the sign, and (2) what sort of birds, having read the sign, would let themselves be bullied into non-nesting by the Department of Parks, and (3) if I encountered one of these birds nesting, could it, and of course would it, be able and willing to tell me how to get out in exchange for my silence on the matter of its forbidden activity?

I met no such bird, though I did encounter two more signs before it turned too dark to read them. When at last I arrived at the tea shop, my friend had left. She later studied dentistry and became a successful orthodontist. For my part, shortly after the park experience, I lost my travelers' checks and boat tickets on a train between London and Southampton where I was to sail for the US. Even after I returned to the US, I continued to wonder about the signs and the birds for whom they were intended until an English friend in Omaha explained to me that the signs weren't intended for the birds at all but for people. 'Bird nesting' which to me meant 'nesting birds', in England means 'robbing the nests of birds nesting'. It is apparently a common pursuit among English egg collectors.

Lost in physical space I did not know where I was in reference to the outside of the park. Lost in mental space I did not understand what the sign meant. Later, in philosophical space after I had encountered a second meaning to the signs, I realized again how relative meaning is even when one recognizes all the words.

Early associations of physical space and thought

Earlier ages connected thinking directly to the physical place in which speaking seemed to originate. For the Greeks, thought was breath and speech and centered in the chest and produced from the lungs and diaphragm. When one thought, one seemed to be talking to oneself. Some of the Pythagoreans believed *logos* to be the 'winds of the soul'.[2] Flute players were in danger of literally blowing their minds away.

Other Greeks maintained that hearing was accomplished via the head which provided passageways for the soul winds of others or the winds of the gods to flow through the ears into the lungs where what had been said was then understood. For Aristotle, the purpose of the brain was to serve as a type of radiator which cooled the passions and the blood and so helped to avoid rash acts. Wisdom came with dry air, foolishness with moist. The Stoics associated wind or breath (*pneuma*) with both the rational order in the cosmos and the rational principle in the human being. The Greek term for lungs and/or diaphragm is *frenes*. When people are confused, disturbed, insane, we call them 'frenetic'. A frantic person (from the same root) is one who is very upset and whose breathing is likely to be intensified and irregular.

The Chinese philosopher of the fourth century BCE, Chuang Tzu, held that the knowledge of human beings as well as of all other creatures, was dependent upon their breathing. And he was amazed that that which is both so essential and so near could be neglected and that people could 'close their pores to it'.[3]

The Chinese *hsien*, which is written as the *heart radical* is often translated as mind was in the heart and chest. In most forms of Indian meditation in order to calm the thoughts, there must be a control and purification of the breath. All of these are reminders of the early association by Greeks, Indians, Chinese, and others of thinking with breath, speech, lungs and heart, that is, with physical space.

The earliest experiences of mental events are thus closely related to being in physical space except that there is a more immediate awareness that this space is in the human body and has to do with the functions of breath and blood. It is the *space in us* in which we talk to ourselves. Today we associate thinking with brain-space. As to whether this association is itself located in the brain, is a question that arises in philosophical space.

GALILEO AND THE LAWS OF PHILOSOPHICAL SPACE

One of the most perceptive modern expositions of philosophical space is found in Galileo's seventeenth-century *Dialogues Concerning the Two Chief World Systems* in the dispute between Salviati and Simplicius as to whether one can rely upon common sense to determine whether the earth rotates or not. Simplicius represents the Aristotelean and Ptolemaic geocentric view that the sun moves about the earth but the earth itself is stationary. He believes this can be clearly established with simple, immediate observation coupled with common sense. Salviati argues for the heliocentric system of Aristarchus, Copernicus, and Galileo himself, in which a rotating earth moves about the sun. He claims this also can be demonstrated with simple observation coupled with common sense.

The Christian position of the time on this matter was clear and was assumed by Roman Catholic and Protestant alike: if the earth moved about the sun, then God should have halted the earth and not the sun at the battle of Jericho. Besides, everyone clearly sees the sun rise in the east and set in the west.

There is not room here to present the history of these two positions, so I will concentrate upon that element that is especially relevant to any attempt to understand and travel in philosophical space; this is the contradiction which the moveable versus immoveable earth conflict presented. This argument involves a discrepancy between sense experience and conception so basic that it ultimately calls all sense experience and reason into question.

We see the sun move across the sky and common sense tells us that if the earth were moving, we would fall off. On a revolving earth, a rock dropped from the top of a tower must fall at an angle because between its point of release and point of impact, the ground should have rolled out from beneath it. Of course none of these things occur within the range of our senses and this proves the earth must be stationary. If any doubt remains, we might take the case of a a cannon-ball shot with equal force in two opposite directions: (a) the direction in which the earth would have to be moving for the sun to seem to rise and (b) the opposite direction away from which it would be moving in order to account for its setting. The ball fired in the one direction would cover far more ground surface because the earth beneath it would be racing toward it. The ball fired in the other direction would travel a lesser distance because as it flew, the earth would roll away from it. However, we know that neither of these phenomena occurs.

It is Galileo's achievement that he too takes common sense and perception to establish that the earth can move, and that the apparent movement of the sun can be explained by a moving earth hypothesis as an optical illusion. The earth is like a ship – a pebble dropped from the mast of a smoothly sailing ship does not fall at a distance behind the mast but rather drops directly down because it possesses the same direction and motion as the deck and the mast when it is released.

To illustrate this point he suggested that a traveler board a ship with butterflies, suitcases, and fish swimming in a bowl. As the ship speeds out of the harbor on its way from Venice to Aleppo, all of these entities will partake of its motion. Inside the cabin, it will not be possible to tell whether the ship is moving or not by checking the relationship of the luggage to the rest of the cargo or by watching the butterflies or the goldfish. Of course with a jerky, quick start, objects may be tossed about until they attain the ship's motion, but once this motion is equally imparted to the contents, it becomes absolute. The swimming fish will not find themselves forced against the rear wall of their bowl. The cargo, though moving between Venice and Aleppo, is not moving in reference to its internal positions in the ship itself unless of course some force external to the ship were to strike it.

Anyone who has ever spilled coffee or juice on a jet flying at several hundred miles an hour knows that the liquid splashes in one's lap and not against one's chest. From similar examples, Galileo reasoned that the earth moves, but we and the coffee and the ship and the goldfish are unaware of this motion because we share it with the earth absolutely.

Galileo tells us that within a closed system, for example, the earth, a ship, an airplane, motion is absolute, and so all-pervading that, though we or the fish may swim in our bowls at great speed, we are unaware of the motion of the system as a whole. Ergo, relative to a system such as the earth, motion is absolute and, therefore, unnoticeable.

However, we do seem to see the sun move. We have also seen docks move, or wondered which column of cars is moving in a traffic jam. There are many occasions when we cannot be sure which entity moves. From this observation comes Galileo's second insight that motion in reference to different systems is relative, that is, the motion of systems can only be observed and established relative to other systems or to a point considered to be motionless, for example other stars, planets, ships, subatomic particles, and so on.

We can reduce Galileo's ideas to the following two principles: Motion within a system is *absolute*, while motion between and among systems is *relative*. On the earth, because the earth's motion is absolute, we do not detect it, but when we contrast the earth and the sun, motion becomes relative. This is why there are those who would see a heliocentric universe and others a geocentric one, arriving from the same observations at two different universes.

We shall now return to Galileo's goldfish – not for what they say about motion, but for what they tell us in philosophical space about basic concepts. Like goldfish in their bowl on the moving ship, the most basic assumptions in which any culture or tradition swims are so absolute that they are often no longer viewed as assumptions but as fixed points which impart a common meaning (motion) to their adherents from which the assumptions of all other traditions and cultures can be judged and found to be meaningful or meaningless. Our views and definitions of reality, logic, the gods, nature, the self, the good, tend to be absolute. But when we honestly try to compare and understand our own world views and those of others or seek to locate other fixed points beyond those relative to our absolute world view, we then discover that our absolutes are relative. This is the relative space between and among absolute assumptions through which the traveler in philosophical space journeys.

This guide is an introduction to *thinking about thinking*, written from the perspective that there are between and among different cultures and peoples different emphases upon various aspects of our thinking processes and these differences are reflected in our varied ways of viewing and explaining ourselves and the world. At the same time, however, there are fundamental paradoxes and questions implicit in human thinking everywhere and common to all of us. One of the most important of these common paradoxes can be illustrated with two analogies.

The first analogy is that thinking and those elements and activities that we associate with thinking like knowing, believing, naming, theorizing, questioning, explaining, when viewed from one perspective are like *mirrors*. As mirrors, our thinking processes reflect the experiential and cultural contexts within which we conceive and perceive. In this analogy, we see and define our experiences in the mirrors of the interpretative possibilities we bring to them. These definitions in turn are reflected in our explanations of the world.

The second analogy is that thinking and all those aspects mentioned above are like windows. And as *windows*, permit us to look through our experiences into our surroundings. In this sense our interpretations and assumptions are the glasses we wear in order to see more clearly aspects of a world that we consider to be *out there*, to distinguish *us* from *them*.

This mirror/window relationship is responsible for the many contradictions and misunderstandings that occur when we emphasize one analogy over the other, even insisting at times in the name of *objectivity* or *subjectivity* that one view is all *mirror* while another is all *window*. Whenever we ask a question, conceptualize our experience, create a model of our environment, choose between and among theories, facts or fantasies, we do so within a union of window and mirror. The offspring of this union will be a three-legged chicken.

Physical space is that world glimpsed through our windows: the there and where and when and then of the objects of our awareness. Mental space, on the other hand, is mirror or thinking space – the *here* and *now* space of thinking processes like conceiving, affirming, denying, questioning. One can conceive an idea, write it down, put it into a book, place the book into a library, but in doing so one moves this idea from the here and now of thinking it in mental space, into signs in the there and then of physical space where the idea as symbol now occupies a slot upon a shelf. An idea on a sheet of paper in a book in a library, is like those little plants and frogs that dehydrate in times of summer drought or winter cold. And these dehydrated ideas like such frogs and plants must be enervated and resuscitated in the here and now of mental space in the thinking of some human being.

Philosophical space is not *there* or *then* space though it is the space in which we think about there and then. It is in philosophical space that Eastern and Western philosophers have historically sought to identify the parameters of thought, establish criteria for reasoning, to attain awareness of *awareness* and an understanding of *understanding*. This thinking about thinking is the source of the wisdom literature, folktales, and paradoxes that cross all cultural boundaries. I as an American can still understand both the humor and the point that the Swahili philosopher and wise man, Abu Nawasi, is making when his neighbor's frying pan dies.

According to the story, Abu Nawasi borrowed a large and expensive pan from a neighbor. A few weeks later when the neighbor asked for it back, Abu Nawasi returned the large pan, inside of which was a smaller pan. The neighbor said that the second pan was not his, since he had loaned Abu only the larger. Whereupon Abu Nawasi assured him that the smaller pan was indeed his neighbor's because while the larger pan had been in Abu's house on loan, it had given birth to the smaller. Being an honest man, he returned the pan and its offspring to their rightful owner. The neighbor was amazed, at the miracle of such a birth and at Abu's honesty in bringing both pans to him.

Later, Abu Nawasi again borrowed the large pan and this time did not return it. When the neighbor became insistent, Abu Nawasi assumed the face of mourning and informed him that his pan had died. The neighbor was incensed because he knew that pans could not die, and took Abu Nawasi to court. Abu Nawasi explained to the judge that when it suited him his neighbor had been willing to believe that pans could give birth, but he refused to accept that they could die. The judge ruled in Abu Nawasi's favor, saying 'everything that gives birth must also die'.[4]

IN CONCLUSION

Our voyage into philosophical space is a critical one; one that individuals and cultures around the world are beginning to make at the end of the twentieth century, for in the midst of our technological advancements, and in great part because of the precision and systematization of experience that these have made possible, the questions of mirror/window relationships have surfaced with a new and greater urgency. These questions occur in two very important contexts.

Firstly, in scientific and technological systems which have become ever more refined and exact, they are the questions as to how observers relate to and influence observations? To what degree or in what sense, do human interpretations determine the world we seek to interpret? This is particularly important in the physical and social sciences as our theories become increasingly abstract and our models become the world. Abstractions are aesthetic constructions created in the thinking processes of observers. We tend to forget that harmony, balance, chaos, order, symmetry, true, false, right, wrong are aesthetic and ethical values and concepts within which we interpret ourselves and nature. How much of any observation is of the *world* and how much of it is observation of some *instrument* designed within an interpretative system to observe the world? If there are no observations without observers, how does observation effect and alter the observed? As, hopefully, every social scientist knows, a group *being tested* is not a group *not being tested*. A human or animal population being observed is an observed population. Our first problem then is the position and relationship of the observer to observation to the observed.

The second set of situations in which mirror/window questions are encountered, with perhaps an even greater urgency, is in the deciding and choosing of what is of value – what should or should not be done or preserved, aesthetically and/or ethically? This is a question applicable to any act or process. It cannot be answered by our ability either to know scientifically or to successfully carry to completion various technical procedures. These are questions that technology and modern science can no more address than a lobotomy can address the moral implications of administering lobotomies, or a can of red paint determine how much red should be used in the painting of a sunset. It is the necessity for exploring the thoughts of the observer *observing* and the chooser *choosing*, rather than the things observed or chosen, that has shaped my purpose here. The guide is an approach to understanding *understanding* as a mental process, utilizing some of the great thought systems of the world and their insights into and methodologies for philosophizing, in order to grasp in a greater totality the position of human thought in and its relationship to the world about which we think.

This exploration of philosophical space is unique in a number of ways, and understanding this is critical to understanding what follows. Perhaps most important is that as far as possible it attempts to treat each of the dimensions examined in terms of the views of the cultures and civilizations that illustrate it. I believe this provides a perspective from which it will be possible to create a flexible yet more comprehensive model of the wisdom space in which knowing and understanding occur. It is my contention that such space must consist of a harmonizing of introspection and extrospection, the speakable and the non-speakable, questioning and answering.

Initially this adventure into philosophical space may prove to be confusing and difficult. But driving a car for the first time for many of us who learned on manual shifts also seemed difficult and confusing. The Neo-Confucian philosopher, Chu Hsi, 1130–1200 AD, compared thinking to digging a well – although the water is muddy at the outset, after much drawing, it clears.[5] I hope that this will also be the reader's experience here.

2 Thinking about Thinking

There is an old joke about the man who lost his wallet and was looking for it under the one bright lamp on an otherwise dark street. A stranger stops to help and after an unsuccessful search asks him if he is sure he lost the wallet here. The man replies that, no, he lost it in the dark down the road but is searching for it here because the light is better. We encounter this *better light* dilemma in any attempt to discuss thinking because the medium we are using for our discussion consists of the written or spoken symbols of a language system. But word recognition is not necessarily word understanding. We may recognize every word someone uses and yet not understand the idea he or she is trying to convey. Unfortunately, *talking about thinking* is easier than *thinking about thinking* because one can see or hear the words.

Language is perhaps the most important tool that we as thinking beings possess, but the words we select to express our thoughts are not the thoughts nor the thinking processes that select them. Anyone who has ever struggled to find the *right* word to express an idea is aware of this difference. And anyone who is bilingual realizes that in traveling between countries, one may check one's language at the border, but not one's thoughts.

Another paradoxical difficulty in thinking about thinking is that that which we seek is the seeking itself. The trick is to try and distinguish the *objects of thought* from the immediate processes of thinking about them, just as we make a distinction in sense experience between awareness of sensing or having a sensation and the object sensed. If one touches a cold surface, this surface is the stimulus for one's sensing, but it is neither the sensing nor the sensation, and the sensing of cold, like our other senses, is applicable to many different objects. We shall try to proceed in the same fashion in thinking about thinking. In this case the surfaces are the words we use to facilitate and communicate the process but are not the process itself and when one has understood an idea one can then express this idea in different terms and languages or apply it in different situations.

In this chapter as we attempt to think about thinking, we shall examine thinking in three related contexts: the first considers *thinking as process*, the second *thinking as meaning*, and the third *thinking as undefinable awareness*. Finally, I shall outline the four critical dimensions of philosophical space through which we shall be traveling with the guide.

Thinking as process

The thinking process has many aspects, but the awareness of two are essential to understanding *philosophical* space. The first is our experience of thinking as a flowing, often chaotic, stream of impressions, idea fragments, and phrases. When one tries unsuccessfully to concentrate in studying for a test or seeks to terminate a stream of disconnected thoughts in order to sleep one can become keenly aware of this flood and discover how disconcerting it can be. I had a friend once who in order to relax at the end of a stressful day would, as he put it, 'place his mind on automatic pilot' and let his thoughts wander. Dreaming too is a form of automatic pilot in which we have little control over the sequences or senses of what moves through the sleeping brain.

In addition to and opposed to this fragmented process, is the stabilization provided by assumptions which connect and relate scattered thoughts and sense data. Most of us have probably had the experience of being overwhelmed and puzzled by disconnected experiences and ideas, when suddenly in a moment of inspiration a basic insight or assumption ties the disconnected pieces together or reorganizes them. Something like this must have occurred to the sixteenth-century Polish astronomer, Copernicus, when without any change in his observations he proposed that the earth and other planets might better be assumed to move about the sun, rather than moving the sun about the earth. Newton took the theories and data of his predecessors, among them Kepler and Galileo, and arrived at his assumption of universal gravity. Most good mystery stories employ a similar organizational technique when at the end Sherlock Holmes, Judge Dee, Hercule Poirot, or Perry Mason identifies for the muddled reader the clear thread that unites a seemingly unrelated diversity of acts and events. The stability in diversity which our basic assumptions provide is one of the most important sources of creativity in science as well as art.

Thinking is an ongoing back-and-forth between flow and stability, between automatic pilot and concentration. These two aspects of fleeting impression versus stabilizing concept are expressed in Indo-European languages in the use of terms for *same* and *different*. Are any two objects or experiences ever the same or is each different and therefore only similar or dissimilar to the other in our thinking? Do we experience *sameness* or do we only assume it? Is experience, particularly sense experience, always of the different as similar or dissimilar? With these simple questions, we confront one of the important problems in philosophical space, that is, how do the *sameness* and *difference* which seem the essence of our stabilizing concepts and their symbolic expressions relate to the *similarities* and *dissimilarities* of the immediate sensing of a changing world? Is it possible for the psychoanalyst to tell us what our dream fragments really mean because he or she assumes certain similar themes always have the same meaning?

The Greek philosopher of the sixth century BCE Heracleitus of Ephesus said that we cannot step into the same river twice. Both we and the river shall have changed. We and the river are perhaps similar from one moment to another, but not the same. He felt this was a result of the changing nature of both the individual and the world. The stabilizing aspect of our thought, on the other hand, reflects the view that both we and the river are the same in some way every time we step into the water. Two statements seem to make equally good sense: (1) All human beings are basically the same, although they are dissimilar. (2) Although all human beings are similar, they are never the same, they are all different. Can you identify the possible assumptions that might be made in each case? How do these assumptions influence our contacts with others? How might they relate to the social and biological sciences?

We recognize just how important the contexts of sameness and similarity are when we realize that recognition is dependent upon them. Sensations of unique moments of experience are connected by focusing upon similarities and dissimilarities. These similarities and dissimilarities then become conceptual sameness and difference and are the essence of those ideas that we tend to associate with what we call *reality* or *being* or *existence* in religion, science, philosophy. The question in philosophical space is whether same and similar describe the world, our thinking about the world, both, or neither? Regardless as to how this question might be answered, the question itself arises out of our experience of flow and fixity, the changing and the constant, the one and the many of our thinking processes.

As we become more aware of the dynamic/static nature of our thinking processes, we also recognize certain characteristics of thinking which enable us to order and stabilize this process. Using our space analogy, we can examine these characteristics as *positional aspects* of mental and philosophical space. They are also incorporated in the techniques that various Eastern and Western traditions have developed for analyzing and organizing experience. The following seem to be implicit in the stabilization of thinking processes in all traditions:

I. *We think in patterns and sequences*. These sequences can be *causal*: from cause to effect or from effects to causes; *temporal*: before and after, now and then; *spatial*: here and there, before, behind, above, between, beyond: *logical*: premisses to conclusions and conclusions to premisses. Sometimes these are categorical relationships and sometimes they are causal ones. When we categorize, label, or name, we are collecting together within concepts of sameness and difference the similarities and dissimilarities of our experiences. This permits us to ask and answer 'What is that?' 'Whose is that?' 'Where is that?' Any descriptive or classificatory system whether of Chinese dynasties or the taxonomy of flower families is an example of categorical patterns and sequences.

When we order our experiences causally, we are less concerned with what things are than we are with why they occur and behave as they do. In causal orders and relationships, we order our thoughts and events in sequences of causes and effects, asking 'Why is that?' 'What will occur if ...?' Predictions can be considered either categorical, for example, if it has six legs and a segmented body, then it will be an insect; or causal, for example if you drop the glass then it will break. The dispute between creationists and evolutionists in the West is categorical in some aspects and causal in others and frequently a confusion of the one with the other.

The ideas of sameness and similarity, difference and dissimilarity are the sources of both causal and categorical sequences and are implicit in our recognition, prediction, and anticipation of events.

II. *We think on planes of abstraction and levels of attention*, that is, moving from particular instances to general ideas, from individual experiences to generalizations and definitions, from details to totalities, from symptoms to causes, from particulars to universals and back again. On one level of abstraction, we define the world and on another level we describe it. One very important aspect of this thinking from parts to wholes is that it represents a *knowing to understanding continuum* as on one level we understand what we claim to know on another. We may know the bits and parts of the tree, but we understand these bits and parts as they relate to one another as parts, aspects and functions of a whole – the tree. And the tree itself we understand as an aspect of the concept of *treeness*. On the other hand we may insist that in reducing the complex to the simple we get closer to *reality*. In Chinese landscape painting, there are many ways to paint the bamboo but only as one practices and masters these many ways does one understand the bamboo, and in the other direction, only as one understands the bamboo, does one know the many specific ways that it can be painted. Every term is a sign for a part of some larger context and vice versa.

The plane of an answer is determined by the plane of the question. The confusion of question/answer levels is a frequent source of misunderstanding. For example we sometimes pose *definitional questions* as though they were *questions of fact* to which we could apply sense verification and make true/false judgments. The questions, 'Is the frog alive?' and 'What do we mean by life?' are related, but not on the same plane. The questions, 'What time is it?' and 'What is time?' occur at different levels of abstraction in our thinking. We probably don't need to think much about the nature and meaning of life and time in order to live our lives mostly on time. However, if in philosophical space we want to examine the significance of our lives or ask fundamental questions about the nature of time, then we discover that neither the clock on the wall nor the biology book on the shelf will tell us much about the meaning of either.

It is in such introspective moments that we can be aware that we think on different planes, and that understanding relates not only to categorical and causal relationships and sequences, but also to these on levels. On one level we make a statement, on another we decide whether this statement is true, significant, or silly. To ask what a term or event means, or how an object is to be used, involves a change of level of attention and understanding.

Another area where this insight into thought levels is critically important is in our distinguishing of *definitions* from *generalizations*. On one level we define frogs, life, time, space, matter, mental illness, society, psyche, art and then on other levels we use these definitions to locate, study, describe, examine, and generalize about the specific entities that our definitions identify for us. We then try to prove or disprove that our generalizations are true or false. However, even this proving/disproving of generalizations on one plane is possible only if we agree on another plane on a definition of what it means to prove.

We can now examine the close and critical relationship between our thought levels and the processes of recognition and prediction. At the level where we define male animals, the cowboy and his horse may be considered the same. At the level where we focus upon cowboys and horses as distinct, cowboys are the same, but different from their horses – which, in turn, are the same in their categorical essence of *horseness*. We may assume on a universal plane that there is a cause for every effect, but may be at a loss as to what caused Andrew's hives and Alice's feet to swell. And we can indirectly study human behavior by observing mice in mazes if we define *behavior* as the same in both cases.

On one plane we may wonder (1) if God, time, or matter exist? On a second we may wonder (2) what we mean by *God, time, matter, exist*? On a third plane we might ask (3) if we must answer question two before we can answer question one? And on plane four, we may question (4) what kind of question is question three? (5) And on yet another plane, we may wonder how the answers to any of these questions might be judged, that is, considered true or false? There are many levels of thought. Some of them may take us beyond ideas that can be expressed in words. The Chinese *Book of Tao* begins with the statement that the *Tao* (nature, path, way), that can be talked about is not the Tao. Most of us have thoughts on one level which cannot be verbalized on another. Understanding is understanding not only of a sequence of inferences but also of the planes upon which the inferring occurs.

III. *We think in directions*, not in the sense of up/down or north/south, but in the metaphorical or analogical sense of direction on a *thinking continuum*, which in one direction consciously involves the thinking, perceiving subject, and in the other direction concentrates upon the objects of conception or perception. In the first direction one may view definitions as *mirrors*, and in the latter view them as *windows*. Thinking in the direction of wholes may lead toward abstract conceptions and thus toward the conceiver, thinking in the direction of parts and details may lead away from the conceiver and toward the specific objects of perception that the perceiver's conceptions identify.

Depending upon the direction of our thought, we will refer to our statements as *objective* or *subjective;* of course, upon the level upon which we define subjectivity and objectivity, these categories may no longer be appropriate. One person might argue in one direction that another person is subjectively defining *objectivity*, while the latter asserts in the other direction that he or she is objectively defining *subjectivity*. This is a good example of the relationship of direction to thought level.

We also think in directions in that every statement has its origin in one set of contexts and has consequences in its implications for other sets. We seek a statement's origins when we ask 'How do we know?' We seek its consequences when we ask 'What does this imply or mean?'

Thinking as awareness and meaning

Although objects and events and our awareness of them may not be distinctly separated from one another in the immediate moment of sensing, it is clear that these are different aspects of our experience. The potential for sensation is not defined by any specific set of sensations, nor are we the objects which we perceive and define. At the same time, perception is always perception of something. When we chance to pass a mirror, we may look to see how we look at the moment, but we cannot look at the looking that occurs. Hindu philosophers in the *Kena Upaniṣad* spoke of the Self, the source of awareness, as the 'unseeable seeing in seeing'.[1]

One of the most important aspects of human awareness, or the seeing in seeing, is that it is also potential awareness of awareness. The *Bṛhadāraṇyaka Upaniṣad* notes that when we concentrate upon the objects of our sensing, we experience a duality of *I* and *other*. But when we concentrate upon the sensing there is a unity. For example, when I look about me, I see a multiplicity of things, but this is always a multiplicity within the unity of my visual field. This reflects the oneness in seeing versus the many in the seen.[2]

I would suggest that it is this potential for awareness of awareness which distinguishes human consciousness from the *sense* consciousness which we share with other living organisms. This potential, for example, provides us with two approaches to the sensing of pain in a toothache. I can increase pain by concentrating on its intensity and repeating how much the tooth hurts until the pain becomes unbearable. Or I can decrease it by concentrating upon lessening it and supplementing my awareness of it with other immediate experiences, for example, the flowers in my window, the new book I bought, the unfinished tax forms on my desk. This increasing/decreasing is possible because I am aware of my awareness of the pain. Most classical schools of Indian and Chinese philosophy recognized this potential and developed meditation techniques, including *mantras* and *mandelas* which facilitated its application. The Fourfold Noble Truths of the Buddha begin with the awareness that there is suffering, and offer its resolution in the techniques and insights of the Eightfold Noble Path. This potential awareness of awareness enables us to ask ourselves what our experiences mean, and thus place momentary impressions into contexts. It is the source of both *responsibility* and *choice* for it makes it possible for us to consciously evaluate and change our thoughts and to modify the way we view the world.

Awareness of awareness is implicit in the conversion of awareness into meaning. I would define *knowing* as the conversion of awareness into meaningful contexts which are the frameworks for recognition. This conversion begins in the human ability to *recognize*, and it is expressed in theories, explanations, speculations, laws of nature, rituals, rites, and so on. Awareness converted into meaning is the essence of the artistic, religious, philosophical, and scientific speculation in any tradition. As the Buddhist might say, it forms the webs with which we connect the points of human experience. It is the maps we make to trace the significance of both personal lifetimes and ages.

The conversion of awareness into meaning is a process with two complementary aspects: (1) It enables us to create the institutions, values, and systems of explanation within which we individually and collectively live and move and have purpose, but (2) it also assists us to a further awareness that these institutions, values and systems of explanation within which we live and find purpose, in turn live and have their purposes in us. We conceptualize the world of our experiences and we conceptualize ourselves – the authors of such conceptualizations. The physicist, Edward Harrison, wrote in the introduction to his *The Masks of the Universe*:

> I hold the view that we alone create and organize the universes in which we live, and no universe is or ever can be the Universe. Yesterday a universe, today another, and tomorrow yet another. Each universe or mask presents a conceptual scheme that organizes human thoughts and shapes human understanding.[3]

On the one hand we define the world and ourselves, but on the other hand we are aware of ourselves as *definers* even when we claim to have *found* ourselves in our definitions. In a sense we are always lifting ourselves by the seats of our own pants. Our capacity for explaining is not a product of any of our explanations.

This awareness of inside/outside, definer/defined, however it is expressed in a tradition, creates an intuitive instability at the core of all conceptual stability. This instability is expressed in an infinite regress of terms and definitions and can be welcomed or rejected, viewed as threatening or liberating depending upon one's basic assumptions. It is the beginning of skepticism and intellectual independence, as well as creative change in the lives of individuals and societies. The Danish physicist Niels Bohr is said to have divided truths into two sorts: trivial ones where opposites are clearly incompatible, and profound ones where two opposites are both profound truths. There is no one truth because intuitively we realize this would require the one true definition of the true truth, which in turn would presuppose a true definition of this truth ad infinitum. Chuang Tzu, a Chinese philosopher of the fourth century BCE described a dream in which he was a butterfly. He awoke and began to ask himself whether he was now a butterfly dreaming it was Chuang Tzu or Chuang Tzu who had dreamed he was a butterfly. To put it into a modern Western context, we might take the imaginings of the physicist who dreams reality to be composed of subatomic particles. He/she then awakens and asks if he/she is a physicist who dreamed of particles, or particles imagining they are a physicist.

Most Indian systems in general and the Jain in particular discuss the difficulties that arise when *being aware* is mistaken for the *objects of awareness*, *choosing* confused with specific *choices*. The Jain asserts that the basic characteristic of *jīva* or self is the potential for consciousness or attention.[4] In this sense, minds like brains might be considered objects of consciousness of which one can conceive, but never the boundless yet immediate process of conceiving them or wondering about their existence. The Chinese philosopher Hsün Tzu of the third century BCE said of mind that it was always empty for it is never exhausted in its nature by what it learns.[5] Nothing we recognize becomes the process of *recognizing* defined by any particular act of recognition.

This insight is found in the Taoist proposition that the 'Tao of which one can speak is not the Tao',[6] the Confucian concern with the relativity of names,[7] Socrates knowing that he does not know, the Eskimo's awareness that the dancing bear in the dance is and is not the bear dancing. One finds it in different approaches to approximation and modeling in modern physical and social science, from Goedel's *incompleteness theorem*, to Heisenberg's *uncertainty principle*, to Poincare's and Deveroux's principle of *multiple explanation* which holds that a phenomenon which has only one explanation is not really explained at all.[8]

If we return to Galileo's two principles of motion as they were discussed in our first chapter, it seems most unfortunate that his analysis of the relative and the absolute was limited for centuries to problems in physics. In the Western world, the insight that some terms always remain undefined wasn't generally recognized until the nineteenth century. It came as a consequence of revolutionary work in the foundations of mathematics as mathematicians began to explore the conceptual flaws in the classical, absolute geometry of Euclid. Within both the philosophical and mathematical tradition of the ancient Greeks, as can be seen with Plato and Euclid, it was assumed that everything, every term, could be defined. It is, for example, this pursuit of ultimate definitions which is one of the themes of Plato's dialogue *The Cratylus*.

In their admiration for precision and order, many of the early Greek philosophers and scientists rejected as unthinkable or inferior that which was uncertain, unclear, or undefined. Except for the Sophists and Skeptics, they preferred axiomatic absolutes. The Athenian Sophist, Protagoras, claimed man was the 'measure of all things', of both their existence and nonexistence. Socrates asked Theaetetus in the dialogue of the same name 'how do we know those universal concepts that we claim to know?'[9] These are the essences of the world, the knowledge of which must be the basis for all other knowledge.

Within this Greek thought system, Euclid organized his geometry around five fundamental assumptions called axioms or postulates which were considered clear, distinct, and self-evident truths, and being so needed no further definition. They were their own meanings. They revealed themselves completely apart from human interpretation.

For these Greeks, ideas, symbols, and things must be in a basic sense synonymous. Thus they were able to avoid the instability of either an infinite regress of definitions or the problems of the meaning of undefined terms. From their Greek forebears onward, Europeans and Americans have developed a preference for positive definitions and tend to see the undefined, apart from the deity, as unknowable and/or useless. They want identification clearly established. Meaning is affirmation. In their taxonomic sciences they make lists of categories, classes and species. In theology, the deity is a naming deity who names nothing into something, although the deity *per se* cannot be named.[10] This view can be contrasted with the view of the deity in the 'Creation Hymn' of the Indian *10th Rig Veda*:

None knoweth whence creation has arisen;
And whether he has or has not produced it:

He who surveys it in the highest heaven,
He only knows, or haply he may know not.[11]

Definitions tend to become the world. This is partly responsible historically for the great successes of occidental science and religion, for it provides a stability of world view. On the other hand, it makes the changing of theory and interpretation a slow and difficult job, and changes in revealed dogma in religion have been accompanied by great violence. It is this affirmative view of meaning that modern physicists have begun to call in question. What were once viewed as the boundaries of nature have become sources of doubt. To know more is to doubt more, not less. 'The penalty of knowledge is doubt' Edward Harrison tells us, and 'The greater the knowledge the greater the doubt.'[12]

In many Eastern thought systems, there is a preference for the undefined and undefinable. One knows what something is if one knows what it is not. The lists, if there are any, are often negative lists – not this, not that, not these, not those. The nameable Tao is not the Tao and the origin of nature is nameless. The Self in the *Māṇḍūkya Upaniṣad* has four aspects and the fourth is beyond both naming and knowledge.[13] The *Bṛhadāraṇyaka Upaniṣad* speaks of the Self as 'not this, not that', ('*neti neti*').[14]

Thinking as undefinable awareness

I would propose there is a *trilogy of terms* central to thinking in all traditions, and would suggest that for the rest of the guide we consider these as terms to be accepted without definition. This doesn't mean we shall avoid them, quite the contrary, for they are the unavoidable contexts of thinking. And I shall take great care to examine how they are defined and related in each tradition as we explore the dimensions of its philosophical space. It is possible to do this, however, only if some *correct* definition is not proposed and the terms are left undefined as points of departure:

1. *REALITY – including the related terms: thing, world, substance, matter, object – object of perception, object of conception, and object of imagination, physical state of affairs, nonself.*

Thousands of books have been written on *reality*. And it is one of the characteristics of the Western tradition from its Greek and Hebrew origins on into our own time that we have equated the real with the true, and viewed the real as that against which all possibilities can be checked. To affirm the existence of things or to deny the existence of things presupposes in either case that we are really saying something and that existence exists.

We most closely associate *things* with sense experience, especially with the tactile sense. However, we also tend to think of *true* thoughts and ideas as things, for example, the concrete versus the abstract, the objective versus the subjective. And not only true and false, real and unreal but most of the dichotomies in which we arrange our sense experiences presuppose things, for example, longer/shorter, older/younger, red/blue, mine/yours. Concepts of motion, space, time, change, progress, life, death all relate to things.

Some traditions *thing* thinking by insisting thinking is something that things like brains do. Other systems will try to *mind* thing by insisting that *thing* is a way of thinking. Both positions express relationships between two undefinables, mind and thing. In order to pursue further how fundamental the concept of *thing* is to experience, one need only deliberately avoid all pronouns for thing: *it*, *that*, *this*, or try to count, without counting things, name without naming things, like or dislike, without objects.

A very important group of secondary terms take their meaning as well from thing: space, motion, time, finite–infinite. We live and move in a world of things, sometimes it rains, the wind blows. Wind, blow, blue cheese, moon, all of these share in common *thingness*. However, it is my intent not to define *reality* or any of these companion terms nor do I feel that a definition of reality is any more necessary for the exploration of philosophical space than is a definition of physical space necessary for traveling to the moon. I would extend to the terms reality and thing the insight of the American physicist Roger S. Jones that

> It is an amazing fact about physics that none of its concepts are ever really defined. What we are given insead of a definition is a prescription for measurement. To build a rocket and send it to the moon, you need only measure space, not define it. The measurement of space is the only specification of it needed for scientfic purposes, and this is called an operational definition.[15]

2. *THOUGHT – including the related terms: mind, mental event, conceiving, thinking, consciousness, awareness, attention, affirmation, negation.*

Almost as many books have been written on *mind* as have been produced on reality. Some of them affirm mind. Some deny it. Some explain how it works; others claim such explanations are impossible, still others say that explaining is the mind. Some will equate it with brain, others with soul. I don't want to become embroiled in any of these controversies; rather, my position is that mind/thinking are undefinable. Affirming the mind's presence is as much a mental act of thinking as is denying its existence. Mind is the responsibility for choosing to affirm or deny, or both, or neither, as well as the act of understanding what it means to affirm or deny.

One of the unfortunate misunderstandings in which we may become involved when we try to think about thinking, is that of assuming *mind* to be some sort of *thing* like a brain, or assuming it to be some sort of physical process which *exists* if it occupies space, and which does *not exist* if it does not occupy space. We do not stop to ask ourselves in what sense *thinking* about occupying space could be said to occupy space? When we conceive of mind and thinking as things and physical processes, we miss the immediate and undefinable experience of thinking which is the essence of the thought that thinking and mind are things and physical processes.

Cultures, including our own, whose thinking is in great part sense oriented, may ultimately try to use the sense organs, the eyes and ears, senses of smell, touch, and taste to poke their fingers or electrodes into brains, and on the basis of these sense probings, often with sophisticated instrumental extensions of the senses, try to define the nature of thinking. One must not forget thereby that statements about our observations of brains, require thoughtful interpretations of what we think we are doing and observing. To understand this, we need only ask ourselves which sense tells us why we should think that we have five senses? We may think that brains and minds are the same, or we can think they are different; the thinking is the constant either way and does the separating of the world into *same* and *different*.

3. *LANGUAGE – including related terms: symbol, sign, word, statement, proposition, sentence.*

If we add the total of books written about thinking to the total of books written about things, perhaps we approach the total of all books written about language. These range from elementary grammar texts to more complex attempts to explain precisely how symbols relate to thoughts and things. Some would insist that where there is no symbol, such as a language, there is no thought. Others would argue that where there is no symbol, there is no thing. Of course this arguing and insisting takes place in and with symbols. A constant question in many thought systems is whether general nouns, for example, space, matter, culture, society, and people are closer to real things, or whether particular nouns are closer to the way things just are. For example, it is the specific distance between my parked car and the curb and not space itself which will or won't get me a ticket. The scratchy chunk of matter in my eye is more real to me than the concept of cosmos as matter in motion. On the other hand, the matter in my eye viewed as matter itself does not really matter at all on a cosmological level.

As with the terms *mind* and *thing*, I shall assume *symbol* to be undefined, and at this time undefinable; this way we can sidestep both the question as to whether any thinking about symbols could take place without symbols, as well as the question of the relationship of the symbols we use to talk and write about symbols, to the symbols we write and talk about. This doesn't mean either question is unimportant. Not at all, but by determining at the outset that there is no definition for *symbol* and its related terms, we can then discuss all of the answers to these questions and others. If we do not become obsessed by the pursuit of the definition from which to criticize all other approaches to symbol systems, we are then not restricted in our considerations nor locked into the absurdity of asserting in some set of symbols, usually one's mother tongue, that the only symbols which could possibly define symbols must come from this set of symbols.

We are so accustomed to operating within certain assumptions about symbols that symbols tend to become like the air we breathe. We have trouble recognizing that we do make assumptions about them. A good example would be the situations in which we apply the terms true and false or fact. If some one waves a grapefruit and asks 'Is this true or false?' most of us will probably ask, 'Is what true or false?' Until a statement is made about the grapefruit, is there a true or false? It is such symbolized relationships that become our facts. We might agree that the sentence 'the grapefruit is round' is true, but we are saying the symbolized relationship of the statement is true. As for the grapefruit, where there are no statements, about it, there are no facts, no true no false. In the same sense, symbolization is neither true nor false until we symbolize it.

If we can resist trying to define these terms, and simply recognize them as aspects of philosophical space, we will be able to examine even radically disparate systems of thought without getting into arguments over true and false, or sense and nonsense. We shall be free to study all positions from the position that the fundamentals remain undefined. We should with equal facility be able to explore the philosophical space of those positions which insist all mental phenomena must be explained by the nature of things, as easily as we can examine the space of those systems which insist that things are only concepts in consciousness. We can discuss differing positions on the nature of reality, often most dogmatically asserted, without choosing sides. This will not be easy and one may find oneself tempted and this is where the intuitive understanding that these three terms are undefined is important and valuable.

Dimensions of philosophical space

Using the spatial metaphor, I propose that travel in philosophical space is a voyage through at least four dimensions, each one of which rests upon a different set of assumptions as to the nature of thought, experience and knowledge. To illustrate this voyage, I have selected several philosophical traditions East/West, each of which has historically developed a perspective upon thinking in general and reasoning in particular in its approach to philosophy and philosophizing. This selection is not exhaustive for in any one culture all dimensions can be found. And most individuals as they think about their own awareness will move from one to the other at different times in their lives. For the sake of a clearer understanding of each of these dimensions, I have selected those individuals and schools in each which would seem to best exemplify it. This means, of course, that more will be left out than is included, but I feel the economy gained in understanding is worth the sacrifice.

1. *THE OBJECT DIMENSION*. This dimension rests upon the assumption that thoughts and statements originate in contact with, or are about things in physical space. In this dimension, an external, object world is the source of sense experience and of the abstractions from sense experience that we call knowledge. In his version of this process, John Locke claimed that 'The senses at first let in particular *ideas* and furnish the yet empty cabinet ...' [16] And science, Einstein claimed '... searches for relations which are thought to exist independently of the searching individual. This includes the case where man himself is the subject.'[17] A popular college biology textbook of the 1970s emphasized this point for students in its discussion of the objects of scientific study and noted that such objects can be observed indirectly or directly, but where there is nothing to be observed, there is no science.[18] In addition to sense stimuli and resulting abstractions from them, the external world is also usually assumed to be the ultimate source of our 'true/false' value dichotomies and the place where answers in nature precede the questions the intellect posses.

The guide will illustrate this dimension using historical elements from Euro/American philosophical, scientific, and religious movements which stress the world as the ultimate source and object of experience, and it will examine some of the corresponding reasoning methods and object logics that have been developed within it.

2. *THE SUBJECT DIMENSION*. This dimension rests upon the assumption that all concepts and statements reflect the mental processes of thinking and speaking subjects, thus observations, interpretations and explanations of

objects and events are made within and express the points of view of thinkers and speakers. Any assumption of *objectivity* is an assumption made *subjectively* by a conscious subject. As the Swiss physician and philosopher, Karl Jaspers noted:

> If we make ourselves into the object of our thinking, we ourselves become as it were the Other, and yet at the same time we remain a thinking I, which thinks about itself but cannot aptly be thought as an object because it determines the objectness of all objects.[19]

This dimension presupposes that consciousness is the final source of knowledge and meaning. Some philosophers limit consciousness to the individual while others see it as a cosmological essence as in the case of *Brahman* in the Indian *Upaniṣads* where 'As the web comes out of the spider and is withdrawn, as plants grow from the soil, hair from the body of man, so springs the universe from the eternal Brahman.'[20] The Austrian Nobel Laureate Erwin Schrödinger as a modern physicist familar with the concept of Brahman was particularly concerned with the nature of consciousness as manifestation of the world's self-awareness. For him 'consciousness is that by which this world first becomes manifest, by which indeed, we can quite calmly say, it first becomes present'.[21]

To illustrate this dimension, a number of Indian philosophical systems have been included, systems in which questions as to the nature of consciousness and its connection with the senses, mind, and brain have been central to speculation for centuries. Of particular importance in these schools is the principle of the *conservation of consciousness* beyond physical change in death. We will examine the Vedānta, Sāṃkhya, and Jain systems in general and then give special attention to the Jain techniques for clear reasoning as developed in a *logic for eliminating ignorance*, and a *logic for acquiring knowledge*.

3. *THE SITUATIONAL DIMENSION*. This dimension rests upon the assumption that the experiences of objects by subjects always occurs in situations at times and in places. Thoughts and statements reflect the encounters of subjects and objects in situations under certain conditions *here* and *now*. These are retained and organized in memories which then define and influence recognition in future situations. The present is always a situation with the past as a situational element in it for it is the *here* and *now* in which we claim to know *there* and *then*. Knowledge and meaning are situational. The only constant is the process of *becoming*. For early Buddhists, for example, there was no essence, either as subject or object, that transcended

situational experience. The beginning of wisdom in the Buddhist *Aṅguttara-nikāya* is the awareness that it is 'a fact and the fixed and necessary constitution of being, that all its constituents are transitory'.[22] Situations follow one another, but there is no permanent nonsituational self or nonsituational world. 'When a man perceives the true meaning of reality as it becomes, he understands that the paths of existence are empty.'[23] And the individual realizes that :

> Misery only doth exist, none miserable.
> No doer is there; naught save the deed is found.
> Nirvana is, but not the man who seeks it.
> The Path exists, but not the traveler on it.[24]

To illustrate this dimension, we will explore parts of two additional Indian schools of philosophy: the Nyāya and the Buddhist. These two schools, though oppposed to one another in many ways, share a common view of the situational nature of knowledge and self-awareness. Both developed profound insights into and techniques for facilitating thinking and then incorporating its situational nature into rules for reasoning.

4. *THE ASPECT/PERSPECTIVE DIMENSION*. This dimension rests upon the assumption that any thought or statement reflects an aspect of an inseparable totality of thinking and the experienced world. Human beings are both *in nature* and *of nature* and so when we speak, what we say is always a unity of the *nameable* and the *unnameable*. Thus knowledge is a synthesis of the knowing of an aspect of this totality, with a perspective upon both this aspect and the whole. Understanding, then, is a combination of aspect and perspective, while failure to understand or to know would entail trying to separate aspect from perspective. Experience should always be accompanied by perspective upon its nature as aspect. Although we define and observe aspects of ourselves and our world, we as *definers* and the world as *defined* do not become our definitions. Implicit in thoughts and statements is a selfreflexive awareness of the limits to thinking and speaking. According to the perspective of the modern Chinese philosopher, Fung Yu-lan, the attempt to think the *unthinkable* is an essential and critical aspect of philosophy:

> Since the universe is the totality of all that is, therefore when one thinks about it, one is thinking reflectively, because the thinking and the thinker must also be included in the totality. ... One needs thought in order to be conscious of the unthinkable, just as sometimes one needs a sound in order to be conscious of silence. One must think about the unthinkable, yet as

> soon as one tries to do so, it immediately slips away. This is the most fascinating and also most troublesome aspect of philosophy.[25]

The aspect/perspective dimension of philosophical space is illustrated with materials drawn from Chinese schools and philosophers, classical and contemporary. Their positions while differing from one another on some points, share common approaches to thinking within nature as changing process and all emphasize some synthesis of aspect and perspective. The reasoning techniques they have employed will be presented as *aspect/perspective logic*.

Each of these dimensions of philosophical space in its most basic presuppositions assigns a priority in knowledge and meaning. This priority is then expressed in the explanations, definitions, descriptions, and reasoning techniques of the dimension. In exploring these four dimensions using different systems and schools, I am in no way emphasizing one over the other. Rather I hope to show that they supplement and complement one another and that their thinking and reasoning techniques when combined can lead to a better understanding of ourselves and the world in which we live. The comparative synthesis of all four unites the strengths of each into a more comprehensive whole that transcends them individually. This is the task of the final chapter in the guide.

Part I

The Object Dimension of Philosophical Space

3 The Object Dimension: Assumptions

> Sticks and stones will break my bones,
> but names cannot hurt me.
>
> Little Ann cannot put on her hat.
> She cannot put her hat on,
> for where her head would then be at,
> there is the head of John.[1]

This pair of children's poems expresses two intuitive ideas implicit in the object dimension of philosophical space. The first verse, which many of us as children were urged to chant back at tormentors, asserts that sticks and stones as material objects have mass, whereas mere names do not and therefore cannot physically injure us. The second poem expresses the idea that objects occupy space and that two different objects cannot occupy the same space at the same time. For centuries these two ideas have defined the real, as having mass and occupying space. 'Whenever there is the body, there is the *ākāśa* [space/ether]. The body becomes related to the *ākāśa* because the latter gives room to the former.'[2]

Object: what?

The term 'object' comes from the Latin: *ob* (in the way), and *jacere* (to throw). An object is that which is thrown or placed in the path of perception. In its simplest sense, the term refers to the source of our sensations which, in the words of Gautama, the Indian Nyāya philosopher of the fourth century BCE, are

> ... that cognition – (a) which is produced by the contact of the object with the sense-organ, – (b) which is not expressible (by words) – (c) which is not erroneous, – (d) and which is well-defined.[3]

For the seventeenth-century English philosopher, John Locke, 'external objects furnish the mind with the ideas of sensible qualities, which are all those different perceptions they produce in us'.[4] However, even more basic than particular sensations, object also refers to what are assumed to be the external sources of these sense experiences as they are, regardless of personal sensing of them, that is what Locke would call the 'primary qualities of things which are discovered by our senses, and are in them even when we perceive them not'.[5] Objective as an adjective is applied to mental processes of recognition, interpretation, and conceptualization when it is assumed that their products conform to actual objects.

Although sensing is a process which requires a sensing subject, always occurs in a situation, and relates to aspects of sensor, sensing, and perspectives on the sensed, priority is given to the directly or indirectly sensed which determines whether the sensing subject is objective, the sense organs normal, the sensing situation typical and repeatable. Just how the perceiving or conceiving subject fits into this scheme varies from age to age and culture to culture. Sometimes the subject is viewed as an object itself, sometimes as an uninvolved, objective observer of an external world. Adjectives like normal, objective, typical, repeatable, relevant, significant, true/false – indicate the primacy of object in this dimension. In the natural sciences, an acceptable experiment must be repeatable, and in the social sciences, samples must be randomly selected, adequate in number, and representative in nature.

Three additional related terms with the Latin *jacere* at their root have implications for theories of meaning and knowing. We tend to think of object and subject and their adjective forms, objective and subjective, as diametrically opposed in meaning. If one is objective one is not subjective and vice versa. We assume that objects have their own identities and are what they are. Objective knowledge reflects these identities and corresponds to them. This is the correspondence theory of truth. Subjects on the other hand, are thrown under, are below, under the authority of. In the case of subjective knowledge when opposed to objective knowledge, it is considered relative, biased, or a matter of opinion, and is true only if it can be objectively verified. Between these two terms is projected knowledge and meaning, for example, that which is thrown forth to be superimposed upon objects by subjects. Objects as laws and essences are assumed to be as they are and can be discovered. They are not projected.

Object: how?

The object dimension of philosophical space rests upon at least five pre-suppositions that co-ordinate the streams of our sensation and thought:

1. *Identity: Object as itself.* This is the assumption that the universe from microcosm to macrocosm consists of objects, events, laws, and processes and so on which possess their own natures and identities independently of

human perceptions and conceptions. This includes a range of things from matter and space to the subatomic particles of the physicist to the fields, black holes, galaxies, and red, white, brown dwarves of the astronomer to the complexes, behaviour patterns, societies, economic cycles, of the social scientist and economist. The idea of the objective is certainly not limited to things for in the object dimension of philosophical space, the interrelationships between and among things can also be considered objective or objects. Perhaps the best known example of such a relationship historically is causality, but a list of such objects would include time, space, motion, behaviour, even death. All of these, when objectively considered, are assumed to have their own essences irrespective of human interpretations, for example, for the Greeks geometry was the science of real space and its axioms were self-evident (and thus objective). As Aristotle suggested in the *Metaphysics*, '... it appears that knowledge and sensation and opinion and thought are always of other objects, and only incidentally of themselves'.[6] When it comes to the active intellect in the human being, which we share 'for a time' with the absolute intellect of the unmoved mover, this intellect is its own intelligible object and stands apart from the other objects of whose intelligibility it is aware.[7]

This *identity assumption* was early formulated by the Greek philosopher, Parmenides (fifth century BCE), when he claimed that what is is and is what it is, what is not is not, and these are absolutely exclusive of one another. Nothing cannot become something, and something cannot become nothing, although we may be deceived by appearances. In the object dimension, one often thinks of objects as entities, (*ens*, from Latin *esse*: to have being, to be, to exist). An object in this sense is in the external world – something of which one is aware. Zeno of Elea (fifth century BCE) claimed that if something were added to or subtracted from some other thing, and this other thing were neither increased nor decreased thereby, then the first thing would be no thing.[8] This proposition conceals a puzzle when it comes to deciding whether mental events and ideas exist or exist as other than physical entities? The Stoics for whom all objects were ultimately material, believed that ideas could be thought, but they did not exist because they were incorporeal. Modern mechanistic psychologists and biologists frequently resolve the problem by insisting that ideas and concepts are electro-chemical processes, and therefore, do occupy space. Perhaps one of the most important implications of the identity principle is the presupposition that correct answers to basic questions in natural or social science exist prior to the human intellect's learning to ask the correct questions.

2. *Duality: Objects as real and apparent.* This is the assumption that there are two interrelated and interdependent categories of objects in the universe:

ones whose natures are real and ones whose natures are apparent but not real in the fashion in which they appear. For example a frog is a temporary and apparent combination of real inorganic compounds and subatomic particles which will continue to be real even after their apparent arrangement in the apparent frog is gone. And frogness continues to occur despite the death of Kermit the frog. Hamlet muses at Yorick's grave upon the real and apparent fates of Julius Caesar (Act V Scene 1):

> Imperious Caesar, dead, and turn'd to clay,
> Might stop a hole to keep the wind away;
> O! that that earth, which kept the world in awe,
> Should patch a wall to expel the winter's flaw!

Experiments and tests in the natural and social sciences are often designed to identify what is really the case versus what appears to be so. The assumption of object identity poses the problem of relating same to similar, real to apparent, conception to perception.

This duality of real and apparent is certainly as old as Democritus, fifth century BCE, who said that contacts with the sense world of color, sweet/sour, hot/cold, and so on were only 'matters of convention' whereas the ultimately real nonconventional world consisted of 'atoms and the void'.[9] The Roman philosopher and atomist, Lucretius, believed that atomic particles do not die, they re-combine, and thus death is apparent but not real.[10] Empedocles, the Pre-Socratic Greek father of chemistry, suggested that both birth and death were but rearrangements of elements.[11] Later in the history of the object dimension this real versus apparent will be expressed in theories of primary versus secondary qualities as was the case for John Locke. The German physicist, Hermann von Helmholtz in his observations on light and color distinguished between appearance and phenomenon. A phenomenon is that which is really there and not 'mere appearance' which is dependent upon the human nervous system and thus relative to sensation.[12] Although the real is the source of the appearances and/or our sensations which depend upon them, it does not appear. For Max Planck the mystical assumption in all knowledge is that

> ... there are two theorems that form together the cardinal hinge on which the whole structure of physical science turns. These theorems are: (1) *There is a real outer world which exists independently of our act of knowing*, and, (2) *The real outer world is not directly knowable.* To a certain degree these two statements are mutually contradictory. And this fact discloses the presence of an irrational or mystic element which adheres to physical science as to every other branch of human knowledge.[13]

In the late nineteenth and the twentieth centuries, this real/apparent dichotomy is often expressed in terms of the simple and the complex, the chaotic and the orderly or determined.

3. *Knowledge: Objects as concepts*. This is the assumption that given the nature of the world as apparent versus real, this difference can be bridged conceptually. Immediate sense experience consists of a great variety of sensations which as sense impressions are unrelated to one another, that is sound to color, to touch, to taste to smell. However, co-ordination of repeated experience in memory enables us to concentrate upon similarities and dissimilarities. In similarity, difference is still preserved, but common characteristics are identified and conceptualized. At the next level of thought, similarity via abstraction of common features is converted into sameness. Difference may now be a subset of sameness, a characteristic of the apparent not the real world, just as dogs and cats are the same in mammalness or as subatomic particles, but different as individuals. With the assumption of sameness, the intellect can return to experience and re-cognize the essences of what before it could only cognize superficially in diversity. The pursuit of absolute sameness is the pursuit of absolute knowledge, for example, the search in modern physics for a unifying field theory which would ostensibly explain both the universe and itself as an explanation.

Aristotle and Plato were searching for a key to conceptual sameness which could connect the differences of experience. Plato located it in innate copies of transcendental forms. Aristotle saw its beginnings in the object world of the sense experience of a mind born empty of content. He maintained, however, that sameness transcended individual sense impressions for 'Sense perception must be concerned with particulars, whereas knowledge depends upon recognition of the universal.'[14] Furthermore 'the knowledge of everything must necessarily belong to him who in the highest degree possesses knowledge of the universal, because he knows in a sense all the particulars which it comprises'.[15] And when observers conceptually disagree, the objects observed as they really are must provide the ultimate resolution of such disagreements. This also applies to statements about objects, which if they correspond to the same things in the same sense and at the same time, cannot be contradictory, that is, both true for one and false for another rational intelligence.[16]

The Stoics held that all existents were bodies, either acting or acted upon. For them, reason was a corporeal principle which permeated and formed specific objects and their interrelationships in a material continuum. In addition, the Stoic cosmos was a physically causal one in which the time and nature of events was predetermined.

In the object dimension of philosophical space, objectification is both an attitude toward, and a methodology for generating knowledge. As attitude, objectification is expressed in value dichotomies: true/false, objective/subjective, relevant/irrelevant, significant/insignificant and so on, which provide the mental contexts for the interpretations of our experiences. As methodology, it is reflected in our techniques for observation and data analysis as well as in structures and rules for consistent reasoning. And it is in a very practical synthesis of attitude and methodology historically that the object dimension of philosophical space has achieved its greatest importance and success in designing within conceptual models, increasingly complex observation techniques and instruments to discover the more subtle and absolute truths of nature.

4. *Objectivity: The object knower as neutral.* This is the assumption that the objective knower, while making true/false judgments about the world, is and can remain neutral. For this reason, justification in the object dimension is usually located in and/or derived from the non-observer, for example, revealed either by the external world via application of a methodology as in science, or by a transcendental deity via sacred texts. This is one of the reasons why arguments over free will versus predestination or predeterminism so frequently recur. Both the *evolutionist* and the *creationist* agree in attitude that an external source must justify each's position and disprove the other's. In both cases the speaker or observer is considered by his/her side to be neutral and beyond subjective opinion.

This presupposition of the neutrality of the objective knower can be illustrated with two analogies based on Euclid's Elements. The first analogy compares the observer to a point. 'A point is that which has position but no magnitude.'[17] A fixed point exists, but does not occupy space. The fixed point from which other positions on a line can be defined is in itself as point undefinable and without dimension in apparent space. Being there, it is affirmative and axiomatic. Like the point, the objective observer in the natural and social sciences, logics and religions exemplifies what the physicist Erwin Schrödinger in a lecture delivered at Trinity College, Cambridge, in 1956, called the 'principle of objectification'. It is this principle which lets us believe that we can '... step with our own person back into the part of an onlooker who does not belong to the world, which by this very procedure becomes an objective world'.[18]

The second analogy is between observers and the relationships of lines. Through a point, according to Euclid, an infinite number of one-dimensional lines can pass without influencing it in any sense, just as the dimensionless definitions and observers in any field accommodate the particular events and observations that flow through them. The more highly trained the specialist in any field, the more dimensionless she or he becomes, and thus the more objective. This presupposes the Greek view that the universe is ultimately homogeneous, for example, the signs of life on Mars will be the same as the signs of life on earth.

At the same time in the Elements, it was assumed that though many lines can pass through the same dimensionless point, no two parallel lines could do so. Their parallel natures are defined by that which itself is dimensionless just as true and false are neutrally defined and like parallel lines do not cross. The path of each is parallel in value to the path of the other, and the observer's point of observation on the one absolutely precludes the other. (Of course the fifth postulate on parallels changes with the idea of curved space.) In the same sense, the question as to whether any definition of truth is itself true does not arise, for this would be to attribute magnitude or a value dimension to that which has position in value determinations, but no value dimension itself, that is, cannot be valued. True is true and not relative to a subjective perspective.

This positioned point without magnitude or value illustrates important assumptions in logics and mathematics too. For example, in the object dimension of philosophical space, it is assumed such systems themselves have position, but no magnitude, that is, that abstractions of language into highly distilled symbol systems and logics continue to retain position, in this case meaning, without reference to the interpretation of experience to which they can be applied. This can be very useful, for it permits multiple applications of a system in the acquisition of knowledge. When we express our observations statistically, we are taking that which has magnitude, shape, form, color and giving it only the significance of statistical position without dimension. Roger Jones claims that 'Herein lies the objectivity of physics and the basis of our objective view of the world. The final retreat, the ultimate stronghold of objectivity, is the fortress of measurement.'[19]

5. *Language: Object as statement and symbol.* This is the assumption that true statements about the existence and nature of objects as things, laws, events, and processes must correspond positively to these independent, self-revealing identities. On this basis, Aristotle clearly distinguished true from false statements:

> A falsity is a statement of that which is that it is not, or of that which is not that it is; and a truth is a statement of that which is that it is, or of that which is not that it is not. Hence, he who states of anything that it is, or that it is not, will either speak truly or speak falsely.[20]

Perceptual and conceptual experiences are the ultimate sources of meaning in sentences about the world, where they translate into subject and predicate classes. The Greek *correspondence theory* of truth, as we have already noted, permits one to equate statement to object via existence and reality. The truths of the world of sense experience, if clearly grasped in essence, enter unchanged and objective into statements about this world. As the German philosopher Ernst Cassirer said of this Aristotelean perspective, 'The conception of the nature and divisions of being predetermines the conception of the fundamental forms of thought.'[21] This objectification becomes a valuable tool. It is efficient and precise and permits the delineation, refinement, and storage of great blocks of experience within names and formulae in books. It is also the source of the literalism in the object dimension which tends to view words as the objects that they symbolize. Certain words are sacred, dirty, magical. During the great plague of 1348, the name of the Virgin Mary when written on a piece of parchment and swallowed without chewing was assumed to protect one from the disease which was seen as a punishment sent by God.

Objectification was and is often accomplished by means of axioms. These are positive, primary definitions which are unprovable and self-revealing. They are the source of other statements whose truths and functions depend upon their acceptance and application. So basic is the predilection for positive definition, that when a negative is assumed to exist, as in the case of abnormal behavior, it can usually be defined positively without defining the positive concept, normal behavior, at all or only vaguely.

In Aristotle's *Posterior Analytics*, one finds the assertion that the nature of any particular thing's essence must be affirmatively grasped.[22] Existence and substance are the ultimate affirmations, that is, *is and is of such a nature* or is substantive. This is the source of noun forms and the variables of both class and propositional logics. This differs from the position of many Eastern philosophies, where the conscious subject is given priority over the objects known. For these philosophers, affirmation may be the absence of negation (the Buddhist) or a matter of convention (the Taoist). Some consider non-existence as much a basic characteristic of experience as is existence (NyāyaVaiśeṣika).

One of the most fruitful consequences of affirmative definition occurs in the quantification of the world developed in science. This is the Pythagorean theorem that the nature of the world can be understood via number, for number is the world's positive essence, the knowable and namable limit. Professor S. Sambursky in his analysis of Greek science and discussion of the 'mathematical formulation of physical laws' suggests 'We do not consider the possibility of formulating such laws of conservation as a coincidence; it is rather a further confirmation of causality.'[23]

It was one of the presuppositions of most of the early Greeks that 'That which is is namable; that which is not is unthinkable and unnamable.' This was implicit in Plato's criticism of Gorgias. Descartes believed one could rearrange in concept that which existed, but never conceive that which did not exist. This is the challenge of his *Cogito ergo sum* – 'I think, therefore I am.' Whatever one conceives, names or speaks must exist in some sense, for example, the parts of the unicorn if not the whole. Non-existence then becomes distorted existence. The object dimension contains an approach to classification which permits one to name existent *non-existents* or *pseudo-existents*. For example, anthropologists and theologians can refer to beliefs in the non-existent as myths, which implies that these beliefs which others hold are existent non-existents and are not to be confused with the beliefs of anthropologists and theologians whose beliefs about the beliefs of others reflect really existent existents.

Because in the object dimension, meaning arises as an aspect of the external world and because clear thinking is 'thinking of objects in the ways in which they truly exist', objective rules for reasoning (deduction/induction) are often considered pathways to reality for '... he whose thought is contrary to the real condition of the objects is in error'.[24] To Aristotle certainly belongs the discovery that certain subject/predicate relationships would seem to provide the objective and consistent structures within which reasoning and knowing occur. In his development of syllogistic, he outlined the forms of thinking which reasonable individuals would employ. And in the history of the objective dimension in the West, formal logics have from Aristotle on played a critical role as the key to objectification of thinking, and in time these formal systems and their rules became objects themselves.

In modern symbolic logics, the existents are the objectified signs and operations which according to the Danish philosopher Jørgen Jørgensen as 'symbols are far clearer and more distinct than ideas and conceptions, and thus less liable to confusion'. And if our symbol systems become too complex, 'we can, by definition set new and simple symbols in their place, thus not only facilitating the work of thought, but extending its scope far beyond what would otherwise have been possible'.[25]

Object: when?

Our historical exploration of the object dimension of philosophical space starts with the Pre-Socratic philosophers who shared a belief in an order in nature that existed independently of gods and human beings. For Thales, a seventh-century philosopher from Miletus on the Coast of Asia Minor, the *archē* (Greek for beginning or rule – thus first principle) of the real world was water.

Anaximenes, one of his successors, said it was air and added that all change was quantitative, a matter of degree according to its density or rarity. Empedocles claimed there were four basic elements held together by love and hate, or attraction and repulsion. Democritus believed the first principles were atoms. For Pythagoras and the Pythagoreans, the essence of all things was number and the universe was a harmonious whole composed of the limiting and the unlimited. Number therefore was the essence of knowledge and understanding for it was the nature of that which the mind sought to know and understand. On the basis of the fragments of their works that still exist, we can assume that most of these Pre-Socratics thought they were inquiring into the nature of nature and not into themselves, except as an individual could be considered as an atomic or elemental manifestation of nature. Of all the questions that the Pre-Socratics asked, the answers to two of them are particularly relevant in the development of the object dimension of philosophical space:

The first question inquires into the relationship of the changing to the constant. One possible answer was offered by Heracleitus of Ephesus, according to whom everything changes and nothing remains the same. One cannot step into the same river twice. He claimed the wise understand this but the ignorant think of things as fixed and constant. The changing world, however, is not chaotic for change is governed by the *logos*, a harmonizing principle in change which leads to a unification of opposites. He praised sense experience as the way of knowing, but noted at the same time that sensing without understanding is empty. Individuals with barbarian souls cannot grasp the significance of what is being sensed.

Opposed to Heracleitus' position was that of Parmenides of Elea. Parmenides was apparently less interested in what might be the ultimate objects of nature and more concerned with being. What is *being*? Can one get being from *non-being*? Unlike Heracleitus, the Eleatics denied change and motion. If there is change, then that which is would change and not be. Being could become non-being and non-being could become being.

The Parmenidean fragments contain a pronouncement by a deity on this matter who explains to Parmenides that there are three ways of knowing, thinking, and speaking about the world: The way of Truth which consists of realizing that what is is, and that what is not is not and cannot be; the way of error and falsehood is the way of is not, that is, thinking and claiming to know that something which really is might cease to be. The third way is the path of the foolish masses. It is the path of mere seeming in which people speak as though real objects came and went, things could both be and not be. This is the path of ignorant belief in the reality of change.

In the object dimension, almost every concept of contradiction, identity, objectivity and truth can be traced back to this absolute demarcation between is/isn't of Parmenides and his Eleatic successors, Zeno and Melissus – positing a fixed existence without beginning or ending in time and space. One finds this view reflected historically in the principle of conservation, as well as in the presupposition of existence as a given. For example, the question 'Does God exist?' would seem to give a primacy to existence over God. A number of Medieval theologians recognized the shift in priority and as a result defined God as pure being.

The opposing poles of these first two philosophers are: (1) The essence of nature is change in which opposites are reconciled in the process of change itself (Heracleitus), versus (2) the real in nature is unchanging, unmoving being in which there are not and cannot be opposites.

The second Pre-Socratic question involves the first but expresses a different emphasis: What is the relationship of the nature of things to their appearances? Under the influence of the Heracleitian/Eleatic controversy the two philosophers we will now examine represent opposing attempts to formulate a unifying essence that would also accommodate the apparent world of change.

The first of these philosophers, Anaxagoras of Clazomenae, was born around 500 BCE, and was the teacher of Pericles and a friend of Euripides. He was later banished from Athens on the charge of impiety, allegedly for asserting that the sun was a burning rock.

His position was that the world of objects was a continuum of all things in all things. Every thing had some of every other thing in it. What a particular entity appeared to be at any given moment depended upon what particular *seeds* or elements were predominant. Gold has a predominance of gold, but it also contains the other elements as well. Only in this way, he felt, can one explain how bread could be eaten and turned into hair and bone. And hair and bone become earth and so on, in an endless process.

In this mixing process, nothing ever ceases to exist, nor can anything ever be completely created or separated out of all other things, that is, cut off from everything else. There is no smallest, only the smaller, no largest, only the larger, and everything is both smaller and larger, depending upon its relationship to its surroundings. And the greater and the smaller have an equal number of parts in this continuum.

In addition to his mix of seeds or elements, Anaxagoras believed it was *nous* or cosmic mind that first set this continuum of mixtures to rotating, producing the syntheses that we perceive as objects. There was mind also in some of these syntheses, but not in all. It is mind which, being different from the elements in the cosmic mixture, recognizes objects, precisely because it is not such objects. For Anaxagoras as for Parmenides, sense experience is not reliable. It mistakes the finite aspects of the continuum, which it separates out by perception, for the infinite, total process.

In Anaxagoras' view, the particular is always defined by the totality of a mixture as continuum. The part is arbitrary, its reality is the totality, and this totality leads ultimately back to mind (a) as the original orderer and mover and (b) as an element in individuals, existing in some things but not in others. Anaxagoras' approach to explanation is one from wholes to parts. To understand the part, one must relate it to the whole and the predominance of the whole of which it is a part. Anaxagoras' view, while conceding fixed existence to Parmenides, is far closer to Heracleitus. Anaxagoras' successors were the Stoics who developed a propositional logic based on empirical experience. And it is Anaxagoras' view that is closest to modern fluid or wave views of matter.[26]

Opposed to Anaxagoras' continuum view was that of Democritus of Abdera. Democritus, like Anaxagoras, accepted with Parmenides the idea that what really exists does not pass in and out of being. And like Anaxagoras he sought to account for change and the apparent coming to be and cessation of objects. His solution has proved one of the most popular and enduring in the history of occidental science and philosophy. Democritus denied that all things were in all things. For him there were three basic aspects to the world and to each one a different nature applied.

Firstly there were the atoms (from the Greek *a* = not + *temnein* = to cut, that is, the indivisible). These were the irreducible, indivisible unique particle building blocks of all that is. The atoms themselves are eternal, they neither come into existence nor go out of it, they simply are. Those things we experience as changing, coming and going, are combinations of unchanging atoms. Some of the atoms have hooks and rough surfaces, and when these collide and become attached to one another, things appear. When they break asunder, things disappear. The atoms themselves in this total process remain unchanged. Some of the atoms are smooth and spherical, and these move others but can not combine with them because of their shapes. Of such atoms was the soul or mind composed. As long as there are sufficient smooth atoms, and these are constantly replenished through respiration, a person lives. When the supply is not or can not be replenished, the individual dies and decomposes into basic particles to reform into something else. Secondly, there was the void or empty space in which the atoms move and combine with one another to form the objects that come in and out of apparent being. Thirdly, there must be motion, for the atoms to move in space.

In contrast to the apparent world, the atoms possess only size and shape. Leucippus, Democritus' teacher, is supposed to have maintained that everything happens as it happens necessarily. There is no randomness. For everything there is a reason and this reason is not to be found in any sort of teleology of gods or cosmic minds, rather it is in the nature of the atoms themselves.

For Democritus, like the other three Pre-Socratic thinkers we have examined, sense knowledge is not to be trusted. One can go only so far with the senses in achieving a kind of obscure knowledge. To know things as they really are in their atomic nature, one must employ a more genuine means of knowing. The senses give us a world of apparent differences, and thereby miss the sameness, in this case, of the real substructure which are the unchanging atoms.

In Democritus' work, there is no continuum, but an infinite complex of particles moving in empty space. In atomism there is a smallest, and to explain an object is to take it apart to arrive at its smallest possible components. The whole is nothing more than the sum of its unique parts. Knowing the parts is understanding the whole.

There is a different direction involved in the knowing and explaining processes of Anaxagoras and Democritus, although both distrusted the senses. The one spoke of totalities, the other of parts. In almost every field in the object dimension of philosophical space in our own time, these two approaches to knowledge appear sometimes as competing alternatives, sometimes as complementary. Can the environment, for example, be viewed in terms of its components, or must its components be viewed as inseparable aspects of a whole? Is a society the sum of its parts, or is it a totality which is greater than the sum of its parts? What is the relation of the forest to the tree? When is a forest its trees? When is the tree a forest?

These Pre-Socratic poles of change versus being, and essence as continuum versus essence as particle provide the object dimension of philosophical space with some of its first limits and values. It is in the ideas of *being* and *essence* that the identity of an object is fixed and this identity is the source of our definitions, our knowledge and our values. In part it has its origins in experience and in part in the very nature of Indo-European subject/predicate languages. In Chinese, as the philosopher and translator Angus Graham noted, '... there can be no essences bridging the gap between *ming* ... "names" and *shih* ... "objects", and there are nominal but not real definitions'.[27]

The object dimension assumes that things exist and that the identity of an object can be expressed in classificatory and causal sequences which the simpler and more abstract they become the more clearly they relate to reality. According to Cassirer this was no 'mere subjective schema in which we collect the common elements of an arbitrary group of things', this dealt with the 'real essences of things'.[28] Existence defines at the highest level of abstraction the most real, that is, atoms, matter, space, God, humanity, which are more real than the particular things manifesting such essences in appearance.

4 Aristotle, Objectivity, and the Unmoved Mover

> Man is the measure of all things: of things that are, that they are; of things that are not, that they are not. (Protagoras 480–411 BCE)[1]

> ... since in fact men have little ability to remember the past, observe the present, or foretell the future, speech works easily; with the result that most speakers on most subjects offer only opinion .... But opinion is delusive and inconstant, and those who rely on it run grave risks. (Gorgias fifth–fourth century BCE)[2]

> Although all of them want to find some entity by which everything in the universe can be explained, they cannot agree on how to name that entity. One of them calls it air, another fire, another water, and another earth; each of them trying futilely to adduce evidence to substantiate his own account. The fact that they give different answers. although making the same kind of inquiry, shows how faulty their knowledge must be. (Hippocrates of Cos 460–390 BCE)[3]

In the fragments cited above, we sense the philosophical situation in the cosmopolitan center that was Athens in the fifth and fourth centuries BCE, where ideas from the entire Mediterranean encountered one another, leaving some philosophers skeptical and others committed to clarifying how one might know with certainty. Is human intellect the measure of all things? Is knowledge only a combination of opinion and persuasion?

As the Hippocrates citation illustrates, the philosophers of the age were operating within the legacy of the Pre-Socratic vision of reality, that is, if there is knowledge, it must correspond in some way to the unchanging essences in the physical world – a view which Hippocrates himself questioned in his practical and descriptive approach to medicine. The Socratic philosophers and scientists, especially Plato, the mathematician (427–347 BCE), and Aristotle, the biologist (384–322 BCE), realized that knowledge as *what*, must be supported by a corresponding *how* of knowing. This is the basis for Aristotle's wisdom hierarchy in which the man of experience is wiser than the man of sensation, the man of art wiser than the man of experience, the master craftsman wiser than the manual worker, and the theoretical sciences higher than the practical ones.

Plato and Aristotle shared the belief that the essences expressed in our ideas are common to all reasoning human beings because thinking represented the divine in man.[4] That individuals disagree with one another is due either to their lack of a common language or to ignorance. Many early Christian Fathers who accepted this Greek position assumed that it was according to essences in God's mind that the phenomenal world had been created, and that from God's mind these essences were placed as concepts in the human mind. The English philosopher, Thomas Hobbes (1588–1679), suggested that 'the first author of Speech was *God* himself, that instructed *Adam* how to name such creatures as he presented to his sight'.[5] Johannes Kepler, the seventeenth-century Austrian astronomer who worked out the elliptical orbits of the planets, believed that God created divine geometry before he created the heavenly bodies themselves. And Albert Einstein claimed he was interested in the thoughts of God behind the phenomenal world.[6]

Plato and Aristotle inherited the Pre-Socratic dichotomy between the real and the apparent. But in their works, the inquiry into the nature of things is coupled with an equally compelling inquiry into the how of the knowing process. In the Socratic dialogues of Plato, for example, there is a clear awareness that the difference between the universal *archē* of nature and its apparent, particular manifestations corresponds in the human intellect to a puzzling dichotomy between concepts and sensations. The former seem stable and constant, the latter seem to change and vary, and as Aristotle maintained in the *Metaphysics*, '... if there is to be a science or knowledge of anything, there must exist apart from the sensible things some other natures which are permanent, for there can be no science of things which are in a state of flux'.[7]

In their analyses of the how of knowing, Plato and Aristotle differed. Plato taught that the forms of our concepts exist in a transcendent mind and are imparted to the human soul before its birth. The soul comes into the world with these *eidos* innate but forgotten in the trauma of birth. Knowing is recollecting. Thus one does not teach answers, one facilitates their recollection by asking questions as in the *Socratic method*. In the *Meno* dialogue, for example, Socrates elicits from a slave an intuitive knowledge of geometry, even though the boy has had no previous training in it. Thinkers in the occident who speak of intuitive and/or pure rational knowledge tend to choose this Platonic direction.

Since in a Platonic view, knowledge is innate and must be recalled introspectively, there might seem to be less need for developing a knowing technique which would generate from the shadows of the external world what one already really knows. But for Aristotle, because the mind is born a blank slate, the techniques and processes that enable us to acquire knowledge externally were very important. It is easy to see why Aristotle was interested not only in logical processes, but also in a system for cataloging the real and apparent worlds in order to establish their interconnections. It was Aristotle who was the father of modern taxonomy.

Aristotle: the nature of the world

Aristotle was both a categorizer of phenomena and the creator of a logical system which could relate his categories in hierarchies ranging from particular manifestations to universal classes, from Rover the dog, to the dogness which makes Rover a dog. He shared with the Pre-Socratics the view that some constant nature must underlie the apparent differences in the world. To truly know is to grasp the permanent nature which determines what it means to be for everything and in everything that exists.[8] For him, this basic nature was expressed in the idea of substance itself. All objects relate to substance either in that they are substances, are attributes of substances, or generate substances. Where there is no substance there is no being. Substance is the positive and absolute essence which neither changes nor has degree in its being.[9] The shift here is away from specific elements like water or air to the idea of substantive being which, while physical, accommodates all elements, much as the early idea of mass does. Although sensible objects change and come and go, that they can do this presupposes an unchanging matter/substance background within which orderly change can occur: ... if matter exists because it cannot be generated, it is even more reasonable for the *substance* which that matter at any time is coming to be, to exist; for if neither *substance* nor matter exist, nothing will exist at all.[10]

If all things can be reduced to essential substances, there is still the problem of the differences encountered in the apparent world. This problem Aristotle resolves by adding to the idea of matter and substance, the idea of a first principle or form. Just as there are many different animate and inanimate objects of awareness but all are substantive in nature, so do these different objects have many different forms but all express the basic principle of form. Substantive nature and forming principle, are different yet inseparable for form does not exist without substance nor is substance ever without form. Form provides the controlling elements in substances and enables them to appear as individuals.

Substance and *form* combined contain potentially all possible individuals which can be generated as matter in all possible forms. But '... neither the matter nor the form is generated, and I mean the ultimate matter and form'.[11] The universal form occurs in particular instances while at the same time the identity of the particular instances expresses the universal form, for example, manness as such in this individual man: '... by the individual we mean that which is numerically one, and by the universal, the one about the many'.[12] If nothing existed beyond the individual, there would be no intelligible objects. We recognize Dobbin, the horse, as a horse because we know from previous experiences what it means to be a horse in general. Without this general knowledge there could be no recognition of objects beyond immediate appearances.

This Aristotelean assumption gives objectivity both to the class and to the individual. *Women* and *woman* are both real, and can both be known objectively, that is, the one as universal, the other as Helena. This presupposition makes it possible to recognize the universal by observing individuals and observe individuals by understanding the universal. This process is implicit in every public opinion poll where different individuals are asked the same questions. Biologists study life via particular, living organisms, but seek to understand it in an essential sense so that, for example, they might send a probe to Mars to check for signs of life there or take DNA samples from dinosaurs and identify their mating habits.[13]

Even though form provides the apparent differences that substance supports, the problem of change remains. Is there an order in this flow of forms in which organisms live and die? When one plants a bean seed, one does not get an oak tree. Mice do not cross with cats. There seems to be a clear line of succession in which substance and form flow from an actual being to potential being to actual being. An egg comes from a chicken that in turn was an egg laid by a chicken and so on. To combine substance and form, Aristotle explained that matter is *potentiality*, and as substance contains all potentials. Form is its realization in the *actual*.[14]

Does this process have a beginning or is it an infinite regress? Aristotle rejects this latter as an impossibility. The universe began with the actual forms from which all further potential–actual sequences emerged.[15] The whole process was set in motion by an unmoved mover, a first, uncaused cause which is itself actuality, exists of its own necessity, and whose intellect is its own intelligible object.[16] Aristotle compares the unmoved mover to the commander of an army. Order exists because of the general. The general does not exist because of the order.[17] This commander is the ultimate substance, is 'eternal, immovable, and separate from sensible things'.[18] With a definition of the unmoved mover as pure thinking about thinking, Aristotle gave to the object dimension, the principle of cosmic intelligibility as the source of things, an intelligibility which corresponds to the potential and actual process in human thinking. The human intellect which enters the world as a blank slate can and does learn to know the world as it is. This perspective appealed historically to monotheists who applied it to the creation stories found in the Hebrew

Scriptures. Charles Darwin was essentially using a modified version of it when he wrote:

> There is grandeur in this view of life, with its several powers, having been originally breathed by the Creator into a few forms or into one; and that, whilst this planet has gone cycling on according to the fixed law of gravity, from so simple a beginning endless forms most beautiful and most wonderful have been, and are being evolved.[19]

The relationship of substance to form, being to becoming, potential to actual are expressed in Aristotle's theory of causality. To him knowledge was dependent upon the grasp of the four causes which account for the four possible actualities of any entity: its material cause, its formal cause, its efficient cause and its purposive cause.[20]

Aristotle: the nature of human nature

Types of soul

The unfolding substantial/formal and actual/potential process is found in inanimate and animate bodies alike. The animate, however, is capable of self-sustenance, growth, and decay.[21] As we read in the *Parts of Animals*, in animate bodies, the animating principle as psyche or soul is responsible for the actualization of varying forms at different levels, and for any creature from ant to elephant 'when its Soul is gone, it is no longer a living creature, and none of its parts remains the same, except only in shape'.[22]

At the lowest and vegetative level of life, this principle as soul manifests itself in a nutritive and reproductive form. On the next higher level, that of the animals, the nutritive and reproductive faculties are supplemented by sentient and appetitive faculties. Some animals also have the capacity to move, others do not. At the highest level, which is the human, the animating principle, in addition to all of the above forms, is the potential faculty of reasoning which exists only at this level and gives humans the form which separates them from the animals with whom they share the other capacities.

The actualizing function of thinking is to produce knowledge and understanding, and ultimately direct and control the animal and vegetative principles. Humans share sensing with the animals, but thinking gives this sensing a higher, non-animalistic dimension for it enables the intellect to discover the forms implicit in the surrounding world. This is a qualitative difference entailing a number of assumptions that are central to the history of the object dimension: (1) The reasoning soul is separable from the body and survives it.[23] (2) As the capacity to reason, it is introduced as principle from outside the body.[24] And (3) given its special nature, the thinking or reasoning principle is not altered when it thinks, anymore than a 'builder is altered when he builds'.[25]

The privileged status of the intellect or soul for both Plato and Aristotle meant that there was a special element in human experience and thought that in some way rose above or beyond sense data and language usage – either as innate forms (Plato), or as universals indirectly sensed by the intellect in experiences (Aristotle). It is this element which guarantees the correspondence of thoughts and categories to the object world. It also provides the perspective on language which makes it possible to create and use language to objectify and talk about language itself, that is, in *meta-languages* or *meta-logics*. Just as the observer is outside and unchanged by his/her observations, so is the philosopher and logician outside and unchanged by language and logic and so can deal with the first principles and basic nature of language and logic.

Sensation and the sensible

'What exists is either sensible or intelligible; and thus knowledge is the knowable and sensation is the sensible.'[26] Given the universal/particular syntheses of substance/form, there will be two kinds of knowing: perceptual knowing which is concerned with the sensing of particular things, and conceptual knowing which is concerned with the recognition of universal identities. Sensation *per se* has only potential existence until external objects of perception actualize it. However, at the completion of the sensory process the sentient subject, has become like the object, and shares its quality. This *likeness* is the ultimate expression of objectivity.[27]

There are five senses, each of which is appropriate to the actual, sensible forms of objects in the sensing process. Relative to each sense, sensation and the sensible are the same in form.[28] Sensation is always true, though what imagination creates may be and often is false.[29] Because sensations are always true, knowledge based on true sensation is always true as well.[30] And it is through the repetition of individual sensations that the knowledge of the universal emerges in thinking.[31]

Conception and the conceivable

The knowing of universal forms which are expressed in class concepts as plants, lions, human beings, and so on begins with sensation but is completed in the intellect by way of the memory which enables the knower to identify that which is the same in varied experiences. Aristotle claims that

> ... repeated memories of the same thing give rise to experience; because the memories, though numerically many, constitute a single experience. And experience, that is the universal when established as a whole in the soul – the one that corresponds to the Many, the unity that is identically present in them all – provides the starting-point of art and science.[32]

It is the universal manifested in the form of the particular that enables us to recognize what we are sensing. At the same time, however, as universal it exists in the intellect.[33] The universal is not a substance for 'the substance of a thing is peculiar to it and does not belong to another thing, but as universal is common; for by "a universal" we mean that whose nature is such that it may belong to many'.[34] For example, we refer to substance as 'this', but to universals as 'such'.

Despite the origins of knowledge in true sensations, to know the universal in the particular one must transcend sensation. Our definitions are never of individuals but of unprovable and indemonstrable essences.[35] Particulars as objects and their attributes get their identities by way of the definitions of the universals for the individuals change and come and go while essences as potentiality in the intellect become actuality in experience.[36] The distinction Aristotle made between substance and form and the encounter of the two in particular individuals as composites, is central to the distinctions that are made in the object dimension between definitions and descriptions. Definitions in this view are beyond sensation for they express ultimate essence and ultimate knowledge while descriptions – not sensations – can be true or false, affirmed or denied.[37]

One can consider definitions as first principles in any operation or system of classifications. They cannot be proven, they are known, as were Euclid's axioms. Though based on sensation, they are assumed to correspond to reality. This is why changing definitions in the object dimension is frequently so difficult. Definitions are often not considered the products of knowledge but its first principles and sources 'which cannot be proved'.[38] Cow as such is defined, but we sense and describe and prove our descriptions of a particular cow.

In order to accommodate this dual process of knowing which begins in sense impressions upon a blank mind and ends with a grasp of universal suchness, the knowing, human being possesses two intellects: one which is passive and records particular sensations, and one which is active and identifies the universals in particular sensations. The passive intellect becomes all things and the active intellect makes all things. It is like light which makes things visible.[39] And when actively thinking, the intellect like the senses corresponds to its objects.[40]

The passive intellect is related to sense perception and perishes as the body and senses perish. However, the active intellect in which universals exist potentially and where reasoning occurs is not in this material cycle for it is unmixed and uncontaminated by the body and sense organs, and survives them.[41] It is this rational principle in human beings that assures correspondence among things, thoughts, and symbols beyond relative and subjective interpretations. It gives the knower a privileged position as other than the known world, and provides the basis for true/false judgments and values.[42] Just as there can be no knowledge *of* that which changes so there can be no knowledge *in* that which changes. The rational soul unaffected by either sense limitations or body is the unchanging knower in the changing world of sense impressions – the dimensionless Euclidean point *in nature but not of nature*.[43] And as the senses in sensing are one with the sensible, so thinking corresponds with the forms in that it makes them. This is why they remain equally true as concepts and as universal classes of things.[44]

Paralleling his theory of form and substance, potential and actual, and active and passive intellects, Aristotle analyzes two kinds of certain knowledge: (1) scientific knowledge which produces facts, and (2) intuitive apprehension of first principles within which scientific knowledge of facts and particulars occurs.[45]

This theory of dual intellects also extends into a theory of significant or scientific questions. There are certain questions which are appropriate to a science, and these have to do with its facts. There are other questions which treat the first principles or presuppositions of a science. The former are appropriate to the content of a science as a science of. The latter are inappropriate, for these are the questions as to principles upon which the science as intellectual knowing process is based.[46]

Aristotle: class and proposition

Class

Early object logic as Aristotle understood it was a synthesis of reasoning structures with the class identities about which reasoning occurs, and which have been identified by the active intellect. Identity, however, is not a consequence of the use of a term in a statement. Rather, the identity of the class refers to that which it symbolizes before it enters a statement and it is this meaning which determines its use in the statement.[47]

The Aristotelean view of universal classes and particular individuals contains at least two classification principles that are central to language use and logic in the object dimension:

1. *The principle of correspondence.* There is a correspondence between and among the objects of experience, their counterparts in sensation and thinking, and their formulation in symbols. This correspondence is the essence of the definitions in any field.[48] The world as a continuum of things and thoughts can be expressed in nouns, (or verbs and adjectives as noun forms) in sentences and statements which assert something about something.[49] *Redness* is as real as is *running* as is human being. And even though different peoples may speak different languages so that the names given to objects may vary and be matters of convention, the thoughts and objects they symbolize are not a matter of convention and are the same for all reasonable, intelligent individuals.[50] This presupposition is also critical to the further assumption that there can be only one logic.

Statements about the world are usually assumed to objectively correspond to it both as universals and particulars. This has been one of the most useful consequences of class logic as it extends from its Aristotelean beginnings to Kant at the beginning of the nineteenth century. Certainty for Kant, however, is related not to the objects of thought but to the objective nature of thinking itself. And in logic, according to Kant as he understood it in his time, an absolute perfection had been achieved, an objectivity in method beyond all subjectivity.[51]

2. *The principle of stability.* Once categories and classes have been identified, these can be applied, stored in books, taught, and in general seem to take on a life of their own beyond subjective, arbitrary or conventional concerns. A classificatory system which integrates thought, language and nature assures stability and consistency in the world of human experience. The more it can be universally applied, the more universal its authority and vice versa. Just as Euclid's work defined all operations in real space for succeeding centuries, so did Aristotle's work define all operations of and in real nature from the divine to the mundane. His unmoved mover as source of the world's intelligibility provided the framework for the development of both natural science and religion in the West. It is both with and against this synthesis of Aristotelean and Christian explanations and interpretations that Galileo argued in his *Dialogues Concerning the Two New Sciences.* Every formulation of natural law owes a debt in its origins to Aristotle's abstraction of essence which presupposes correspondence among term, formula, thought, and thing.

Proposition

Thinking as identifying, affirming, denying, defining, describing, and so on can be viewed as an including and excluding activity in which the identities of objects and their attributes are included in or excluded from categories both as names and as subjects and predicates in statements. In Indo-European languages, when one speaks one links categories to one another in simple sentences in which the predicate portion predicates certain attributes of the subject in that it either includes or excludes the subject portion completely or partially, for example, 'All aardvarks are mammals' (complete inclusion of subject by predicate). 'No aardvarks are camels' (complete exclusion of subject by predicate). 'Some mammals are aardvarks' (partial inclusion of subject by predicate). 'Some mammals are not aardvarks' (partial exclusion of subject by predicate).

Aristotle, given his view of the active intellect and of nature, associated this process of inclusion/exclusion with the world itself as actual and potential. The certainty of knowledge stems from its absolutely inclusive/exclusive definitional nature. It is on this basis that knowledge differs from opinion, for according to Aristotle knowledge is both necessary and universal, while opinion '... is concerned with that which is true or false and which may be otherwise'.[52]

Logical reasoning whether inductive or deductive presupposes certainty which applies to the identity of the classes about which one reasons. On the other hand, the inclusion/exclusion relationships asserted by generally accepted opinions is not logical but dialectical and rests upon the acceptability of the sources of the opinions.[53]

Language reflects the perceptual detail of the passive intellect and the conceptual sameness of the active intellect. These are symbolized in the universal and particular classes and categories that are the subject and predicate building blocks of statements. Aristotle distinguished between sentences and propositions in that he attributed meaning to both, but claimed that only propositions made assertions about subject/predicate inclusion/exclusion that were true or false, that is, had a truth value.[54]

The clearest expression of the principles of inclusion and exclusion is to be found in what has been called the 'three laws of thought'. Aristotle understood logic as a bridge from the unique and individual to collective sameness, and he sought to distill from ordinary language the fundamental patterns and rules of logical reasoning and to connect the universality of reasoning structures to the universality he felt was the forming nature of the external world.[55] For him, logical consistency reflected a natural consistency in the world of things, a consistency set in motion by the unmoved first mover. Thus the three laws of thought which are attributed to Aristotle and are to be found in his texts in various forms, are laws that apply to the external world as well.

The first law is that of 'identity' which holds that a thing or class is what it is, its identity does not change, and a true term or proposition reflects this identity. By extension, a logically consistent or valid line of reasoning preserves this identity flow from premiss to conclusion.

The second law is that of 'non-contradiction' which holds that no thing can be what it is not. Every class or attribute divides the world into two sets – those objects, and so on which are included in the set established by the category and/or attribute, and those which are excluded from it. The former are members of the class, the latter are members of its complement or the non-class. No class is a member of its class complement or the non-class and it would be a contradiction to assert that any member of a class is a member of the non-class and vice versa. Thus if a proposition is true, it cannot be false and vice versa. Zebras are not both zebras and non-zebras. Two statements or thoughts which contradict one another can not both be true, and a logically inconsistent or invalid line of reasoning would be one where the identity flow of inclusion or exclusion either contains a contradiction or conceals the possibility of one.

The third law of thought is that of the 'excluded middle' which holds that every object is either a member of a class or a class complement, but never of both at the same time. And every proposition is either true or false but not both. By extension, this means that a line of reasoning which contains ambiguity, is potentially a violation of the law of the excluded middle and is invalid. And a class which fully includes a second class and is itself included fully in a third, includes the second in the third.[56] These laws form the basis for assigning truth values to propositions and consistency values to lines of reasoning, that is, a true proposition is true and to say it is false is a contradiction for no proposition is both true and false, and every proposition is either true or false.

In modern logic texts the term 'distribution' is applied to classes which are completely included or excluded in a proposition, for example, 'all dogs are animals' distributes the subject class dogs but not the predicate class animals. This explains why in certain proposition types the subject and predicate orders cannot be reversed without changing identity and thus violating the three laws of thought. For example, 'all mothers are females' does not imply that 'all females are mothers' for this would change the class that is distributed and be contrary to both definition and experience. A line of reasoning requires clear class identity. The inclusions/exclusions entering the syllogism in its premisses are also those which must emerge in its conclusion.[57]

Within this categorical view, there are four possible kinds of inclusion/exclusion relationship and thus four kinds of proposition. Each proposition is *qualitatively* affirmative or negative and *quantitatively* partial or universal:

1. *Universal affirmative.* These are propositions in which it is universally asserted that all members of the subject class are included in or predicated by the predicate class. 'All porcupines are mammals.' To be a member of the subject class is at the same time to be a member of the predicate class. In such a proposition the subject class is distributed and its predicate class is undistributed. Because the identity of only one class is distributed, the positions of the classes cannot be reversed, that is 'all mammals are porcupines'.

2. *Universal negative.* These are propositions in which it is universally asserted that all members of the subject class are excluded from the predicate class. 'No porcupines are birds.' In universal negative propositions, the subject and predicate classes are both distributed. To be the one is not to be the other and vice versa. Because both classes are distributed, the classes can be reversed in the proposition and the intent would remain the same. This is a characteristic of universal negatives, that is: 'No birds are porcupines.'

3. *Particular affirmative.* These are propositions in which it is asserted that the predicate class includes some (at least one member) of the subject class. 'Some females are mothers.' In particular affirmative propositions, neither the subject nor predicate class is distributed, thus the position of the classes can be reversed without change in intent, that is, if some mothers are females, then clearly some females are mothers.

4. *Particular negative.* These are propositions in which it is asserted that all of the predicate class excludes some (at least one member) of the subject class. 'Some males are not fathers.' In particular negative propositions, the predicate class is distributed, for the entire predicate class excludes the individual/s which form/s the subject class in the proposition. However, we are speaking only of some of the subject class in this case, that is those that are excluded from all of the predicate. Therefore the subject is not distributed. The two classes cannot be reversed without changing intent, for if the predicate class excludes some of the subject class, it is not necessarily so that some of the subject excludes the predicate class, for example, some males are not fathers does not mean some fathers are not males.

On the basis of the three laws of identity, noncontradiction, and excluded middle, each of these proposition types has an identity relationship to all others. Sometimes this relationship is clear and sometimes it is not. If for example we assert that a universal affirmative proposition is true, then the corresponding particular affirmative will also be true according to classical interpretations. And if a universal affirmative is true then both a universal negative and a particular negative would be false. And if we claim a universal negative proposition is true, then a particular negative would also be true, but both a universal affirmative and particular affirmative would be false. In induction we would go from particulars to universals if we were to insist that our particulars produce *definitions* and not *generalizations*. On the other hand, if we claim a particular affirmative is true, then we do not know whether the universal affirmative is true or false nor do we know whether the particular negative is true or false. The universal negative would of course be false if the particular affirmative were true.

Aristotle began to diagram these inter-propositional relationships. In the sixth century AD the Roman philosopher, Boethius put his diagram into a square of opposition that was used for centuries to illustrate the interrelationships of these four proposition types to one another:

SQUARE OF PROPOSITIONAL RELATIONSHIPS

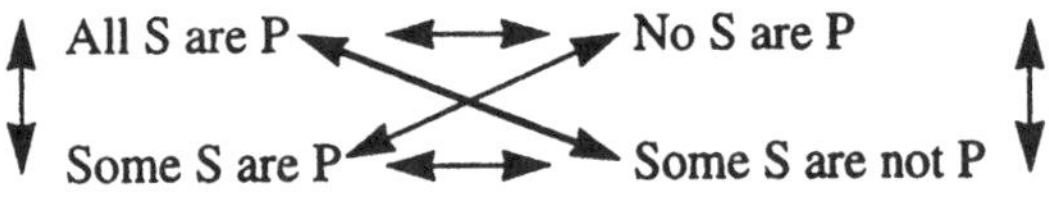

On this square of opposition, the particular affirmative was considered a 'subalternate' of the universal affirmative, for if the universal was true the particular would be also, although the reverse was not the case. And the same subalternate relationship applied to universal and particular negative. The universal affirmative and negative were considered 'contrary' to one another in intent because they might both be false, but could not both be true. And the particular affirmative and negative were considered sub-contraries because although they could both be true, they could not both be false. The propositions that were always contradictory in the Aristotelean/Boethean interpretation are the universal to particular diagonals. The universal corners and their diagonal corners can never have the same truth values. If one is true the other is false and vice versa.

If one accepts the *correspondence principle*, one can see the square of opposition as a divine blue print of both God's reason and of the human mind. Some of the most important modern modifications of the square deal with the relationship of the universals to the particulars. In such interpretations, the universal is not necessarily presumed to imply existence, while the particulars do imply existence. Thus a universal affirmative would not make a particular affirmative true. For example, the statements that 'All centaurs are good horsemen' or 'No centaurs can be domesticated' do not imply that centaurs exist. Particular propositions, however, are usually presumed to imply the existence or *existential import* of at least one member of the class. Thus the following line of reasoning is invalid in the modern interpretation: 'All centaurs are good horsemen', therefore 'Some centaurs are good horsemen', therefore 'Some good horsemen (at least one) is a centaur.'

This idea of *existential import* shifts objectivity from universals to particulars, conceptions to particular perceptions. It does not eliminate objectivity nor its source. It does raise the question as to whether objectivity can ever be applied to any definition – and of course if definitions are not objective, then can the particulars those definitions enable us to identify be considered objective?

Compound and compound complex forms of propositions can be reduced to their essences in simple inclusive/exclusive statements.[58] The principle of inclusion/exclusion can be applied to sets of these four types as they are expressed in additional propositions that can be inferred from any true statement. For example, the consistency of class identity becomes apparent when the position of subject and predicate are reversed so that the predicate class becomes the subject and vice versa. If all dogs (subject class) are animals (predicate class), then some animals must be dogs. NOTE that the converse of the proposition no longer expresses any universal identity. In addition to reversing the order of the subject and predicate of a proposition (called 'conversion', or the converse in logic), one can maintain the original order, but identify the class relationship between the subject and the non-predicate class (called 'obversion', or the obverse in logic). And finally, one can on the basis of the given proposition try to relate both non-classes if possible (called 'contra-positioning', or contra-position). The following examples illustrate these three possibilities for maintaining identity. Not all of these possibilities are still accepted, but the original idea of *conserving identity* is still agreed upon by logicians:

Proposition	Conversion	Obversion	Contra-position
All S is P	Some P is S	No S is non P	All non P is non S
No S is P	No P is S	All S is non P	Some non P is not non S
Some S is P	Some P is S	Some S is not P	(none)
Some S is non-P	(none)	Some S is non P	Some non P is not non S

These four possibilities become quite important when one realizes that in Indo-European languages a class's non-class or *complement* can be expressed in many different ways which take on identities of their own, for example, finite versus in-finite, rational versus ir-rational, American versus un-American, normal versus ab-normal, intelligible versus un-intelligible, moral versus im-moral, and so on.

Aristotle: logic and syllogistic reasoning

Aristotle's logic is an extension of his theory of nature and his theory of the passive and active intellects into an analytic method whose function is to demonstrate and clarify the definitional and descriptive relationships between and among the objects of experience as these relationships are expressed in definitions and descriptions.[59] In this sense it is a class or categorical logic. He believed that experience once it had become certain knowledge in the active intellect, could then be processed unaltered as premisses and conclusions through the rational sequences of either inductive or syllogistic (deductive) logic.[60]

This is also a *formal logic* in that it clearly identifies forms of reasoning which are distinct from its class content. For example, many different classes would fit into the 'All subject is predicate' propositional structure just as a Euclidean postulate might apply to many different figures that one might construct. Aristotle knew too that it was possible to separate form from content so that one would have a syllogism but not knowledge.[61]

In the following brief discussion of class logic I shall incorporate a number of the refinements that have evolved in its development from Aristotle through the Scholastic Middle Ages and into the nineteenth century. Hopefully this will facilitate both understanding and useful application and provide an incentive for the interested reader to refer to more comprehensive introductions to and histories of classical and symbolic logics. There are a vast number of specialized texts and histories available, some of which are referenced in the bibliography. My purpose here is a cursory examination and exploration of syllogistic reasoning as an example of a very basic deductive object logic using the assumptions that Aristotle and his students made as to the nature of world, language and the process of deduction.

The standard syllogism contains three propositions and relates three classes. The justification for the inclusion/exclusion of the subject class and the predicate class in a conclusion is their inclusive/exclusive connection in the premisses to a common, third class which appears in the premisses. For example: (premiss) if all monkeys are primates, and if (premiss) all primates are warm-blooded animals, then (conclusion) one is justified in concluding that all monkeys are warm-blooded animals. The three classes in this example are monkeys, primates, and warm-blooded animals. The syllogism connects these three classes in three propositions. This is a form which would seem still to accommodate most of the class arguments in which we are reasoning about identity relationships. We can and do most of our relating of classes like communists, taxpayers, violent criminals, schizophrenics, good Americans, Christians, Moslems, Republicans, Democrats, and so on in syllogistic structures in which definitional assumptions are basic.

In the syllogism each premiss shares a class in common with the other. This class which appears only in the premisses as the relating class but does not appear in the conclusion is called the *middle* or *common class*. In a syllogism the predicate of the conclusion relates to this middle class either as subject or predicate in the first premiss of the argument. The subject of the conclusion relates to the middle class as subject or predicate in the second premiss. In the following argument the predicate of the conclusion is the subject of the first premiss and the subject of the conclusion is the predicate of the second premiss: (1) All Parrots are Birds. (2) No Birds are Snakes. (3) THEREFORE: No Snakes are Parrots. Out of these three sets of propositions and three classes, Aristotle constructed the first and one of the most important of object logics, the *syllogism*.

Sometimes in an argument a proposition or the common class is assumed but not identified. This is called a partial syllogism, or enthymeme, and the missing proposition and/or common class must be supplied in order to use the syllogistic form. Any proposition or statement of fact can be treated as a conclusion to an argument. To do this one needs only ask 'How do I/you know this to be so?' or, 'Why/how can this be said?' For example 'John is a criminal.' How can this be said, on what basis can it be asserted? When one asks such questions, one is seeking the common class or middle term which would permit including John in the class of criminals. 'Because he has spent time in jail.' The answer to the question has given us the common class which is 'people who spend time in jail'. The complete syllogism is now: Premiss: Those who spend time in jail are criminals. Premiss: John spent time in jail. Conclusion: Therefore John is a criminal.

Of course, there can be all sorts of disagreement as to whether a common class is acceptable or not. The value of the syllogism is often to bring this middle term into the open where it can be discussed. The syllogism cannot determine its acceptability. However, this *producing the middle term* is critical to the question of acceptability, and if one is an Aristotelean, acceptability relates to reality as we know it as universals and particulars.

Syllogistic structure

Because syllogism is a system for relating two classes in a conclusion through a common class in two premisses, it will consist of only three classes, three propositions, and four structural possibilities called 'figures'. In the following table, S = subject term of the conclusion, P = predicate term of the conclusion, M = middle term or common class through which S & P are related. It occurs only in the premisses:

	Figure #1	Figure #2	Figure #3	Figure #4
PREMISS	M P	P M	M P	P M
PREMISS	S M	S M	M S	M S
CONCLUSION	S P	S P	S P	S P

The structural consistency of a syllogism does not arise in the truth of its propositions, but rather in its patterns of inclusion/exclusion, just as the consistency of 2+2=4 does not depend upon whether one is counting grapefruit or water buffalo. For example the syllogism All C is P and All F is C, Therefore All F is P, is structurally valid. And its structural validity would not cease if we were to let the letters stand for: C = Chevrolets, P = Plymouths, and F = Fords. We might insist that each of these statements is now untrue, but the syllogism remains valid. In modern object logics, truth is applicable to an argument's content, and validity is applicable to its structure. Aristotle was clearly aware of the difference between truth and validity, but it was part of his faith in the rational nature of human beings, that he believed individuals would not use valid arguments to knowingly convey un-truths or half-truths. In modern formal logics, there is a complete separation of validity from truth, structure from context.

Rules

For the syllogism, using a modified Aristotelean perspective as a guide, we can identify a series of rules. These rules can also be explained and illustrated with an appropriate use of content. For after all Aristotle (and all logicians and mathematicians) did not start thinking with formal structures, but rather learned in time to analyze his thoughts and streamline them into such structures. It is part of the beauty of the classical syllogism that it can be so easily seen to reflect in everyday terminology basic speaking and thinking patterns. The following rules are all that are required to make it work:

1. There can be only three classes in a valid syllogism.
2. There can be only three propositions in a valid syllogism.

3. A conclusion can never contain more of a class than is contained in the premisses. This means that in the conclusion, one cannot refer to all members of a class, either negatively or affirmatively unless all members of that class were referred to in the premiss in which the class appears. (No class can be distributed in the conclusion which is not distributed in a premiss.)
4. The middle or common class must be referred to universally, either affirmatively or negatively in one of the premisses. (If this does not occur, there is no certain basis for relating the subject and predicate in the conclusion.)
5. From two negative premisses no conclusion can be drawn. (If both premisses were negative their classes could not be related in the conclusion.)
6. If one premiss is negative, the conclusion must be negative (Exclusion takes precedence over inclusion.)
7. From two particular premisses no conclusion can be drawn.

(This illustrates the emphasis upon definition in deduction versus emphasis upon particular descriptions in induction which result in generalizations. It is more or less accepted today that generalizations are probable and not certain, while we still tend to use definitions in an absolutist sense.)

Two arguments which violate the above rules indicate how important the objective existence of universals and definitions is for certain knowledge and deductive reasoning with the categorical syllogism:

(Premiss) Some animals are bears.
(Premiss) Some animals are lions.
(Conclusion) Some lions are bears.

In the above example, there are no universals which could connect the classes in the conclusion. It violates rules #4 and #7.

(Premiss) All bears are animals.
(Premiss) All lions are animals.
(Conclusion) All lions are bears.

In this example, there are two universals present, but the common class is not a universal, therefore the classes in the conclusion still cannot be connected. It violates rule #4. When one tries to reason without universals, one appreciates the significance of Aristotle's attempts to identify them as fundamental aspects of the real world.

CONCLUSION

Logical sequences whether *deductive* (definitional and demonstrative) or *inductive* (evidential and leading to generalizations) can be either or both categorical and causal, and the the syllogism can be used in constructing both kinds of arguments. Aristotle's combination of category/causality in a hierarchy of classes with the ideas of first cause and the four causes of identity have been historically invaluable in establishing in the object tradition both the *principle of intelligibility* of the world of objects, and the *principle of the privileged position* of the observer and reasoner. A valid syllogism does not rely upon the points of view of subjective observers.

5 Objectivity and Ataraxia: Epicurean Gardens, a Stoic Porch and Skeptic Scales

That man, O Parmenon, I count most fortunate
Who quickly whence he came returns.
While he that tarries longer, worn, his money gone,
Grows old and wretched and forever knows some lack,
A vagrant he, the sport of enemies and plots.
Gaining no easy death the transient guest returns. (Menander)[1]

Socrates' lifetime spanned the Athenian Golden Age of Pericles, the construction of the Parthenon, and the devastating Peloponnesian wars with Sparta. His trial and death in 399 BCE can in part be credited to the instability and chaos in the city by the end of the fifth and beginning of the fourth centuries.

For Plato the time of Pericles was the immediate past. He was born at approximately the same time that Pericles himself succumbed in 429 to the plague raging through the streets of an overcrowded and besieged Athens during the second Peloponnesian War. By the time of the death of Aristotle in 322 BCE, Athens had fallen to Macedonia. And when Alexander died from a fever in Babylon in 323 BCE upon his return from India, the independent, Greek cities were absorbed in the kingdoms established by the warring generals he left behind. The dynasties they founded, the Seleucids, Ptolemeys, and the Antigonids continued their conflicts until the Romans eliminated them or reduced them to vassals.

But if the moment of the city state had passed, Greek culture itself became international, influencing alike Indian sculpture and Egyptian literature, Roman dress and Persian religion. In this Hellenistic period, the entire Mediterranean was a Greek sea, with great libraries and cultural centers outside of Greece proper at Pergamum and Alexandria. It was a time of increasing material prosperity, trade, and commerce, despite the disruptions of almost constant warfare. But in contrast to the city state, it was also an age of decreasing individual significance in the larger social masses of the great kingdoms. A world, as Menander (343–291 BCE), its most popular comic playwright, suggested, in which at times an earlier end seemed better than a later.

Nowhere is the loss of identity which the autonomous city state had provided its citizens, so obvious as in matters of religion and philosophy. The Olympian gods, although still celebrated in festivals, no longer provided a stability in the lives of the subjects of these great kingdoms who saw around them a chaos of practices and beliefs encouraged by monarchs who also called themselves divinities and demanded state worship. In his play, 'The Girl from Samos', Menander has the character Demeas remark: 'I can name you by the thousand persons strolling in our midst who are sprung from gods ... '[2]

Some still saw the great deities of Olympus as participating in the affairs of men and controlling natural phenomena. Others like the atomistic Epicurians believed the gods existed in ethereal isolation, unconcerned with the world where events followed their natural courses. But it was a world, according to Epicurus, where the temptation to believe that the gods controlled events was an ancient habit and one that the superstitious tended to fall back upon in their ignorance.[3] Sextus Empiricus, a Greek physician and Skeptic of the second to third century AD, suggested 'with-holding judgment' in such matters for he felt that both claims for and claims against the existence of the gods would be impious.[4]

Human existence seemed to be at the mercy of the capricious whims of fortune who, as the goddess Tyche, was worshipped in temples and palaces around the Mediterranean. In a fragment from one of Menander's plays, a character declaims: 'Fortune ever holds the tiller. This goddess alone we ought to speak of as both intellect and forethought unless we perversely take pleasure in empty names.'[5]

For those who would escape Tyche or the oppression of meaningless being, a mixture of Egyptian, and Near-Eastern mystery religions offered initiates a promise that fate and luck might both be circumvented by identifying with and participating in the mysteries of special saviour deities and demigods like Dionysus, Osiris, Sarapis, Attis, and Mithra who promised paradise and life everlasting to their followers, helping them to avoid after death those terrible torments which some predicted.

Another view of and approach to the meaning of human existence was offered by philosophical schools which, as the historian Peter Green points out, offered refuge in negative ideals of being: '*aponia*, absence of pain; *alypia*, avoidance of grief; *akataplēxia*, absence of upset; *ataraxia*, undisturbedness; *apragmosynē*, detachment from mundane matters, *apathia*, non-suffering ...'[6] Of these ideals, *ataraxia* or the unperturbed mind, was one or the most important and its achievement was the central concern of the Epicurean, Stoic, and Skeptic schools of the post Socratic age. These philosophies emphasized stability in changing circumstances, not by denying change or destiny but by trying to objectively understand it and come to terms with it in so far as it lay within one's power to do so.

The idealized concepts of Plato and Aristotle in the Academy and the Lyceum were rejected for positions more immediate and realistic. Arcesilaus (c.315–240 BCE) as head of the Academy is credited with developing Socrates' 'knowing that he did not know' into 'knowing that one cannot know'. The Lyceum became a center and model for the more specialized scientific research that spread abroad to the great museums in royally subsidized programs where the emphasis was increasingly on empirical observation and mathematics. For example as early as the third century BCE, Herophilus of Chalcedon dissected cadavers at Alexandra; while his pupil Erasistrates, studied the relation of digestive processes to the circulatory system.

A garden, a porch, and balanced scales

Aristotle's teleological identification of substance, form, and final cause in universals and particulars, genus and species was derived from the external, objective world by an active soul which was in essence separate from that world. This Aristotelean view of knowledge was modified by the post Socratics who sought to describe objects and events as they appeared, as they related to one another, and as they could be accommodated in daily affairs.

These Epicurean, Stoic, and Skeptic thinkers did not agree and were one another's sharpest critics. Taken as a group, however, they offer three different and fundamental approaches to the object dimension of philosophical space. Each begins with an affirmation of the world of immediate experience and then proceeds to develop its own perspective upon perceptual and conceptual reality. For each of them *ataraxia* was to be attained by way of an appropriate understanding of nature and one's own limitations.

I. Epicurean gardens

The first objective path to *ataraxia* that we shall examine is that provided by Epicurus who was born in 341 BCE in the Athenian colony at Samos. One account of his life suggests that it was his encounter with the works of the atomist, Democritus, that turned Epicurus' interests to philosophy.[7] In any case we know from Epicurus' works that he saw in atomism an explanation of the world that would lead one who understood it to an unperturbed mind. In an atomist's view there would be no room for superstition, fear of the gods, fear of death, fear of hell or even the frustrating and uncertain longing for eternal life after death – all of which were sources of confusion and suffering for the living. When the body dies, sensation ceases, the compounds that were the individual disperse, and an awareness of this process and its end '... makes the mortal aspect of life pleasurable, not by conferring on us a boundless period of time, but by removing the yearning for deathlessness'.[8]

Atomism focuses attention upon the pleasures and pains of the moment without ephemeral and useless promises and threats. The same applies to strivings for power, wealth and political position. These all come to an end in death, while in life they generate more pain and suffering than pleasure and happiness. The Roman atomist, Lucretius, over a century later compared the politician to a Sisyphus ever pursuing unattainable ambition or to a maiden trying to fill a sieve with water.[9] Consistent with this philosophy, one of the first requirements of the Epicurean way was withdrawal from active participation in the affairs of the city.

Consistent with his rejection of an active, public life, Epicurus purchased a garden on the outskirts of Athens and there lived with a group of friends and disciples engaged in what one might call humanistic atomism discussing the universe as it seemed to them it really was.

The atomic world

Reality consists of (1) bodies which are singular or compound, (2) the space within which these bodies move, and (3) motion. The singular bodies are the individual atoms which are solid, unchanging and indestructable. Compound bodies are formed from these immutable particles in combinations within which the individual atoms always preserve their identities even when the compounds as animate and inanimate beings come into and go out of being. The motion of the atoms is primarily perpendicular, though swerving at times and oscillating at others. It is this combination of motions that generates the objects of our sense experience of bodies changing in compounds but unchanged in essence.

Human nature

If something exists it is a corporeal body, for to exist is to be body, and to be body is to exist extended and moving in space. Two concepts are particularly important illustrations of this: The mind which is the source of thinking and understanding is a body part as much as are hands and feet. In addition to mind there is also a vital spirit which in one respect is the same as mind, and in another is distributed throughout all parts of the body. The portion of this bodily unity which is intelligence and understanding resides in the chest. The portion that is *vital spirit* is the source of life and feeling and is located in all parts including the extremities.[10] Both portions are body and composed of particles so fine that their dispersal in death cannot be detected either by observation or weighing.[11]

The senses, as the source of contact of intellect with the external world are also bodies as are the impressions that they receive. The difference between a perceived object and its perception and conception is only a matter of density.[12] Sensation of objects is thus a form of *body containing body*. For the Epicurean, reason is simply an extension of the senses which always provide a check upon it.[13] The check upon the senses in turn is body. And on the basis of perceptible bodies we can infer the existence of imperceptible ones or atoms.[14]

In hearing, we hear bodies. Sounds, including words, are bodies because '... every sound and voice is heard, when creeping into the ears they have struck with their body upon the sense'.[15] We taste bodies for '... we perceive flavour in the mouth while we squeeze it out in munching the food'.[16] We smell bodies, although '... it may be seen that smell is made of larger elements than voice, since it does not penetrate through stone walls'.[17] We are able to see because '... semblances and thin shapes of things are thrown off from their outer surface which are to be called as it were their films or bark, because the image bears a look and shape like the body of that from which it is shed to go on its way'.[18] This Epicurean body theory both illustrates and emphasizes, perhaps in a naive way, why in the object dimension, a tactile definition of reality dominates all others.

Ataraxia in practice

Given this atomistic view of nature, human nature, and sensation, it might seem that human beings are as trapped in a deterministic and universal *atom shower* as are rocks and trees and other animals. But for the Epicurean this is not the case. For them, even a superstitious belief in capricious deities was preferable to belief in a deterministic universe because with the former one could try at least to influence the gods with prayer and sacrifice.[19] Epicurus suggested that some events are determined, others are accidental and others are in our control. It is with our attitudes toward the accidental and our responsibility for that which is in our control, that *ataraxia* and ethic are possible. The exercise of this control is the task of intellect and reason.

But what is it that is in our control and how is the requisite freedom to determine our responses and actions possible? The answer for Epicurus and Lucretius goes back to the *swerving* of some atoms in their essentially perpendicular descent, for

> ... while the first bodies are being carried downwards by their own weight in a straight line through the void, at times quite uncertain and at uncertain places, they swerve a little from their course and in this swerving, varying from the given direction, human freedom is born.[20]

The *swerve* in human existence is both responsible for and becomes the responsibility of the intellect. Lucretius claims it is this which enables the mind, itself a body, to influence and move the rest of the body in the directions and paths it chooses in its swerving. *Free will* as the outgrowth of the swerving motion and interaction between and among bodies too is corporeal. Discussions of aberrant behavior in some modern schools of psychology while denying a conscious, free will, still presume that using pleasure and pain stimuli, one can be brought to swerve from a behavior pattern.

Having established the existence of free will, whatever its origins, the next step was to arrive at courses of action that would lead to *ataraxia* and a moral life. For Epicurus the idea of good and evil is equated with the idea of pain and pleasure. The pleasure principle more than any other has been the source of a general misunderstanding of Epicurean doctrines. As Epicurus proposed it, it is inseparably connected to sound judgment, desire to help and not hurt others, the joy of pleasant company, the happiness of self-respect, and peace with one's self. He asked whether one can imagine any individual who is more moral than one who '... realizes that the goal of the good life is easily gained and achieved and that the term of evil is brief, both in extent of time and duration of pain? Or the man who laughs at the "decrees of Fate," a deity whom some people have set up as sovereign of all?' On this basis he catalogued human desires for his followers that they might gain a perspective upon their swerving.[21] At its simplest, pleasure is the absence of pain, and in its most profound sense it is an affirmation of a peaceful life followed by a peaceful death, at which time the simple atomic components of our complex bodies are once again dispersed.

II. The Painted Porch: Stoa and Stoics

The second path to *ataraxia* that we shall examine is that of the Stoics, so named because they met at the '*Stoa Pokile*' or Painted Porch in Athens where Zeno of Citium, the founder of Stoicism, lectured. Zeno (333–261 BCE) had been at one time a follower of Crates, the Cynic, who probably provided him with his first contact with philosophy. He also studied with the logician, Philo. These contacts may have encouraged an austere and critical view of the world around him. Zeno arrived in Athens within a decade after the death of Aristotle – stranded there perhaps as result of a shipwreck.

According to Diogenes Laertius, he was the first philosopher to divide philosophy into three parts: 'physics' – the philosophy of the physical world, 'ethics' – the philosophy of morals and customs, and 'logic' – the philosophy of reasoning. This division was said to be like an animal: logic was the skeleton and sinews, ethic was the flesh, and *physis* was the soul.[22] This comparison is quite appropriate as far as the Stoic view of nature (physics) was concerned. The Stoic cosmos consisted of an inseparable unity of two principles: an active *archē* which was an inherent, divine ordering principle; and a passive *archē* which consisted of the inert matter which was ordered and acted upon.[23] Things from rocks to plants to animals to human beings were manifestations of these two inseparable essences. The objective world is known and experienced, not in classes or definitions, but dynamically in observable relationships. These relationships are always particular and our apprehension of them is expressed in simple statements.[24] All else is constructed from these building blocks. Because reason is responsible both for the content of these simple statements and their linking in complex lines of reasoning, one can see why Zeno and the Stoics maintained that logic was central to both physics and ethics. For the Stoics, the rational represented the divine in nature and man and provided the human intellect with the techniques with which truth could be grasped.

Probably the best known and most widely read Stoic philosophers today are the later *Roman three*: Epictetus, (50–130 BCE), an educated Greek and one-time slave in a Roman household whose thoughts are found in the notes of his pupil Arrians; Seneca, (4 BCE to 65 AD), Roman statesman, dramatist, and philosopher; and Marcus Aurelius, (121–180 AD), the Roman Emperor.

Unfortunately the logic of the Stoics for which they were famous in their time has fared less well. Neglected and misunderstood, its texts are mostly to be located in the works of others like Diogenes Laertius, the Greek biographer of the Greek philosophers; the texts on Skepticism of Sextus Empiricus, who frequently criticized it; Cicero, who objected to its formalism; and Plutarch, who stressed what to him seemed paradoxical in it. It is only recently that logicians, mathematicians, and philosophers have begun to rediscover the logical achievements of the Stoics, particularly of Chrysippus, of whom it was said that if the gods practiced dialectic, it would be that of Chrysippus of Cilicia.[25] According to historical records, Chrysippus wrote more than 250 books on logic – no single one of which still exists.

Nature

As did their Epicurean contemporaries, the Stoics viewed nature as material. However, unlike the atomists, they were physical monists, accepting the world as a material continuum directed and maintained by an implicit, divine, rational order which manifested itself in individual physical forms and events. As material monists, they rejected Aristotle's idea of an unmoved mover who stood outside of the cosmological process. To the Stoics, this corporeal unity of active and passive principles formed and shaped the qualities that we detect with our senses because it manifested itself in individual things and events.

The Stoic system is harmonious and deterministic in whole and in part. For example, Seneca, the Roman playwright and philosopher/politician, spoke of the rule which binds gods and men. He suggested that the deity which first ordered everything ' ... obeys for ever, he decreed but once ... It is impossible for the moulder to alter matter; to this law it has submitted.'[26]

Human nature

As with nature, so with human nature. What happens to individuals is destiny and cannot be judged except in the totality of the universe which contains both the pleasant and unpleasant in a mixture beyond human ability to alter it. Thus Marcus Aurelius suggests that

> ... a man should take heart of grace to await his natural dissolution, and without any chafing at delay comfort himself with these twin thoughts alone: the one, that nothing will befall me that is not in accord with the Nature of the Universe; the other, that it is in my power to do nothing contrary to the God and the 'genius' within me. For no one can force me to disobey that.[27]

In the human being, the soul is the active, rational aspect of the body just as the divine is the active, rational aspect of passive nature. According to Epictetus, this ability to perceive and experience was the most important quality that man shared with the divine reasoning which was in nature, and so was the source of all truth.[28] God is the cosmos and man as a part of the cosmos is God. From this perspective, as Diogenes Laertius noted, no sharp line can be drawn between nature and the human.[29]

There is, however, a difference of degree for the Stoics which distinguishes the rational from the irrational, human beings from animals, and from one another. It is the mark of the rational and virtuous individual that he/she recognizes that he/she is determined and welcomes this determination as destiny.[30] In some modern genetic theories as well as in nineteenth-century Spencerian ideas of social evolution, a similar view suggests there is an objective explanation of the status quo and the social, intellectual, and economic differences within it. What changes one can make based upon environment are ultimately conditioned by genetic equipment and destiny.[31]

Chrysippus equated the active force in the cosmos and in man with *pneuma* or breath, which in both cases performs the same four basic functions: it provides order and unity in the corporeal substance of the human and cosmic; as nature it is responsible for development and growth; as the soul it is the source of sensation and movement; and as mind or intellect it is the source of rationality. The inanimate world has only order and unity, the plant world possesses unity plus growth. Animals have unity, growth, sensation, and movement. Only in the human being does the *pneuma* as mind add rationality.[32] The nature of *pneuma* as the rational principle is still corporeal for air is a physical force with variations in degree that are almost unlimited.[33] In the human intellect the essence of *pneuma* is remembering, analyzing, distinguishing, and thus it empirically and logically knows the world based on presentations from the objects of experience or the objects of reason. Diogenes Laertius noted that some of these presentations come from sensation and others from the reasoning, but ' ... that which comes from a real object, agrees with that object, and has been stamped, imprinted and pressed seal-fashion on the soul, as would not be the case if it came from an unreal object'.[34]

Knowledge and logic

The world consists of both possible and necessary relationships between and among events and things. Thus, in anticipating the future, the mind derives the necessary from the experience of the possible and this empirical state is expressed in the inferences of a conditional if–then logic. The possible is that which can occur and is true when external events do not obstruct its occurring. The impossible cannot occur and therefore cannot be true. A proposition which is necessary is one which as true cannot be false. And a non-necessary proposition is capable of both true and false, depending upon external conditions.[35] Stoic logic is not a class or categorical logic. It treats with specific relationships for this is the way things happen and are experienced in a vast array of presentations. This accounts for the Stoic emphasis upon the relationship of sense experience to reasoning in the development of its logical system.[36]

According to Chrysippus, each sense was specialized in the material quality of the particular objects it encountered, for example, as taste, touch, sight, sound, smell. A sense impression was a wind (*pneuma*) proceeding from the sensed object and entering the *pneuma* of the soul as a presentation.[37] The *pneuma* of the soul was thus influenced by the physical qualities of the object and modified accordingly in response to the presentation. In a true presentation or impression, the qualities of object, sense, soul would coincide. The task of the ruling *pneuma* or soul, located in the heart, was to distinguish true impressions from false.[38] So concerned with the particular object is the Stoic, that the general often seemed irrelevant or mere linguistic form.[39]

Sensation, when one is aware of it, becomes perception. Perception in turn becomes recognition when one consciously assents to it and it is expressed in a true proposition, or complete *lekton*, for example, 'The dog is barking.' One should remember, however, that a proposition is that which is signified, and neither the object, nor the symbols used to state it. It is in this condition of signifying that it is true or false but this value is clearly dependent upon the objects and relationships signified.

Chrysippus divided statements or propositions into simple and complex, and held that a simple proposition (roughly a simple sentence in form) like 'John is six feet tall', is intelligible and true or false. It merits or does not merit assent. But a complex proposition, a combination of simple propositions, may not be intelligible. If it is, it must reflect real possibilities.[40] (In modern symbolic logics, propositions are called *atomic* if simple, and *molecular* if complex.) Propositions are simple if their subject and predicate terms are non-propositions, that is, if they have no logical connective which links them as clauses. A complex proposition contains two or more simple propositions joined by logical connectives such as and, either/or, if/then. The simple proposition represents the Euclidean dimensionless point at which the individual, natural occurrence, sensation or presentation, and language coincide in the first stages of knowledge.[41]

In the simple proposition, the connection of its subject and predicate occurs in the *pneuma*'s recognition of the perception of a relationship. For example, red skies in the morning indicate storms at sea. The truth of this for the sailor is a matter of experience. A complex proposition is, however, quite different, for it asserts a relationship between two or more individual propositions, via the term used to connect them. Whereas, the simple proposition could be said to arise in nature, the connective as well as the decision to connect arises in human reason and reflects conscious choice and assent based on experience. Thus skies that are red in the morning and afternoons and evenings that are stormy are co-joined to express observations, that is, skies are red in the morning *and* sailors take warning.

A complex proposition is true if its individual simple propositions are true and the way in which they are connected is true. Here the emphasis, as far as truth is concerned, clearly shifts from proposition to connective. At this point the objective nature of experience gives way to the objective nature of reason which connects and relates simple propositions. Here, too, one sees why reason itself can be viewed as objective as the physical *pneuma*. Note the obvious difference between the following three complex propositions, where the only changed terms are the connectives. 'John is my brother and Mary is my sister.' 'Either John is my brother or Mary is my sister.' 'If John is my brother, Mary is my sister.' Propositional logic as developed by the Stoics, especially Chrysippus, is a *connective logic* constructed of simple and complex propositions.

Propositions in Stoic logic, like the logic itself are descriptive and not definitional. The laws of reason are themselves reflections of the laws of the corporeal world. Reasoning structures, or connectives, facilitate the reasoning *pneuma* in assenting to the way things are and anticipating how they may occur in the future. And in this respect the *pneuma* could be said to have three rational functions: (1) The *pneuma* knows, senses, perceives the world of individual bodies and their qualities. (2) It understands the world. And (3) It adopts an appropriate attitude toward the world. How it accomplishes each of these is determined by the rational principle implicit in the world body itself. One of the most important consequences of this use of logic by the soul or intellect was the attempt to predict or divine future occurrences on the basis of past experience. This approach is central to modern empirical science where any hypothesis is fundamentally a linking of at least two propositions in a complex predictive statement.[42]

The next task in reasoning about experience is to place complex propositions into argument structures, or *connective syllogisms*. A complex proposition alone is not an argument. The argument begins when one has a premiss/conclusion sequence. For example, Fred has the car keys. George needs the car to get home. These two propositions combined in a complex proposition might enable us to construct the argument: If Fred leaves, George can't get home; Fred just left: therefore George won't make it home. Logic at the level of argument has two functions: (1) In reference to physics (nature), logic facilitates empirical divination – that is in a deterministic continuum, it helps one to anticipate future events by knowing and linking together specific present or past events. This is certainly the beginning of the hypotheses of empirical science.[43] (2) In reference to ethics, within nature as a determined continuum manifesting itself in individual bodies, both the human being and its *pneuma* are determined as well. However, one's attitudes are not determined. The *pneuma*, using logic in understanding events, their nature and inevitability can give or withhold assent. One can fashion one's attitudes toward the world even when one cannot fashion the world itself. Recent developments in the field of psychosomatic medicine have shown how self-destructive our attitudes can prove to be, producing physical illness.

Propositional arguments: objectified content and form

The Stoic interest in the relationships expressed in complex propositions is said to have produced literally thousands of such possibilities.[44] Of these possibilities, two were of major significance: The *hypothetical connective* which connected simple propositions with 'If' – If the boat leaks, it will sink. And the *disjunctive connective* which connected simple propositions with either/or – Either the battery is dead or the car will start.

The truth of a complex proposition for the Stoic depended upon two factors: (a) the truth of each of its simple components, and (b) the truth conditions or requirements imposed by its logical connectives. This is an important insight in the object logic of the Stoics, and it also defines modern symbolic propositional logics in which one must identify and understand the truth conditions of the connective/s used in formal reasoning. The hypothetical if/then was true for Chrysippus when the first simple proposition, or antecedent, was true and the second simple proposition, or consequent, was also true. For example, the complex proposition 'if the boat leaks then it will sink' would be true for Chrysippus only if both events occur. There was disagreement among logicians of the time as to the conditions for the truth of if/then (hypothetical) statements. The important alternative interpretation was that of Philo of Megara which was essentially that of modern material implication. Philo began with the assumption that when the implication of a hypothetical is not false, it can be deemed true. And a hypothetical complex proposition is false when its antecedent (if) is true and its consequent (then) is false or does not follow. For example, the hypothetical, if skies are red in the morning then a storm will follow in the afternoon, would be false only if the morning skies were red and a storm did not follow in the afternoon or evening. Otherwise it would be considered true (1) if the antecedent and consequent both occurred (the skies are red in the morning and a storm followed); (2) if neither antecedent not consequent occurred (the skies were not red and no storm occurred); and (3) if the antecedent did not occur, but the consequent did occur (the skies were not red and afternoon storms did occur).[45] Philo's idea also expresses the basic assumption involved in the formulation of a hypothesis in science where one assumes that the hypothesis is true until it can be proven false, that is, the antecedent occurs and the consequent result does not follow. Under all other circumstances, testing and observing will be continued because its truth is still presumed.

The either/or was true when either the first or the second simple proposition was true but not when both were. This is referred to in modern propositional logic as the exclusive use of the disjunct. Modern propositional logics tend to use an inclusive interpretation that either one or both parts may be true, for the total to be true, and only if both parts are false is the disjunctive complex proposition itself to be considered false. For example, using the inclusive interpretation, the complex proposition 'Either John leaves or Mary stays' would be true if both occurred, and false only if neither occurred. Just as Aristotle had organized classes into syllogistic argument structures, the Stoics devised a distilled sign system for identifying the relationships of statements and their connectives in arguments. The propositional logic of the Stoics did not replace class logic, but rather supplemented and complemented it as an objective reasoning technique. In his argument structures, Chrysippus used the terms first and second to represent propositions and their positions in arguments. And he identified five argument forms in which propositions are related to one another as premisses and conclusions. The element of prediction here is very important. Accepting or rejecting one event or state of affairs permits one to predict another. NOTE: the variables in these arguments (the first, the second) stand for propositions and not classes:

A. First argument form:
If the first, then the second.
(If the sun is shining, then it is day.)
The first.
(The sun is shining.)
Therefore: the second.
(Therefore: It is day.)

B. Second argument form:
If the first, then the second.
(If the sun is shining, then it is day.)
Not the second.
(It is not day.)
Therefore not the first.
(Therefore: The sun is not shining.)

C. Third argument form:
Not both the first and the second.
(It is not both the case that the sun is shining and it is night.)
The first.
(The sun is shining.)
Therefore, not the second.
(Therefore, it is not night.)

D. Fourth argument form:
Either the first or the second.
(Either the sun is shining or it is night.)
The first.
(The sun is shining.)

Therefore, not the second.
(Therefore, it is not night.)
E. Fifth argument form:
Either the first or the second.
(Either John is running or John is walking.)
Not the first.
(John is not running.)
Therefore, the second.
(Therefore, John is walking.)[46]

In these argument forms, Chrysippus' logic applies the relationships established in complex propositions to relationships between and among complex propositions in arguments. Although modern propositional logics have become vastly more complicated than these original forms of Chrysippus', they reflect his insights.

The logic of classes represents a *taxonomic* approach to reason; the logic of propositions represents a *process* approach. Both belong to the objective dimension of philosophical space, for both claim to begin with the object world and sense experience and to translate it, via intellect using logic, into true statements and valid arguments which identify patterns in the relationships between and among things and transcend situational encounters. Both are incorporated into modern science, mathematics and logic as categorical and propositional logics. For example, the English mathematician, George Boole (1815–1864) worked out an *algebra of classes* which is very important in computer programing. And the German mathematician Gottlob Frege (1848–1925) produced a *propositional calculus* for use in both logic and mathematics. Each approach has a particular usefulness, depending upon the aspect of the object world that one would objectify and the procedure that one would select. However, it is important to remember that in their origins, these two logics accommodated two different views of the world: The Aristotelean saw the world stabilized in concepts and categories. The Stoic saw the world stabilized in sequences of events and relationships.

Ataraxia

Epictetus' *Encheiridion* begins with a discussion of that which is within the power of the individual and that which is not. To the former belong '... conception, choice, desire, aversion ... everything that is our own doing'.[47] To the latter belong our bodies, possessions and positions in the world. In reference to the former, we are free. In reference to the latter we are not. Individuals cannot change the world in which they live but can as rational beings change their attitudes toward it, and thereby assume responsibility for the way they act in it.[48]

Human beings are not born rational although its potentiality is in human nature. Rationality itself is learned through time just as virtue and self-control must be. One is not virtuous until one has acquired the virtues of the wise person: moral understanding, courage, self-control, temperance and justice. The Stoics felt these could not be learned before the age of 17, because of the time and experience required.

It is essential in achieving emotional equilibrium or *ataraxia*, that emotional and rational judgments be clearly distinguished, especially as these relate to the possible and necessary. The emotional is the irrational in nature and to be avoided by the tranquil, wise individual who occupies the highest position in ascending rationality in a rational and physical universe. It is this individual who distinguishes what is possible and what is impossible, understands the necessary, and reasons out his/her attitudes accordingly.[49] The truly ethical or wise individual need no longer, nor perhaps can no longer choose between good and evil, for he/she is by nature virtuous and thus evil would never be a choice.[50]

Acts in themselves are neither good nor bad, it is the intent of the actor that is so. Life itself is as objectively neutral as is the world. In a fragment sometimes attributed to Chrysippus he is reported to have said: 'If to sail well is good and to sail badly is bad, then to sail is neither good nor bad. And if to live well is good, and to live badly is bad, then to live is neither good nor bad.'[51]

It is in reasoning that we are free individuals and can choose, not our bodies, but our attitudes. This contrasts with the twentieth-century modern who is constantly trying to choose the body via surgery, face lifts, liposuction, silicone implants, youthification treatments, drugs, transplants, gland injections, all the while enslaved in this process by an intellect whose attitudes are determined and defined by the world.

III. Balanced scales and the Skeptic

Sextus Empiricus introduces the origins of skepticism and its approach to *ataraxia* quite simply as 'the hope of attaining quietude'. Its fundamental technique was 'that of opposing to every proposition an equal proposition; for we believe that as a consequence of this we end by ceasing to dogmatize'.[52]

The starting point of our discussion of the Skeptics is with Pyrrho of Elis (c.360–270 BCE). According to Diogenes Laertius' *Lives of Eminent Philosophers*, Pyrrho was a painter, a student of philosophy, an honorary citizen of Athens, and a traveler who was reported to have had contacts with

Persian Magi and Indian wisemen.[53] These travels and contacts must have influenced his own philosophical position which was that one was to suspend judgment when one was confronted with conflicting views and theories for he was said to have believed that '... custom and convention govern human action; for no single thing is in itself any more this than that'.[54]

The world

The term 'skeptic' comes from the Greek *skeptesthai* = to look, consider, inquire, and for the Greek Skeptic the relationship of doubt to inquiry was clear: one does not inquire where one does not doubt, and if one does not doubt, one does not inquire.[55] It is one of the great misunderstandings in the history and development of the object dimension that skepticism is often thought of as opposed to objectivity instead of as one of its most important adherents. The Skeptics' position from Sextus Empiricus to Hume to Wittgenstein has always based itself on and in the object world. The Greek Skeptics' arguments with what they considered the Epicurean and Stoic dogmatists was that although these claimed to start with the world of appearances, they quickly subsumed appearances under some doubtful and unprovable opinion which became as absolute, indefensible, and objectionable as those that the Stoics and Epicureans themselves criticized in Plato and Aristotle. For the Skeptic, if one initiates inquiry, one either arrives at the inquiry's object, or one realizes that the object cannot be found, or continues to pursue it. The latter was the Skeptic's way.[56]

For the Skeptics, *epochē* (from *epi* = at or on plus *echein* = to hold or pause, thus suspension of judgment) was the essence of *ataraxia*. But *epochē* does not negate the world of experience, rather it begins in and affirms appearances. It is in evaluating the interpretations which philosophers and scientists judge to be the real world that skepticism is to be practiced.[57] Thus it is with judgments and explanations as to the true nature of things that *epochē* is to be applied.[58]

That Sextus Empiricus was writing within the object dimension of philosophical space is clear from his discussions in various texts of truth and true for he deals with truth as it relates or must relate to the external world.[59] The problem implicit in the object dimension for the dogmatist and the Skeptic alike is that of locating truth in the external existence of real or apparent sensible or intelligible objects without entering either upon an infinite regress of *true* truths, or arguing in a circle. He distinguishes between truth as an essence, and true as an attribute. In reference to the essence, he recommends a balanced scale between those who claim truth exists and those, like

Xenophanes, who claim there is only opinion.[60] This raises the problem of a definition of truth which would be decisive because it was not an opinion, which would require that decisive also not be an opinion, which begins an infinite regress of opinions and/or decisive definitions of *decisive*.[61] And if one cannot arrive at the definition of truth, then the application of true is problematical.

Human nature

For the Skeptic, man is a mix of sense and intellect and so we '... can have no other instrument by means of which he will be able to judge except sense and intellect'.[62] These can be taken separately or together. The problem is that we do not conceive what we sense, and we do not sense what we conceive. The relativity of sensing and the impossibility of directly sensing our conceptual world, presents us with a mixture of existence and non-existence as the sources of our concepts and statements. One must remember that skepticism is a development within the object tradition where identity *is or is not, not both is and is not*, and always *either is or is not*, as suggested by the Aristotelean three laws of thought. The identity of objects determines the Skeptics' position too, which is to withhold judgment when not knowing which identity is *the identity*.

The problem is not with identity as it equates with appearances, but with the possibility of knowing which interpretations of appearances are true and so exclude all other interpretations. What is the criterion which will enable one to apply true to the non-apparent abstractions of the theologians, physicists, philosophers, logicians, and mathematicians for whom knowledge of the real world is conceptual?[63] Sextus claims that even if one grants the independent existence of the intellect, it is still not possible to know objects beyond appearances for it is dependent upon sense and cannot even judge or know itself.[64] How can one know objects if one does not know that which claims to do the knowing? One might read out of or into Sextus Empiricus the idea that judging accurately means to identify an object as it is independent of human interpretations. So before the intellect can apprehend or know itself, it must somehow appear as an object, objectified beyond intellectual relativity.[65] One can hear Menander's echo from the *Thrasyleon*: 'In many ways the saying "Know thyself" is not well said. It were more practical to say: "Know other folks".'[66]

Method

The Skeptic in the object tradition clearly comprehended that the problem of knowledge of the world is the relationship of sensation via inference to the intellectual processing of sense experience into concepts and statements. But as empiricists, the Skeptics refused to give an unrestricted, dominant role in the final product to the reasoning intellect as Plato and Aristotle earlier had done or as the Epicureans and Stoics continued to do.

Reasoning and intellect rely upon axioms, and axioms, or Aristotelean universals quickly take on lives of their own and may even in religion and science, modern or classical, abrogate their roots in sensation by claiming the existence of all sorts of absolute dogma. Sextus Empiricus warns '... if reason is such a trickster as to all but snatch away the appearances from under our very eyes, surely we should view it with suspicion in the case of things non-evident so as not to display rashness by following it'.[67] The Skeptics in their criticism of the dogmatists remain true and consistent to their empirical origins in a number of ways:

1. They insist that the ultimate check upon and definition of truth both as an essence and true as a criterion rests upon the perceivable being of the apparent world and not upon some dogmatic and unlimited abstraction from it.[68] The problem is the connection of the conceived to the the existent. Is one prior to the other? Few individuals would argue that no matter what one conceives, it exists as one conceives it. Does existence refer to perception, conception or if to both, what is the mixture?

2. The Skeptic did not deny what could not empirically be denied about the world for they realized that such a denial would be dogmatic too. Atheism is as dogmatic as theism, and so from Pyrrho on they suspend judgment or balance the scales when confronting two equipollent propositions, adding nothing more than can be empirically said for one side or the other, preferring to continue the inquiry if possible while in *epochē*, attaining *ataraxia*.[69]

3. Language for the Skeptic is also tied to the apparent world and expresses our sense experiences. As with concept, once released from its connection to appearances, there are no limits upon what can be expressed in symbols. For example, one may make assertions as the dogmatists claim they can do about both pre-evident and even non-evident objects. The difficulty in doing so is that they must then rely upon expressions and symbols to assert that one can express such assertions in symbols and that these assertions correspond, as Aristotle assumed, to reality. It is a hopeless attempt to solve the problem with the problem.[70] The Skeptic holds that definitions and names are a matter of convention and as conventions change, so do their meanings.[71] The objects sensed or apprehended cannot be expressed as they are experienced, in language, nor communicated to someone else. That which we speak with others is speech but not the experience nor the object experienced.[72]

4. The Skeptic claims that proofs and rules for inference presuppose the very sort of inference for which they are to be proofs and rules. Induction

depends upon particular experiences and appearances for its generalizations. But a generalization cannot become on an inductive basis a definition and thus a premiss in a syllogistic argument.[73] Induction thus provides the check upon deduction. But since one uses the deductive universal or definition to establish the inductive particular, the inductive also provides a check upon itself because definitions by definition entail an infinite regress.[74] Or else they involve us in circular reasoning. In either case judgment should be suspended.

5. The Skeptic does not dogmatize, nor does he/she dogmatize his/her non-dogmatism for this would be to fall into the trap of dogmatism.[75] Thus, in a final act of homage to his empirical roots in sensation, the Skeptic also places both method and *epochē* upon the scale, so that the criticism of dogmatism should not become itself dogma and prohibit further inquiry. It is for the Skeptic neither a matter of true nor false, but a matter of noting 'what appears' and 'not to make any positive declarations as to the real nature of external objects'.[76]

The task of the Skeptic's method is to keep the intellect as close to its source in sense experience as possible. And when it escapes sensation in dogmatic flights, then to suspend judgment – which is also an intellectual activity, but a braking of intellect by itself for the senses cannot do this any more than they can decide to inquire.[77] Sextus Empiricus realized attributing to the intellect the power to separate itself from the sensations is a product and trick of intellect, a sort of illusory *peep-hole* into nature.[78] Aristotle felt that he had solved this peep-hole dilemma with his theory of two intellects, the passive which took wax impressions, and the active which extracted the identity of classes from the passive.

One can approach the methods of the Skeptics in two ways. The first is to see them as a general synthesis of sense experience and conceptualization which can find neither in concept nor sense a basis for separating one from the other, or giving one priority over the other or dividing knowledge into sensibles and intelligibles. All of these lead either to dogmatism or an infinite regress. An excellent explication of this was developed by the Skeptic philosopher Agrippa and is cited in Sextus Empiricus' *Outlines*.[79] Agrippa's five modes or *tropes* for suspending judgment are based on (1) *Discrepancy*, that is, disagreement, variety of view, different opinions on the matter at hand; (2) *Infinite regress* of criteria, the true truth, real real, certain certainty, atoms claiming they are atoms in statements that are atoms, and so on; (3) *Relativity* to cultures, individuals, times, places, and so forth, of every observation, statement, proof, test, and so on; (4) *Hypothesis* which is the unquestioned assumption of some position as a starting point for a sequence that in all its extensions and applications remains based on unquestioned dogma; (5) *Circular Reasoning* which uses that which is being asserted as proof of the assertion.

Ataraxia *in practice*

We now have explored an objective view and reasoning methodology which stresses the empirical elements of sensation over the abstract products of the intellect. Upon encountering these latter, the thinker withholds judgment, neither denying or affirming the non-evident or pre-evident assertions of the dogmatist, and this not dogmatically, but for the sake of continuing to inquire. Skeptic logic is both a critical thinking technique and a way of life. Sextus Empiricus suggests '... it is, I think, sufficient to conduct one's life empirically and undogmatically in accordance with the rules and beliefs that are commonly accepted, suspending judgment regarding the statements derived from dogmatic subtlety and furthest removed from the usage of life'.[80] Hume in the eighteenth century echoed this position when he wrote 'If we carry our inquiry beyond the appearances of objects to the senses, I am afraid that most of our conclusions will be full of skepticism and uncertainty ...'[81] As for the finality of the Skeptic position, it too is susceptible to all the criticisms of dogma if taken dogmatically. Like a purgative, it removes both itself as final truth along with all other final truths from the intellect.

In summary

We have now briefly explored four classical systems within the object dimension: the Aristotelean, the Epicurean, the Stoic, and the Skeptic. All of them begin with the presupposition of a world of objects and events external to human experience and awareness. All agree that whatever knowledge or understanding human beings may have of this world, it must come, at least initially, through sense experience of it. The conceptual products of our intellects, minds, souls, or *pneuma* are derived from sensation and must correspond with the sensed.

However, I believe that there is in all of them an awareness that this assumption itself is not a product of simple sense experience, but rather created by the intellect within which it is made. And so, as with Plato earlier, in order to maintain their objective positions, they must in some fashion objectify intellect and the thinking processes. It is in their approaches to the possibilities of the latter that they begin to differ, raising in the course of their differences, many of the most important questions and problems of the object dimension.

1. Aristotle objectifies intellect in two ways: Firstly, by its division into active and passive elements in which the passive part, like wax, receives sense

impressions and the active then discovers in these passive contents the categories and classes of a universal and unchanging reality which can be understood and demonstrated logically using the categorical syllogism. Secondly, the thinking and reasoning soul of the human being is inserted into the individual in some unexplained fashion by the unmoved mover who is pure thought, its own essence, and the first cause of the phenomenal world. Because the intellect shares reasoning with this absolute intellect, it does not die when the body dies, and occupies a privileged position in matters of experience and knowledge which assures its objectivity as observer.

2. *The Epicureans*, while emphasizing sense experience, stress the sense of touch above the other senses. What exists, what can be seen, smelled, tasted, heard, must somehow be a body just as the organs or sense and the sensor are body. Only sense organ and sensor as body could sense the world as body.

3. *The Stoics* began with sensation in a necessary and determined world of experience. They certainly realized that questions as to this world's nature must originate in some unsensed source of sensing and the sensed. This was an inherent *logos*. Because the *logos* was implicit in the sensed objects, their presentations, the sensing process, and in the sensor, it could account for the correspondence between perception, conception, propositions, and the objects and events of the world.

4. *The Skeptics* stopped at sense experience of the object world. However, they realized that the decision to stop was not a product of sensation but of intellect, and so they turned intellect upon itself via the *tropes* for withholding judgment and insisted that one must be skeptical of the Skeptic method itself lest it lead to dogma beyond sensation. Because they start within the object dimension of philosophical space, they do not see infinite regress as more than incomplete or limited reasoning and criticize the dogmatists who believe they can extrapolate something more knowable within and about the object world from the object world.

6 The Handmaiden and the Handiwork

The nineteenth-century French social philosopher, Auguste Comte (1798–1857), claimed that the human intellect had historically evolved in three different stages: a *theological* one, a *metaphysical* one, and finally, in his own time, had entered into a *positive* and scientific stage.[1]

The theological stage, according to Comte, consisted of a fallacious and supernatural accommodation of experience and observation. In it, observed facts were explained by invented facts. The metaphysical stage was a bastardization stage in which explanations were neither completely supernatural nor completely natural as the intellect constructed abstract metaphysical interpretations of experience. The third and final stage was a definitively positive stage in which the intellect had at last abandoned all metaphysical fictions and begun to pursue a purely descriptive approach to nature. At this point, positive observation and verification determined all facts which were connected by positive laws which in turn were simple facts elevated to the status of universal principles as in the case of gravitation.[2]

It was as a resident of this positive stage that Comte felt he could objectively identify and review the preceding stages. The distinctions which appeared so obvious to Comte are as much ideological as historical. While he clearly placed the source of real knowledge in the external world, he dreamt of a new social order created by men of science who were by origin and nature European alone.[3] And to these new European men in this new age, *positivist religion* would be as necessary as *positivist science*, for positivist religion corresponds to positivist science and completes it morally and spiritually.[4]

Despite vast political and technological changes that have occurred over the centuries in the development of the object tradition, two fundamental beliefs expressed in Plato's *Philebus Dialogue* have endured. In the Dialogue, Socrates ask Protarchus whether all that we call the universe is a matter of irrational chance, or whether it is the product of a wonderful and wise intelligence. Protarchus considers the first possibility blasphemous, and the second obvious to anyone who looks at the order of the heavens and stars.[5] This Greek belief in order and a divine source of it merged easily in the Hellenistic age with Near Eastern monotheism which gave it a more stable form and a linear direction. This union has provided the framework for philosophy, science, religion, and art in the object tradition into the nineteenth century. And it will, according to Comte, become in a new positivist age a truly 'human religion' uniting science and 'human religion' in the worship of the 'Great Being'.[6]

One of the early and most important centers of the mixing of philosophy and theology was the city of Alexandria where astronomy, mathematics, mystery religions, Neo-Platonism, Neo-Pythagoreanism, Christianity, and Judaism encountered and influenced one another in an openness matched only later in the Italian Renaissance. This chapter examines some of the elements of that divine – cosmic – human complex that emerged in this Egyptian center of the Hellenistic world. We are particularly concerned with it as it provides a new theological basis for an object world which was to be progressively revealed to those who had the faith as well as the knowledge to understand it. Twenty centuries later the Nobel physicist, Max Planck, can assure an audience that this complementary union of religion and science in seeking to know the rational and orderly universe is alive and well, and that it still provides the foundation for knowing indirectly that which cannot be directly perceived.[7]

The analysis of this philosophical and theological mix has been separated into two parts in this chapter. The first part, *The Handmaiden*, covers some of the critical attempts to combine monotheistic religion with classical philosophy in such a fashion that Greek philosophy would serve as both a precursor and handmaiden or servant of Jewish and Christian theology. This was a theological whole in which Augustine could affirm that even though the Greek philosophers were not Christian, they should be exalted for having recognized the changeless in the changeable.[8]

The second part of the chapter, *The Handiwork*, discusses the consequences of this philosophy/theology synthesis and its implicit or explicit assumptions in classical and modern knowledge theory, especially in physical science where by the sixteenth to eighteenth centuries even the atoms had been given a divine origin and organization in the works of Gassendi (1592–1655), Boyle (1627–1691) and Newton (1642–1747). Boyle, for example, while accepting the atom theory, still objected to the ideas of Epicurus and Lucretius of fall and swerve as the origin of things, and suggested that this was even more unlikely than that a dropped box of printer's letters would spell out the creation story.[9] And Isaac Newton declared in his *Mathematical Principles of Natural Philosophy* that such a splendid system as that of the solar system could only be the product of a supremely great and intelligent Being.[10]

The handmaiden and the possibility of knowledge

We might well begin our journey back to Alexandria with the assistance of her most famous astronomer, Claudius Ptolemaeus (c.100–178 AD) who charted a divinely ordered and earth-centered universe observable from a divinely ordained and man-centered earth. This view was embraced by Christian and non-Christian alike, and clearly lent itself to the intertwining of Greek philosophy and astronomy with Christian dogma. Later, Luther and Galileo both discovered how difficult it could be to alter the one or the other.

Claudius Ptolemaeus introduced his cosmological *Almagest* with a separation of knowledge onto three interrelated planes: the highest was the theological, the lowest the physical, and between these two was the mathematical and rational which linked them.[11] These three planes might well stand for the three domains in one that was Alexandria. There was the domain of intellect composed of books and libraries, research and education. There was the physical domain of wealth and commerce which attracted merchants and their goods from around the known world. And there was the domain of the religious which brought together Neo-Platonism and Neo-Pythagoreanism, Judaism and Christianity in addition to the traditional gods of the traders. In this city of domains, within a period of two centuries, Christianity became philosophic and philosophy became Christian.[12]

Alexandria was the home of mathematicians and astronomers from Eratosthenes to Aristarchus to Ptolemaeus. The place where Archimedes studied as a young man and where Euclid compiled Greek mathematics (300 BCE). Here the Greek translation of the Hebrew scriptures, the *Septuagint*, was completed for a Jewish world more fluent in Greek than in Hebrew. Here the Neo-Platonist, Plotinus (205–270) was educated in the school of Ammonius Saccas, who had abandoned Christianity for Platonism, and among whose other pupils was Origen (c.182–251) who, like Augustine and Justin, abandoned Platonism for Christianity. Here one encounters the works of Philo Judaeus (c.20 BCE–40 AD) whose *logos* might be compared to the logos at the beginning of the Christian Gospel of St John because Philo believed God created the world and related to it by way of the divine *logos* which was both the image for the creation and its governing principle.[13] Philo was a Jewish philosopher who held Greek philosophy to be as divinely inspired as were the Moses Mysteries and he provided an allegorical analysis of Hebrew texts which justified this position by demonstrating that God had given to Greek and Jew alike the same revelation but in different philosophical terms. This was an idea continued a century later by the Christian, Clement of Alexandria (c.150–213).[14] Clement in his *Stromata* described two ways to one truth, the Greek and the Christian, and stressed their indispensability to one another.[15] Many Christian philosophers, like their Jewish counterparts, believed that Plato must have plagiarized insights from the Hebrew Moses.[16]

This Alexandria of the Ptolemeys possessed a library reported to have contained over 700,000 rolls. The destruction of the great library mirrored perhaps the destruction of the intellectual and political world that created it. The first fire was set accidentally by Caesar's forces in 47–8 BCE when Caesar found himself trapped in the palace at Alexandria and ordered the burning of the Egyptian fleet anchored in the harbor. The flames swept uncontrolled into the main section of the library. What was left was destroyed ultimately and completely by the Christian Patriarch, Theophilus, in 391 who established a monastery on the site.

The handmaiden synthesis had its origins in the common assumption of the Jew, Christian, and Greek that the universe is rational and intelligible because it was created by rational intelligence. For the seventeenth-century British physicist and chemist, Robert Boyle, in looking backward it was clear that most of the early Greek philosophers were believers in a deity.[17] This deity, however, as the source of first principles could itself have no first principle according to Plotinus (205–270 AD).[18] It was the 'Universal Principle' of all else and as such it was the beginning of existence into whose existence one cannot inquire. It is the answer which precedes all questions. Philosophy as handmaiden to theology can lead this far and no farther.

It is this view of an unknowable knower and uncaused first cause which most closely links Plato, Aristotle, and Plotinus to Hellenistic Christianity and Judaism. In Plato's 'Timaeus dialogue', Timaeus tells Socrates that although the creator of the world is beyond discovering, within his creation man can and must inquire into the patterns that the creator had in mind when he created all things.[19]

Circulating in Alexandria around 100 BCE was a Jewish apocryphal text entitled *Wisdom of Solomon* which claimed to outline God's revelation to Solomon via the divine Wisdom. It contains an excellent outline of the knowledge of nature that the object tradition has pursued in the centuries since:

> ... he hath given me certain knowledge of the things that are, namely, to know how the world was made, and the operation of the elements.
> 18. The beginning, ending, and midst of the times: the alternations of the turnings of the sun and the change of seasons:
> 19. The circuits of the years, and the positions of stars;
> 20. The natures of living creatures, and the furies of wild beasts: the violence of winds, and the reasonings of men; the diversities of plants, and the virtues of roots;
> 21. And all such things as are either secret or manifest, them I know.[20]

Plotinus believed that the creator and creation formed a hierarchy of levels of existence. At the highest level was the Divine which *is its own existence*. Like Augustine's view that God who created time could not be said to be in time, Plotinus' Divine can not be said to exist but is the source of the nature and existence of all things.[21] Einstein seemed to have been suggesting something similar when he claimed to be a 'pantheist', accepting like Spinoža a belief in a human unity with the whole.[22] For Plotinus, between the unknowable and what we might call the apparent world was the level of *Nous* or Mind. *Nous* is not the Divine, but within the Divine and it is *Nous* which engenders the world by 'thinking it'. This creates a harmonious whole which unites both thought and object of thought, that which thinks is mind, that which has being is the object of thought. This totality of thought and object is the source of 'otherness' and 'sameness'.[23] To the degree that the human mind and the Divine via *Nous* correspond in spirit, the human intellect can define time and existence without concerning itself with the time and existence of its definitions of 'time' and 'existence'.

The principle of otherness and sameness is implicit in the intellectual knowing of the world. There is an unbroken line from the '*One*' to the world Mind or '*Nous*' as the synthesis of thought and object of thought. On this line, the intellect occupies a middle ground as thinking being. It has thought objects but is not a thought object. The individual is like oil and water – a temporary mixture of two different natures, the soul and the body or 'beast'.[24] And so man is in the world physically, but not of the world spiritually. St Gregory of Nyssa affirms this mystery, even as he wonders at it. To Gregory, the material body cannot surround the non-material intellect, nor can the non-material intellect be contained in the material body.[25]

Despite the readiness with which Greek philosophy was welcomed by many early Christians as the handmaiden of theology, it brought with it a *handmaiden dilemma* which is implicit in the relationship of faith to reason in the object dimension. Does faith follow reason and thus one has reasonable faith, or does reason follow faith, and so one must have faith in order to reason? Augustine offered an interesting circular solution to this problem when he suggested that one must begin with faith, the faith that faith itself is reasonable, and this faith that faith itself is reasonable is reasonable, and so reason precedes even faith. This reasonableness of faith, he attributed, as did Plato, Aristotle, the Stoics, and the Neo-Platonists to the rational soul with which humans are endowed by the divine.[26] Gottfried Wilhelm Leibniz (1646–1716) later argued this view as well. Leibniz maintained that if both faith and reason were given to man by God, they could never run counter to one another because this would have God contradicting God. However, for Leibniz, if there does seem to be an irresolvable conflict, then faith must take precedence.[27]

In a modern resolution of the handmaiden dilemma, the German physicist, Max Born, in responding to a letter from Einstein, also noted that even physics with all of its exactness ultimately rests upon and cannot be reduced beyond acts of faith.[28] And for him three such acts were fundamental: faith in 'causality', faith in 'probability', and faith in 'objective facts' beyond subjective interpretations.[29] Albert Einstein too in reflecting upon modern physical science and its successes, was greatly moved by the rational order behind all that exists.[30]

This marriage of faith and reason is one of the most important characteristics of the handmaiden synthesis. For much of the object dimension, to believe that the world is intelligible and to identify intelligible orders in it is to have faith in a transcendent source of this intelligibility. The alternative would be to assume that intelligibility is a human projection upon sequences of events in history, science, social science, and philosophy. Leibniz disposed of this possibility for the early modern period by distinguishing the truths of reason into two types: (1) those which are mathematical, metaphysical or logical and which are absolute beyond doubt, and (2) those which are imposed upon Nature by God's laws. Neither of these is dependent upon the human intellect for its objective identity and existence.[31]

The handiwork: methods for knowing

'God saw everything that he had made, and behold it was very good.' (Genesis 1:31) The incorporation of Greek philosophy into Christianity tended to give philosophy and reason a clear advantage over the mystical and non-rational in theology. This distinction may not have been apparent to many Christian theologians. However, it was certainly clear to Tertullian (c.160–c.220), a Christian with a strong Stoic orientation, who asked 'What has Athens to do with Jerusalem?' He criticized this marriage of philosophy and theology as the product of men and demons done to satisfy the world's curiosity.[32] This position is echoed later in Luther and Calvin, and it retains a place among contemporary Jewish, Christian, and Moslem fundamentalists.

But for Clement of Alexandria in his *Exhortation to the Greeks*, reason can serve as a guide to God's handiwork, both the supernatural and the natural.[33] According to Augustine, the divine which is beyond reason and sense and yet is the source of reason and sense created a world amenable to reason and sense and then placed the human as the rational and sensible being in it to enjoy His handiwork.[34] Gregory of Nyssa taught that the rational and the sensible are the two keys to knowing the world as it is both directly and indirectly.[35] In possibility of indirect knowing, the handmaiden synthesis of faith and reason plays its most important role in the handiwork view of the world. And this has been one of the most important presuppositions of the object dimension over the centuries. It is this role of faith in knowing the unknowable that Max Planck believed permits us to find the rational in the irrational of experience. According to Max Planck, it is faith that helps the scientist to deal with the irrational and unknowable which he/she encounters in nature. At the same time, it is the unknowable which comprises the challenge to scientists and is the source of their interest. Without faith, there would be no science.[36]

In the *Summa Theologica*, Thomas Aquinas (1225–1274) affirmed that there were a number of ways of knowing the deity's existence, and one of these was through the creation itself. The *Summa*, written under the influence of the Aristotelean theory of universals and particulars, gave a new impetus to the study of particulars. In Aquinas' proofs for the existence of God, he sought to establish that the human intellect by reasoning through causal relationships and matters of contingency can achieve a reasonable proof of such an existence. In so doing, he gave to the law of causality both a natural and a divine sanction.[37] He does not deny the route of faith, but he separates natural from revelatory theology. Four centuries later, Newton will echo this emphasis upon observation when he claims that we know God through the excellent world of the things of creation and in understanding their ultimate causes.[38]

Thomas Aquinas does more than separate faith, reason, and observation. He counters the skeptics' questions as to the nature of truth and the possibility of knowing it. For the rational individual, truth is clearly self-evident for if one denies there is truth, this very denial depends upon truth for its truth and so confirms it.[39] In this position, neither truth nor reason is nor need be defined beyond true and reasonable usage.

Like the faith/reason dilemma of the handmaiden view, the assumption that the world is the deity's handiwork also contains a *relationship dilemma*. In this case it is the relationship of the meaning of scriptural texts to the meaning of natural phenomena. This is a critical problem. Both are often accompanied by an insistence that statements about either are to be taken literally. For example, this literalism is part of the sharp division between and among positions on evolution. The Aristotelean principle of identity objectively unites thing, thought and symbol. The very symbolization of nature presupposes not only that nature can be symbolized, but that human sign systems correspond to the deity's natural signs in some fashion. One view of this assumption is succinctly expressed in the twentieth century by the philosopher Seyyed Hossein Nasr who has written extensively both on Islam and the history and philosophy of science. According to Nasr there are two complementary texts of the world: nature and its laws, and the *Koran* and its rules and values. Both speak of God.[40]

Another version of the same assumption is found in the position on sign systems of many modern physical and social scientists. This is a view which holds that mathematical signs are the ultimate tools of rationality. In fact, within this perspective it may be assumed that, as the physicist James Jeans suggested, number is the only sign system in which the patterns and nature of the world order can be expressed.[41] This would seem to indicate, at least according to Jeans, that God is a 'mathematician'.

The mathematization of the world as God's handiwork presupposes that it can be mathematically described. And mathematical descriptions are possible, especially in a science based on observation and experiment, only if one can set aside universals, as absolutes in a Platonic or Aristotelean sense. This is essential if one is to shift identity from a divine category to a mathematical expression of a divinely established relationship. In this transition, the position of the Christian theologian, William of Occam (1285–1349) is of great significance.

Occam actively participated in the the Scholastic debate as to whether universals existed and if so how they related to particulars.[42] This dispute was a basic one, for the deity's handiwork was assumed to be the essence of universal classes and categories which defined particular individuals in reason and sense experience. Aristotle's position was that although awareness of universals begins in particular experience, science itself should be of universals for these carry the identity of the particulars.

According to Occam, experience is of individuals, but the human being possesses two kinds of cognition: one is *intuitive* and enables the mind to immediately cognize that an object exists, the other is *abstractive* and creates conjectures and assumptions from the data of the intuitive. These latter are the source of universals which exist only as concepts in the human intellect. Their origin, however, is in the objective particular. The problem for him was not that of discovering universals inherent in the world, but rather of deciding how individual objects can be designated in universal, abstract propositions. For Occam, logic is the rational science of names and propositions. Propositions in turn are composed of terms of first and second intention, that is, names which refer to individuals and names which refer to class concepts.

If one accepts Occam's position, universals are no longer the source of individual identities. The potential question this position introduces is that unless there are universals in the world as objective laws and existing common natures, can one assume that concepts have real, objective extension beyond their immediate sources in our individual interpretations? The physicist Sir James Jeans provides an interesting perspective on this universal to particular question when he compares the particle/wave positions of quantum theory by suggesting that the particles are indeed physical and move in physical space while waves are mental and move in 'conceptual spaces'.[43]

The implications of Occam's position on universals and particulars is apparent in the experimental and observational sciences of the sixteenth to eighteenth centuries where the laws of nature are related to increasingly specific observations facilitated by the invention of more sophisticated observational devices and technologies like telescopes, microscopes, vacuum chambers, pendulum clocks, and the creation and application of the mathematical analyses which observation and experiment required. One of the most famous examples of this latter was the simultaneous invention of the Calculus by both Newton and Leibniz.

Objectifying method: certainty and truth

If one assumes the reasonableness of nature as divine handiwork, then the next step is to identify methods of observation and analysis which rationally and/or empirically disclose the world to the objective observer who is now equipped to measure it. This is a world view in which answers precede questions, and it is one of the most important and useful consequences of the melding of Greek philosophy and monotheism.

One of the early leading proponents of empirical method, Francis Bacon (1561–1626) looked backward, as August Comte would later, to the Greek world. For Bacon, the Greeks represented the 'boyhood' of knowledge.[44] Bacon believed that the world needed a new method which could produce inevitable conclusions drawn from experience itself.[45] And he would claim for the application of his new method of induction that he had successfully ended the 'divorce' between reason and sense experience and saved the 'human family'.[46] His contemporary and one of the great modern methodological scientists, Galileo (1564–1642), saw the world as an 'open book', which anyone might read who had mastered the mathematical language in which it had been written.[47] Galileo's conflict with the church over the geocentric versus the heliocentric universe is an illustration of the signs of nature versus the signs of scripture dilemma. Charles Darwin's theory of evolution as God's handiwork will also encounter this 'textual' conflict in the nineteenth century.

The view of the world as God's handiwork and the view of man as its rational master committed to objectively knowing that handiwork, is one of the most important factors in the development of modern science. And the beginning of modern science is the beginning of the search for the methods which would reveal to the trained mind of the observer and experimenter the secrets that God had planted in this world. In the middle of the twentieth century, Wernher von Braun, one of the most successful masters of technological method and its application can wonder both at the success he has achieved in understanding and applying the laws of the divine in nature, and at the glimpse of the divine that nature and its laws permits him. This is a particularly important observation coming as is does from von Braun who was instrumental in the development of the German V2 rocket program during World War II and afterward of its successor in the United States.[48]

No process of objectification so clearly separates the post Renaissance and scientific age from the Greek and Medieval worlds as the discovery and application of objective observational technologies and methodologies and the resultant mathematization of the world. In Voltaire's *Philosophical Dictionary*, a philosopher asks Nature just who or what she is. Nature replies to the effect that she is just what is, and not a mathematician. Therefore, how would she know. She also suggests that if he is interested, he might try guessing.[49]

Two great examples of the axiomatization and justification of method occur in the sixteenth and seventeenth centuries. One is born on the Continent in the *Discourse on Method* of Descartes (1596–1650), the French philosopher and mathematician. The other occurs in England as the 'Rules of Reasoning' in *Newton's Mathematical Principles of Natural Philosophy*. Supplementing and complementing one another, these served as a basis for objective philosophy and science in the following centuries. Descartes is more concerned with reason, Newton with observation.

Descartes, upon completion of his studies, surveyed what he had learned and decided that there was nothing that could not be doubted. In this spirit he set about designing a method which would permit him to critically evaluate whatever passed for knowledge. He first rejected the Aristotelean and Scholastic syllogism as simply a system for restating what one already knew. In its stead he outlined his own four analytic steps in the *Discourse*: (1) He would accept nothing as true which was not obviously so. (2) In achieving this, he would divide any problem or possibility into as many parts as necessary for the sake of clarity. (3) He would then begin his analysis with the simplest parts and gradually work in an orderly way to the most complex. (4) Finally he would list all the steps he had taken in his line of analysis and re-examine them to make sure he had left nothing out.[50]

The *Cartesian method* was a rational one in which the restrictions of reason were presumed to take precedence over both sense and faith, and it produced for him the absolutely certain *Cogito ergo sum* whose very doubt would prove its truth. He claims that until he discovered the divinely instilled, rational principle in himself, he could in no wise distinguish himself physically from all other life forms. Once he grasped this principle and the certainty that it brought, he realized how different the human intellect is from the rest of the world.[51]

Newton as an astronomer and observer was interested in the phenomenal world and would have nothing to do with *hypotheses* which could not be related back to *phenomena*. As a result, his four rules are far more closely related to empirical analysis of the scientist: (1) His first rule was that one should accept no more causes of natural phenomena than are true and adequate to explain their appearances. (2) Then to the same effects one should seek to apply as completely as possible the same causes. (3) As one observes, one should take as universal qualities of bodies, those qualities which could be neither increased nor decreased by degrees. (4) Finally, in all experiments one should look upon the inductive propositions that have been inferred from observations as accurate and true, regardless of contrary hypotheses, until such time as they can be completely demonstrated, or until exceptions can be found to them.[52]

Modern puzzles and problems of the object dimension

Skepticism and certainty

No philosopher of the eighteenth century so clearly identified the limitations of knowledge and the implications of the handmaiden and handiwork dilemmas as did the English philosopher, David Hume (1711–1775), who believed that all ideas can be traced back to simple impressions.[53] Hume titled part iv of his *Treatise of Human Nature* 'Skeptical and other systems of Philosophy', and in it, like his Greek and Roman predecessors, he argued for a skepticism which withholds judgment for the sake of further inquiry, urging that his contemporaries confess their ignorance when matters go beyond our limited ability to know.[54]

Hume believed that impressions and ideas could be divided into two classes, simple ones based on particular sensations, and complex ones composed of parts as in the case of an apple which combines smell, taste, color, texture.[55] From these simple impressions and complex ideas derived from them, all else proceeds as matters of fact and relation of ideas. For example, any discussion of mind or soul must go back to the impressions which are its source.[56] He believed that the basic laws of thought which govern the association of ideas are firstly the resemblance of different impressions, secondly, the continuity of objects and events in time and space, and thirdly, cause and effect.[57]

Of course many concepts are products of the imagination which is free to combine impressions in the creation of myths and legends. But imagination is not free in that even in its myths, it must return to specific sensations.[58] Like Sextus Empiricus, Hume affirms the object world and impressions of it, while he questions the nature of explanations and interpretations.

What then is knowledge? Hume's answer has become the answer in contemporary physical science for it suggests that all knowledge is ultimately only knowledge of probability and experience.[59] Hume realized that probability is never certain knowledge but rather the beginning of a mathematical and statistical regress of perception and conception and of knowledge and doubt. This is a process in which on one level one examines what one has asserted to be probably true on another.[60] Thus, all branches of knowledge are, as Protagoras had earlier suggested, matters of 'human knowing'. Affirm or deny whatever we will, we cannot escape that it is man that affirms of denies, sees and interprets.[61]

Hume claimed that logic and reason, which have historically co-ordinated faith in an intelligible world with sense experiences of it, do not give us the world, but only probabilistically relate impressions and matters of fact to abstract concepts and relations of ideas in linear sequences. Two historical positions of the object dimension of philosophical space were called in question by Hume's *Treatise*: The first is the assumption of an intelligible world created by a transcendental intelligence in such a fashion that the orders superimposed upon it correspond to the orders that the human mind projects onto it. The second assumption is that the human intellect occupies a privileged position in the world and can separate its ideas and explanations from that which it observes.

While accepting as a starting point Hume's critical assault on the certainties of *natural philosophy* and *religion*, his continental contemporary, Immanuel Kant (1724–1804) was disturbed by the relativity and subjectivity that its emphasis upon sensation implied. Kant's first concern was for the restoration of the position of the human intellect, a position which for him was the source of *a priori* and, therefore, *certain knowledge*. Without this privileged position, mathematics would not exist nor would logic, or if so, their operations too could only be probabilistic. Basic physical concepts like time, space, substance, causality, would also be called in question for they cannot be found in sense experience. Kant examines both pure reason and sense experience and arrives at rational categories which he claims are both prior to experience and necessary conditions for it.

In the *Prolegomena* in answering the question as to how nature itself is possible, he decides that the *human possibility* of knowing nature is the *possibility of nature* in the human mind and senses. Therefore in seeking to understand nature's possibility we must turn our attention to the conditions of knowledge and experience that are the givens of our minds and senses. It is in conformity of our ability to perceive and conceive and the nature of the world as it conforms or corresponds to our abilities, that the synthesis of empirical knowledge is possible.[62]

Kant divided nature into the *phenomenal* world which we know through our senses, and the *noumenal* world which is what nature is in itself and is therefore unknowable. But the rational intellect does possess certain a priori categories which are never empirical but provide the objective framework for thinking and our interpretation of sensation. These extend in a progression of ideas from the idea of the unity of the thinking self to the absolute unity of the series of conditions of phenomena to a unity of the condition of all objects of thought in general. These three unities provided the intuitive basis for three sciences: the science of the soul or psychology, the science of phenomena or cosmology, and the science of the possibility of the totality of all that can be conceived, which is theology.[63]

Certainty for Kant moved from the world of sense to the world of pure reason, from whence it makes empirical knowledge possible. In this respect, syllogistic logic as the product of reason had attained perfection beyond all subjectivity.[64] The question was, as with Descartes, can the certainty of reason be extended to empirical knowledge? Kant's answer was a qualified 'yes', for he believed we possess 'certain cognitions a priori' which relate thought to sensation. For example, were one to remove all ideas and actual experiences and interpretations of a physical object, the one idea that could not be removed would be that of 'substance'.[65] As with Descartes, the *privileged position* of the reason is preserved. The pure reason does know with certainty its own operations and by extension, knows the world of experience as it conforms to these.

From a Kantian perspective, the emphasis upon observation and experiment in the object tradition strengthens the belief in the power of human reason, for it seems to clearly demonstrate how the senses, under the leadership and control of reason can probe into the nature and behavior of the physical things as they relate to experience, and he saw this as Isaac Newton's great achievement.

This *reason/sense distinction* persists even when reason is assumed bestowed upon man by nature slowly through evolution and not by a creating deity. An evolutionary biologist can maintain that human rational faculties and the parameters of their contents as orders of space, time, and causality provide the frameworks for all experience and interpretation and are objective because, as survival mechanisms in the object world in which human beings have evolved these mechanisms are products of that world and its evolving nature. For example, Friedrich Cramer at the Max Planck Institute for Experimental Medicine suggests on the one hand that our brain and the faculties and techniques that it has evolved in successfully surviving must therefore reflect the world as it is. Thus if our 'worldview apparatus' did not correspond to the world we would not have survived.[66] When asking himself if this view of evolution and survival includes the possibility of a divine source of the world's meaning, he answers with a clear affirmative, and emphasizes that it is not the business of science to prove or disprove the existence of God. This is beyond its capabilities.[67]

Objects as parts and wholes

The intellect versus object dichotomy that the object dimension of philosophical space inherited from Plato and Aristotle has historically facilitated observation of nature by reducing it to specific parts and systems. Such a reductionist approach has allowed simplification of very complex wholes into their constituent elements. One then assumes that the predictability of isolated elements applies to the wholes from which they have been isolated. The advantage of this assumption as the physicist Joe Rosen points out is that it has greatly simplified nature by permitting the human intellect to remove itself from it. Rosen suggests, however, that relative as this assumption of observer versus observed may be, it generally works and has made the advancements we associate with science over the last 400 years possible. But for him, we have arrived at a point in our knowledge and understanding where, at least at the *micro level* it cannot be made anymore for regardless of technical precision and advancement, we are clearly part of the whole.[68]

In the other direction, the potential chaos of dynamic wholes like weather changes, turbulence in fluids, interacting environmental forces, erratic heart filibrations seem to defy attempts to arrive at specific orders and predictions. Objectivity is preserved in this direction by concepts of *deterministic chaos* and *chaotic determinism*, *fractals* and *feedback loops*. These theories express both an infinite regress in the search for specificity and at the same time, indicate possibilities for accommodating and avoiding such regresses in practical observation and experiment. Thus one can accept the theory of a determined world while emphasizing the predictability of phenomena in the short term but recognizing their unpredictability in the long term because even the smallest error, change, or uncertainty when amplified though a system renders unpredictable that which may seem to be predictable in the short term.[69]

Using the models and techniques for observing and analyzing chaos, scientists and mathematicians now seek the objectivity of a 'predictability horizon' rather than a specific effect or consequence. This horizon is then considered the limit of the predictable. Beyond it one cannot attain predictive certainty.[70] One of the best illustrations of this possibility is the idea of the fractal which expresses unlimited potential variation within the ultimately limited as in the case of branching within a growing head of cauliflower, the variations on a coastline, or the computer modeling of the 'Mandelbrot set'.

It would seem at the end of the twentieth century that the separation of observer from observed, and reason from body no longer holds. Rather, such distinctions are much like the infinite 'feedback continuum' of a video camera broadcasting itself into a monitor as it records its own broadcasting of its broadcasting of its broadcasting, ad infinitum. As the biologist Friedrich Cramer like the physicist, Joe Rosen, stresses we can no longer separate ourselves as observers from the world observed. We are the biological organism that studies and thinks about biological organisms. We are evolution studying evolution.[71]

Now what?

What are the possibilities for objectivity and objectification if we are no longer privileged observers of a clear and distinct handiwork world of things, events, and processes? A number of possibilities suggest themselves. They are not mutually exclusive and they presuppose some version of the unity of faith and knowledge which is the Alexandrian heritage.

1. One might retain objectivity by transferring it from the objects observed to the instruments and methodologies employed in observation. This would assume that the objectivity of the method reflects the nature of that to which the method is applied thus setting aside concerns as to the relationship between objectified method and methodological objectification. However, Hume's skepticism of observation and reason, Kant nothwithstanding, leads in an increasingly relativitistic quantum universe to questions as to whether there really is a method, a 'scientific method' upon which one can rely in order to know. Karl Popper's answer is an emphatic 'no' in three fundamental respects: There is no method which discovers scientific theories and principles. And when one has such theories and hypotheses, there is no ultimate method of verification. Finally, there is no method of determining whether a hypothesis is even probable.[72] Popper, however, claimed that his rejection of the 'illusions of a scientific method' is not a rejection of objective knowledge, but rather perhaps a necessary condition, for it permits us to see science as a 'social institution' which reflects the lives and goals of scientists who are interested in the growth of knowledge.[73] In this respect he then developed an approach to verification which depended upon looking for those instances

and conditions in reference to a hypothesis or theory which would falsify it.[74] The method then is not one of proof but of disproof.

2. A second possibility rests upon a Neo-Pythagorean belief in a universe, which if not mathematical *in essence*, at least is mathematical *in form*, and so ever amenable to the number theories and systems we devise to capture and express it. This would mean that objective data reflect the latter rather than the former. This approach, for example, is more concerned with computer and mathematical models and the objectivity of these, than it is with the correspondence of these models to actual states and conditions.

If the computer model permits projection of probabilities, these need not necessarily take into account the actual identities, variations, and/or even perhaps existence of that which is modeled. The model possesses its own identity and it is this which is the source of its predictive value. This approach would suggest any system is its relationships to other systems and not to something called the world. One can then concentrate upon and explore variations and connections between models and systems of measurement.[75] Within this approach it is clear that the problem or question around which a model or theory is constructed becomes the source of solutions and answers provided. One can use the *Newtonian model* of space to perform certain operations and the *Einsteinian model* to perform others without asking which is 'correct'. Each represents a different vocabulary and model suited to a different objective view of space. This is what Bruce Gregory, Associate Director of the Harvard-Smithsonian Center for Astrophysics, terms 'inventing reality'.[76] This objectification of instrument and methodology in models does not imply that these models are arbitrary. They work and their very success (depending upon how work may be defined in the object tradition) verifies their objective natures. As Bruce Gregory suggests, physics is not arbitrary, but it also only indirectly refers to nature. Thus Einstein and Newton are *complementary* and *compatible*.[77]

In this view of a modeled reality, the relationship of observer to observation also changes, for after all it is the model and measurement which defines 'reality' and not immediate observation of specific objects. The model now carries its own identity, and in part this identity is given to it by its creator, the mathematician, the computer programmer, the scientist for whom it is a sign system, a way of speaking. There is no longer an observer separated from the 'real'.[78] This is a mathematician's reality and rational in this sense. In this mathematical universe, we find the mathematician's answer to Nature's question in Voltaire's *Philosophical Dictionary*: Clearly since nature does not 'know' mathematics, there must be some other supreme intelligence who is responsible for her patterns and operations.[79] Perhaps there is a 'Grand Mathematician', James Jeans might say, who is both the inspiration and colleague of his/her/its human counterpart whose brain was made in this God's mathematical image.[80]

3. A third possibility, which is an extension and necessary condition of the former three, entails what could be called objectifying by 'de-subjectifying' the thought processes of observers. The mathematician, Gottlob Frege, for example made an important distinction between the *subjectivity of thinking* and the *objectivity of thought*. The former is the act of thinking, the latter its objective content which transcends the individual thinker.[81]

If one is to construct objective models and experiments, one must turn the thinking processes into thoughts, or logical structures and assure that these are themselves objective. This is to insure that reasoning processes carry their own identities, are clearly understood, are universal, and thus neither relative nor arbitrary. This view goes back to Aristotle and even beyond, and historically has tended to equate logic with particular expressions of formal and two-valued systems. Since it is the intellect's faculty of reason which from its privileged position as observer, reduces sense experience to rational forms and mathematical expressions, it is in the final analysis reason itself that must be objectified. This objectification of reason in the nineteenth and twentieth centuries has taken a formal direction which seeks to separate syntactic structure from semantic content.

The formal or syntactic objectification of reason was presumed to require a *precising* of logic which would enable one to identify and use logical structures more effectively to identify and establish consistency and freedom from contradiction, not necessarily, Ernst Mach suggested, to produce new knowledge.[82] In this sense, using a mathematical model, the precision of logic might ultimately lead to the fulfillment of Leibniz's dream that an 'alphabet of human thought' might be created that would reveal all that can be thought and judged.[83] This has led to the attempt to bring mathematics and logic together by mathematicizing logic into special abstract symbol systems or symbolic logics, while also discovering the logical relationships that underlie the axioms of mathematics as Russell and Whitehead suggested. This was the goal of the *Principia Mathematica*.[84]

Modern symbolic logic is a computing logic. The view of thinking as computing certainly goes back into Greek antiquity. The Pythagoreans believed the nature of the world to be *number* and believed that thinking itself was bound by number.[85] Plato emphasized geometry as a preparation for philosophy. The concept of thinking as computing appears in the *Ars Magna* of the Spaniard Raymond Lull (1235–1315), who tried to devise a technique for automatically establishing the truth of judgments by combining them on a series of overlapping disks which when rotated would mechanically connect positions and determine truth. Three hundred years later, Leibniz (1646–1716), inspired in part by Lull's work on a 'combinatory chart of judgments,' tried to provide a calculus of propositions which would make syllogistic logic as accurate as 'mathematical reasoning'. The goals or Lull and Leibniz were renewed in modern times in attempts to distinguish between meaningful and meaningless statements. The late English philosopher, A.J. Ayer, for example, tried to devise such criteria of meaning, and settled upon 'verification'. A proposition would be meaningful if it could be verified either logically or empirically. The first would involve mathematics, the second sense data. If a proposition were not verifiable, it was meaningless.[86]

As to how successful this synthesis of mathematics and logic has been, there is considerable disagreement with representatives on both sides suggesting that despite certain achievements in understanding, the two can only be artificially forced together and cost each more in clarity than is accomplished. Formalists like Hilbert argued for its value, intuitionists like Brouwer and Weyl rejected its formal limitations.

Questions at the End

As we prepare to leave the object dimension of philosophical space, perhaps it would be well to raise some of the questions that the dimension currently faces in light of changes in science, international relations and economics, religion, philosophy, art. I make no claim that these are comprehensive, but do see them as most important.

1. Is the world *rational* in some sense? For example, is nature rational/mathematical and the human intellect as a natural product is thus rational in the way in which nature is? Or is the human intellect alone rational and thus nature as a product of the human intellect is so? Is this question even relevant at the end of the twentieth century? Has objectivity perhaps become *ideology*?

2. Can *skepticism* provide a basis for objectivity and objective knowledge because it claims to entertain no or few subjective dogmas?

3. Is the assumption of a *transcendental source* for the intelligibility of nature necessary to the objective analysis of nature, particularly when this entails choices between and among explanations, interpretations, and theories as these apply to man/nature relationships? Does the object dimension without an external co-ordinating and/or creating source of objects and objectivity confront a world of infinite sense details and fragments in which the apparent not the real is real? If so can wholes be objectively retained or are these subjective interpretations?

4. Would or could a modern *Stoic/Einsteinian pantheism* provide an objective view of nature by placing reason into nature as a natural element

originating and upholding the principles of identity, non-contradiction, and excluded-middle? And might there also be a corresponding innate, circular or multi-valued logic which transcended individual linear logics?

5. Are the *value systems* of the object dimension – ranging from true/false dichotomies, to ethical issues to environmental choices and planning – which confront the object dimension of philosophical space, dependent upon an objective metaphysics and epistemology? And if this is the case, then would they still hold within a relative view of the world?

6. Does the human intellect occupy a *privileged position* as observer, mathematician, interpreter of nature? If so, is such a position possible without a soul or special quality which separates the human from the animal, the animate from the inanimate, a position which enables it to apply, define, understand, and explain this natural order? If not, then how are objective propositions, understanding, knowledge applications possible? Can this question be asked? Can it be answered?

7. Can we *objectify* at the same time in the same sense *wholes/parts*, waves/particles, mind/brain, logical content/logical form, observer/observed without reducing one to the other? If so, how? Does the difference in identity in each case call for a different process of objectification or treat a different object? Is there a principle in these pairs which unites them all?

Part II

The Subject Dimension of Philosophical Space

7 Consciousness: One Chariot and Two Views of the Galaxy

The dimensions of philosophical space are like optical illusions in which one clearly sees one figure but not another until a sudden modification of attention makes the second visible and the first disappear. With practice, one can move ever more quickly between the two but cannot see both at the same instant. We encounter this characteristic of optical illusions when we try focusing our attention in the object and subject dimensions of philosophical space. The object tradition tends to speak of subjects from the perspective of the objects of knowledge. The subject tradition tends to speak of objects from the perspective of knowing and interpreting subjects for whom objects are perceptions and conceptions. The early Greeks inquired into the relationship of the real to the apparent world of experience. Much of Indian philosophy is concerned with the relationship of consciousness to the perceptual and conceptual objects of consciousness. These two positions complement one another.

In a well known analogy, the *Kāṭha Upaniṣad* takes both dimensions for a chariot ride in which the body is the chariot, the traveler is the self or consciousness, the intellect is the driver, the mind is the reins, the senses are the horses and the desires and inclinations are the highways over which the vehicle is drawn. When an individual lacks understanding and discrimination, the reins are loosely held, the senses seize the bits, and the chariot races out of control. But when an individual has understanding and discrimination, then there is control, the horses obey the reins and life has focus and direction.[1]

Following as it does upon our survey of the object dimension, perhaps our introduction to the subject participant in the chariot ride might best begin with modern science where, due to changing theories and to ever more precise observations, there is an increasing sensitivity to the nature and position of the knowing subject. The comments of two physicists illustrate the paradox of objective awareness in which either no subject occurs or the subject is irrelevant. Erwin Schrödinger noted the 'remarkable situation' in which: '... the stuff from which our world picture is built is yielded exclusively from the sense organs as organs of the mind ... the conscious mind itself remains a stranger within that construct, it has no living space in it, you can spot it nowhere in space'.[2] His English contemporary, Sir Arthur Eddington, questioned both the use and source of the idea of objectivity:

> Objectivity is not a defining property, but a property which we had (wrongly, as it happens) expected the thing defined by other properties to possess. That being so, we must examine open-mindedly whether the physical universe possesses objectivity, and not try to smuggle in the objectivity as part of its definition.[3]

In both the subject and situational dimensions of philosophical space, *consciousness* or self is considered fundamental as the origin of attention toward and awareness of things, for the subject provides the unity in the multiplicity of experience. Things are not the origin of attention and curiosity, though they may constitute the objects of attention on the part of a subject. In traditions which emphasize the subject aspect of experience, a world of external, non-mental things and thing relationships would still presuppose attention and intention, not vice versa.

One difficulty in trying to talk about consciousness is that because so much of our knowledge originates with sensation, and since our concepts often seem constructed entirely from sense experience, we thus assume that consciousness is limited to or is defined by sensation and must be experienced as an object of sensation if it exists and is to be experienced at all. This confuses the process and possibility of perceiving, conceiving, and knowing with the end products of the processing. The Indian philosopher, Dr Sarasvati Chennakesaven, describes self as both *essential* and *contingent*. The essential is the observing self, the contingent depends upon observations and sensations as in our experience of pain, color, sound.[4]

The self as essential is the source of the meaning and interpreting of experience. As contingent, it knows and acts and is dependent upon external events. The essential self is the same in asking as in answering, in telling lies as in telling the truth, in explaining as in defining and describing. And because this self is the source of all these processes but the product of none, it is both *processing* of meaning and its *possibility*. Consciousness as processing and possibility, conceiving and the possibility of conceiving, seems to liberate one from things and fixed mental states, for it is the possibility for reflecting upon one's actions or changing one's mind and attitudes.

As the source and possibility of meaning, function and purpose, consciousness is meaningless. Or put another way, the meaning of self is *ascribing* meaning, its function is *determining* function. This explains our search for our own meanings in the objects of awareness to which we have assigned meaning, and, when we do not find our selves in our possessions, meaning anxieties often ensue. This is the paradox of self which in one direction gives significance to the ideas and things it encounters, and in the other direction tries to find its significance in the institutions and events to which it had assigned significance. It does this by joining groups, acquiring possessions, submitting to belief systems, misunderstanding thereby that the meaning of self is ascribing meaning not finding it. Thus we mistake interpretations for interpreting, explanations for explaining, objects of consciousness for consciousness. And in the chariot ride, the driver and horses and reins become the passenger, while the passenger tries to pull the vehicle along the road from birth to death.

Several Indian *Upaniṣads* tell of an argument among the various elements of the human body as to which was the most indispensable.[5] In order to resolve the dispute each organ agreed to leave for a year. At the end of this test, that element and its capacity which had been missed the most would be the most valuable and therefore worthy of the greatest respect from the others. The absence of each of the senses certainly diminishes the quality of life of the individual who is blind or deaf or without touch for that period. Even when the mind goes, life continues in a vegetative state. But when the self-consciousness, the vital-breath or *prāna* departs, the *Upaniṣads* tell us all else perishes.[6]

Perhaps we can avoid confusing self with the objects of awareness if we realize that the terminology we select for any statement about either consists of a set of linguistic conventions which as words are written symbols or spoken sounds with two objective qualities: they are used to name objects and experiences of objects, and they are themselves symbol objects which can be placed in dictionaries and passed from one individual to another as the physical representations of our thoughts.

But is self-awareness or consciousness of consciousness possible outside of language conventions, and if so how? To understand consciousness, but not to objectify it into some thing or term is to turn attention inward to one's being conscious. This is the function of various Indian techniques for facilitating self-awareness via meditation, and yogic practice which help distinguish between states of consciousness of objects and consciousness without objects.

The root meaning of the Sanskrit term *manas* is measuring, just as it is the root of the Greek *mensas*. Can that which measures be measured either by that which it measures or by that which it uses to measure? Can the true meter or kilogram or yardstick be measured by itself to determine its true length or weight, or is there a quantum leap outside any system which defines the system – a leap which entails consciousness, not as awareness of the length of a 'piece of string', but awareness of length and of measuring.

Consciousness as awareness of one's surroundings is directed outward via the senses as in 'the light is blinding', 'the air is cold', 'the music is too loud'. Most Indian systems view mind as a sense too and its objects are also external or outside, at least in their sources.[7] But consciousness as the field of all these kinds of sense awareness including mind sense is an internal unity which travels with one from room to room and experience to experience.[8]

Consciousness as awareness of one's mental states as in 'I know that I know', is the possibility of considering what one knows and even of changing of one's mind. Dr Sarasvati Chennakesaven, in her study of the concept of mind in India, maintains that: 'Consciousness is not mere knowing, it involves transcendence of the objects known and the knowing process. Mind is that which has a locus in time and space, whereas consciousness is that which is not limited either by time or space, but is that which gives a meaning to these.'[9] And she adds that 'It is because Indian thinkers have realized from very early times that manas is only an instrument of knowledge for the self, that Indian psychology has taken a different line of development than that of Western psychology.'[10]

As consciousness I am not what my body and mind have become, nor can I become my mind and body. As subject, I cannot objectify *I* or self or awareness because I would be mistaking mirror images for looking into the mirror. I do not see the seeing in seeing, the function of functioning. Consciousness has no function and no meaning – only so can it be the source of 'functioning' and 'meaning'.[11] Perhaps the purpose of asking 'what is the meaning of life' questions is becoming aware of 'life as purposing'.

If we understand awareness as the immediate and undefinable state of being aware, we can then begin to grasp the Indian concept of conservation of consciousness, as the constant self in all changing states of awareness. This can also be extended to transmigration of consciousness (not ego). Just as the principle of the conservation of matter holds that matter is never limited to or by any of its apparent forms, so is awareness as self not limited to or by any of its objects, nor any of the individual points from which it would seem to emanate. As death of the body in materialism is not the death of matter, so the end of ego states which arise from ideas of possession, like my, mine, is not the end of consciousness. This is perhaps best grasped if one attempts to define death and then examines as introspectively as possible what aspect of one's consciousness makes such defining possible, and what aspect of one's experience remains undefined in any definition of death?

The *Kāṭha Upaniṣad* begins with the story of a young man, Naciketas, who has been sacrificed to Yama, the God of Death, by his father in a fit of anger. Naciketas proceeds to Yama's dwelling, but must wait three days for Yama's return from his travels. As compensation to Naciketas for the delay,

Yama grants him three requests. His first two wishes are simple: to return to life and be reconciled with his father. He then asks to be taught the fire sacrifice which will carry him to the gods. Yama grants both of these. The third request, however, is quite different, for Naciketas wants to know what death really is. Yama does not want to grant this request and offers him instead all sorts of alternatives: 'Whatever desires are difficult to attain among mortals, ask for them according to thy wish ... but do not ask me about dying.' Naciketas, however, replies: 'Shall we possess wealth, when we see thee? Shall we live, as long as thou rulest?' To all of Yama's attempts to discourage him, Naciketas points out that: 'another teacher like thee is not to be found'.[12]

The West has spent centuries seeking to identify and utilize the laws governing the physical world and the nature of motion, direction of heat flow, physical causal relationships. Many Indian scientists and philosophers have spent centuries turning *being aware* upon states of *awareness* in order to better understand the nature of understanding. The modern world needs both.

The Indian world view is one in which consciousness or the potential for being aware of one's self and of the world of things is a unifying and central concern.[13] This does not mean that there are no disagreements. There are, particularly when Indian philosophers discuss the relationship of self to the world of which we are aware.

General historical background

In this and the next three chapters, we shall examine schools that have for centuries explored the possibilities of incorporating consciousness into analyzing and experiencing the object world. A number of them have developed special reasoning methodologies to facilitate this process, and we will discuss these methodologies in the subject logics of the Jains and the situational logics of the Nyāyas and Buddhists. However, before we explore these particular systems and logics in greater detail, it is important to introduce some of the general historical and philosophical parameters of the classical world view within which they developed. These systems reflect a civilization contemporary with that of the Pre-Socratic Greeks. And as with the Greeks, this is a period in which the first great questions as to the nature of the world and the place of human awareness in it are posed.

There are a number of tensions in the early history of India. Some of these are the consequences of the Āryan invasion from north some time between 2500 and 1000 BC. The Āryans were warring, nomadic worshipers of sky gods who were often warriors too. These gods, although transcendent, could be invoked with appropriate rituals to participate in the affairs of the world. In the Āryan hierarchy, the priest who communicated with the gods was above the warrior who needed this divine help. This is reflected in the respective place of priests and warriors/rulers in the caste system.

The conquered, indigenous, Dravidian peoples were farmers and traders who had built great cities at Mohnejo Daro and Harappa. Like agricultural peoples in many areas, they worshiped the Mother Goddess and celebrated her in rites and rituals related to the cycling and repeating seasons.[14]

The early history of India is the history of both conflict and cultural synthesis. The *Vedas* which were the sacred hymns of the early Āryans consist of incantations, chants and rituals, prayers, and supplications to a pantheon of deities. These texts can be compared to prayers and hymns to sky gods in other cultures. However, in other ways some of the Vedas were quite different from their counterparts, for in them was the beginning of a critical doubt. An excellent example of this is found in the 'Creation Hymn' from the *10th Rig Veda* which asks after the origins of the world:

> Who verily knows and who can here declare it, whence it was born and whence comes this creation?
> The gods are later than this world's production. Who knows, then, whence it first came into being?
> He, the first origin of this creation, whether he formed it all or did not form it,
> Whose eye controls this world in highest heaven, he verily knows it, or perhaps he knows not.[15]

This hymn shows an attitude that will be central in many of the texts (*Upaniṣads*) of the forest hermits, or *Riṣis*, who probably represented a resurgence of Dravidian cyclic nature perspectives. For example where Indra appears as the supreme warrior in the *Rig Veda*, in the later *Chāndogya Upaniṣad*, he has become a humble if divine pupil seeking to understand the cosmic cycles of suffering, birth and death, to the end that he too might be liberated from the process of transmigration.[16] Many historians have seen this cyclic view of life and death in Indian thought, as a triumph of the indigenous Mother Goddess over the Āryan Vedas.[17] From this point on, the cycle of births and deaths becomes a major concern of all schools, even those who ultimately reject it.

Histories of Indian philosophy usually divide it into four periods: (1) The Vedic age from approximately 2500 to 600 BC. This includes the Vedas, the *Brāhmaṇas*, and the *Upaniṣads*. (2) The Epic period from approximately 600 to 200 BC, which produced the two great Indian Epics, the *Mahābhārata* and the *Ramayana*. This is also the birth period of the nine schools of philosophy that have encompassed Indian thought since. Three of these were systems which rejected the *Vedas* completely: the Cārvākas, the Jains, and the Buddhists. The six remaining schools considered themselves essentially part of the Vedic tradition. These six are generally grouped into three pairs based upon affinities between and among them. There are the Nyāya–Vaiśeṣika, Sāṃkhya–Yoga, and Pūrva Mīmaṁsā–Vedānta. (3) The Sūtra period from 100–400 AD. In this period the texts of the various philosophical schools are written down. Finally, (4) the Commentary period from the Sūtra period to the seventeenth century in which vast number of commentaries and commentaries upon commentaries were written on these sūtras.

There is also a difference between those schools which denied the existence of the gods, or viewed them as irrelevant as was the case with the Cārvākian materialists, the Buddhists, the Jains, the Sāṃkhya; and those schools which accepted deities in some form as in the Yoga, Vedānta, Mīmaṁsā, Nyāya, and Vaiśeṣika. Although all systems discuss consciousness and awareness, there is disagreement as to the nature of individual self. The Jain and Sāṃkhya view the self as unique and individual. The Cārvākians and the Buddhists deny there is a self. The Advaita Vedāntins see the individual self as an emanation (*Ātman*) of the cosmic Self (*Brahman*). Since each of these positions, except for the Cārvākians and perhaps the early Sāṃkhya was concerned with transmigration and liberation, their paths to liberation were different.

The Indian social and religious world contains in general four castes: priest/teacher, ruler/warrior, merchant/farmer, laborer/slave. In the *Rig Veda X*. 90, in which the story of the division of the *puruṣa* or person that is the essence of the world is discussed, a number of questions are asked in reference to caste: Firstly, in how many parts was *puruṣa* divided, and how were these parts arranged as the mouth, arms, thighs, and feet? The answer is that each of these parts became the foundation of one of the castes. The mouth produced the priestly *brāhmin*, the arms the warrior *kṣatriya*, the thighs the merchant/farmer *vaiśya*, and the feet the laborer *śūdra*.

An individual's life span in a caste was divided into four stages. To each of these stages a code of behavior and responsibility was associated: The first stage of life was that of the child, student, and dependent (*brahmacarya*). The second was that of the parent, founder, and supporter of the family (*gārhasthya*). These first two stages involve familial and social responsibilities and ethics.[18] They take the individual consciousness out into the world as an active participant – learning as a student and later providing a living and founding a family as a householder. The third is the stage of the elder (*vānaprastha*) in which consciousness is increasingly concentrated upon self-awareness instead of the world. The individual is gradually withdrawing from worldly affairs and leaving them to her/his descendants. The final stage is that of the completely withdrawn person who is preparing for death and liberation (*sannyāsa*). The performance of these last two stages is not required by ethic and duty, but rather relates to preparations for death and balancing one's obligations to the wheel of life (*Samsāra*). There is an awareness of self and the world which is appropriate to each stage. The young do not have the wisdom of the old; the old should not have the desires of the young.

In most Indian philosophies, the world, like the individual who is aware, is a living process. Birth and death are principles in nature. Death leads to life. Life leads to death. There is no view here of a first inanimate basic principle. Hindu temple walls are decorated with the infinite forms life takes, and the central altar is often the stylized *liṅgam* and *yoni*, or male and female genetalia.

Time is cyclic. Physical space and physical nature are moving, changing, living, dying, becoming in form as objects of sensation. Although future lives are determined by the Karma or good and bad actions accumulated in one's past, this sequence can be terminated by the awareness of its nature and the controlling of desires.

If consciousness is never dissolved in the objects of awareness, then it possesses a unity even when directed at many different objects at different moments. Subjectivity in this sense represents both an attitude toward experience and a methodology for dealing with experience in attaining understanding and enlightenment. The philosophical systems within which attitudes and methodologies developed in India are dualistic with clear demarcations between subject and object, or they are non-dualistic and demarcations dissolve on higher levels of knowing, or they are pluralistic in which case situational encounters of a multiplicity of subjects and objects occurs. In this chapter, I want to examine more closely two philosophical traditions, the Sāṃkhya which is dualistic, and the Advaita Vedānta which is monistic. I selected these two because they offer two different but closely related explanations of consciousness and its role in experience and interpretation in the knowing process.

Dualism and proximity

One can think of subject and object as two unique and separate natures, neither of which is reducible to the other. The question of course in such a dualistic assumption is 'how do these two natures relate to one another?' For example, if man is a body and a soul and they are qualitatively different, how can they influence and determine one another? Is one in charge of the other as Plato and Aristotle believed? How can the material encompass the non-material or the non-material be contained in the material as Gregory of Nyssa wondered?

A thorough subject/object dualism might resolve a number of epistemological paradoxes which juxtapose the knowing consciousness and the known object as in the case of Sir Arthur Eddington's mind stuff discussing physics stuff.[19] Subject/object dualism in the West is usually justified on some theistic basis as a divine creation of a soul inserted and/or imprisoned in a body. The meaning and value of the soul, or subject half of such a dualism is then defined by a deity who is outside this soul/body dichotomy but supervises it and holds the soul accountable. In this linear view, there is no return.

I have selected Sāṃkhya to introduce dualistic presuppositions for two reasons: Firstly, Sāṃkhya clearly distinguishes between the subject consciousness and the material objects of knowledge, and treats both as practical and immediate in human experience. Secondly, Sāṃkhya philosophers in their exposition of the nature and relationship of consciousness to matter developed a theory of evolution of physical nature that fits in well with modern biological theories but supplements these theories by providing room for the biologist as both evolved organism and a conscious observer observing evolved organisms. Thus Sāṃkhya discusses the central consciousness paradox in biology, which Sir John Eccles and Daniel Robinson call the 'skeleton in the closet of orthodox evolutionism'.[20] However, the Sāṃkhya position offers a very different approach to the skeleton from that of Eccles and Robinson whose view is dualistic in the Western soul/deity context discussed above.[21]

The subject/object dichotomy of Sāṃkhya is presented in such a way that it reflects individual experiences of both consciousness and the objects of awareness. The central text of Sāṃkhya, the *Sāṃkhyakārikā* of Iśvara Kṛṣṇa (fourth or fifth Century AD), is based on older texts which no longer survive. But Sāṃkhya origins go back to and even beyond the *Upaniṣads*. For our exposition of the system here, we rely on the *Kārikā* as well as contemporary interpretations of it, the most important of which is Gerald J. Larson's *Classical Sāṃkhya.*[22]

Iśvara Kṛṣṇa understood human experience to consist of two qualitatively distinct principles: primal nature or *prakṛti*, and *puruṣa* which is the unique consciousness or self of an individual. Each of these basic essences is uncreated and neither is reducible to the other.[23] The Sāṃkhya system is atheistic and there is no transcendental origin of either *prakṛti* or *puruṣa* which are the unevolved, absolute presuppositions of the system.

The root from which the term Sāṃkhya comes probably meant numbering or reasoning and so implies an analytic emphasis which was applicable to the evolving stages of the basic *prakṛti* and to the stages in understanding of the observing, but unchanging *puruṣa*.[24] Knowledge of the world comes from three sources: the senses, inference, and reliable authority. The most basic of these are the senses. The Sāṃkhya, like many other Indian systems, consider the mind (*manas*) to be a sense. To concentrate with the senses, including the mind sense, upon the world of objects produced by *prakṛti* is to analyze it. To concentrate upon concentrating is to begin to understand and to intuit *puruṣa*.[25]

The tendency in any discussion of relationship in dualism is to see one element as influencing or causing the other, and this element, whether idea or matter, emerges as the dominant and essential one and defines the other via the relationship. This happens, for example, in most discussions of mind/brain. For the Sāṃkhya, neither *puruṣa* nor *prakṛti* is more basic and therefore neither can define or explain the other. *Puruṣa* does not 'cause' *prakṛti* to appear as the organs of sense and their objects. These are simply evolved out of *prakṛti* according to its own material causes and principles. And *prakṛti* does not 'cause' *puruṣa* to be, it is simply given, uncreated and uncreating. Thus there is no relationship in any usual causal sense between them. It is in the proximity of *puruṣa* and *prakṛti* that explaining occurs and one might view all explaining in science, philosophy, or religion, as the consequence of this proximity. It is also proximity that makes experience possible. One might think of *prakṛti* as the possibility of being observed and *puruṣa* as the possibility of observing. Neither possibility is reducible to nor has its origins in the other.

In the *Sāṃkhyakārikā* texts these two principles are explained analogically as wick and oil in a lamp, which combined in fire, produce illumination. But the light is neither the one nor the other in isolation.[26] How then do they relate? The *Sāṃkhyakārikā* says that their relationships are of 'proximity' alone.[27] And this proximity of *puruṣa* and *prakṛti* produces an evolved world of descriptions, definitions, interpretations, explanations, which result in an intuitive awareness that these are neither the subject doing the explaining, describing, defining, interpreting, nor the objects being analytically described, defined, interpreted and explained.

To the question as to how one realizes there are two such givens, the Sāṃkhya philosopher responds that it is a combination of perception, of understanding of the texts of ancient philosophers, and of our experience of suffering – not physical suffering alone, but also and more importantly the suffering that arises in our awareness of and attempts to attribute meaning to life and/or death. Eccles and Robinson ask at the end of their *Wonder of Being Human*: 'Is it that this life of ours is simply an episode of consciousness between two oblivions ...'[28] That this 'episode between oblivions' contains a great deal of suffering is one of the clear insights of Indian philosophy in general and Sāṃkhya in particular. It is also the first of the Buddha's Fourfold Noble Truths. For Sāṃkhya all sufferings arise in and are related to *prakṛti*.[29] One can suppress pain or drug the senses and the intellect but none of these solutions can treat *puruṣa*. When one intuitively realizes that *puruṣa* is not *prakṛti* nor any of its states, then one is free, and suffering as it appears to relate to consciousness, is terminated. One is not one's suffering, but if one is unaware of this, the suffering can seem to define one's whole being.

Prakṛti as nature and knowledge

Sāṃkhya treats the intellect, the five senses and the mind sense as elements of the material universe and so accounts for impressions and ideas within a strictly physical and empirical framework much as David Hume and other Western empiricists have done.

The world might be seen as a drama in which spectator (*puruṣa*) and spectacle (*prakṛti*) achieve proximity to one another in individual beings, but neither is transformed into the other.[30] The material world provides the objects for the *puruṣa* and the physical senses for perceiving them, but does not thereby become consciousness. The difference between brain and mind is one of evolutionary development, but not one of qualitative difference for both evolve from *prakṛti* and it is mind as mental event that enables brain as physical process to do brain surgery. The Spanish painter, Goya once wrote: 'In nature color exists no more than line, – there is only light and shade.'[31] Out of this 'light and shade', *prakṛti* produces the world of form and color. Consciousness or *puruṣa*, however, is neither brain nor mind, form nor color. It is both the recognizing of brain and mind and the recognizing that it is neither.

The evolving material world is like a three-stringed instrument upon which a melody is played that harmonizes the positions on each string with one another, but never abandons or neglects any string entirely. These three strings in Sāṃkhya are called *guṇas* – constituents or strands.[32] Translated into contemporary terminology, they are *tamas* – matter, mass, that which is extended; *rajas* – motion, energy, and activity; *sattva* – light and intellectual awareness. According to historian and philosopher, Surendranath Dasgupta, these *guṇas*:

> ... though co-operating to produce the world of effects, these diverse moments with diverse tendencies never coalesce. Thus in the phenomenal product whatever energy there is is due to the element of rajas and rajas

> alone; all matter, resistance, stability, is due to tamas, and all conscious manifestation to sattva.[33]

Neither *tamas* and *rajas*, nor *sattva* are the *puruṣa*. They are the source of sight, sound, taste, touch, smell, and mind which are the basic forms of the evolving world, and they produce the gross elements that we encounter as objects.

The *Sāṃkhyakārikā* (xxxiii) teaches that in the manifesting world of *prakṛti* there are 13 instruments of knowledge, each of which is related to a particular aspect of the evolving and changing world of experience. These consist of the three inner organs, intellect, ego and mind (*buddhi shaṃkāra, manas*) which operate in the past, present, and future, the five senses, and the five organs of action: voice, hands, feet, and the organs of excretion and reproduction, which operate only in the present. However one views these areas of human nature and experience, their purpose and relationship is that of awakening an intuitive consciousness in the proximity of *prakṛti* and *puruṣa*.[34] *Prakṛti*, though unevolved, evolves further into additional evolving entities. This resembles classical materialism too which tends to start with matter or big bang as unevolved, from which the animate and inanimate universe then evolves.

Puruṣa as understanding and consciousness

The Sāṃkhya would say that the meaning of the body is not found in the body, but in that which ascribes meaning to it. The body doesn't create meaning, it is given meaning. But in ascribing meaning, *puruṣa* is *meaningless*. In a world of things it is no thing and so is the nothingness in our experience.[35] A paradox then occurs when, confusing itself with the body to which it gives meaning, *puruṣa* tries to derive its own meaning from this body.

With the non-material consciousness, Sāṃkhya maintains an observing center which is the here and now of the spectacles produced by material nature as *prakṛti* in its changing manifestations while *puruṣa* experiences itself as constant and unmanifested. For this experience of *puruṣa*, non-*puruṣa* is a necessary condition.

In the Sāṃkhya theory of evolution, the evolving and the evolved occur in endless apparent changes before the uncreated and uncreating consciousness in its nature as understanding. As a result of this spectator/spectacle performance, there are different levels of ignorance. There is the ignorance associated with understanding the processes and consequences of the material world as these are related by the outer sense organs to the inner awareness organs (not *puruṣa*) of intellect, ego, and mind. And there is the ignorance which arises from the confusion of consciousness with its objects.[36]

The dualistic proximity of *prakṛti* and *puruṣa* creates philosophy, mathematics, scientific theories, works of art. Leshan and Margenau express a similar position in different passages in their comparison of Einstein and Van Gogh. For them: 'Today, science is beginning to view the nature of consciousness quite differently. Classifying and organizing the world are seen as human activities. What we can observe of reality is our own organization of it. Reality is a compound like water, with consciousness one of the elements. But we can never hope to know what the compound would be without consciousness.'[37]

The French mathematician and physicist, Henri Poincare, in comparing beauty and usefulness in science suggested that the scientist observes the world because: '... he takes pleasure in it; and he takes pleasure in it because it is beautiful. If nature were not beautiful, it would not be worth knowing and life would not be worth living ... I mean the intimate beauty which comes from the harmonious order of its parts and which a pure intelligence can grasp.'[38]

A dualism, like that outlined by the Sāṃkhya and expressed in contemporary science and philosophy is a view which enables our awareness of the world to develop toward a deeper awareness of and respect for *puruṣa* as one's self and the self of others as the source of the world's meaning. It accomplishes this in a dichotomy, which permits the objective/subjective dualism which has been so important in the history of science, to be used without confusing *puruṣa* with *prakṛti* or relying upon transcendental forces. Kārikā lii tells us: 'Without the "subjective", there would be no "objective", and without the "objective" there would be no "subjective". Therefore, there proceeds two-fold evolution, the "objective" and the "subjective".'[39]

Non-dualism and superimposition

To return to the chariot ride ... given the Sāṃkhya dualist interpretation, the traveler as observing *puruṣa* is neither the carriage, its driver, reins, horses nor the road over which it travels for these are all *prakṛti*. But from a non-dualist perspective while the carriage and its parts seem to exist for the passenger or observer at the level of objects of awareness, they are not different from the passenger at a higher level as awareness of objects. As objects of perception, they are for the perceiver and as objects of consciousness they are the perceiver. This is the position of *Advaita* (*a* = not, *dva* = two, that is, non-dualistic) *Vedānta* (end of the Vedas). This is the philosophical school founded by Gaudapada (seventh century AD), whose greatest proponent was Śankara (c.788–c.820 AD). The most important and widely read of all classical Advaita Vedānta texts are the *Vedānta Sūtras of Bādarāyana* with the commentaries of Śankara. It is a position which resolves the dualities and multiplicities perceived on one level of awareness into the non-duality of consciousness on a higher level. Here there is no question of the proximity of *prakṛti* and *puruṣa* for here all is consciousness which in sensation and conception superimposes an illusionary dual nature upon what is in essence one.

In Advaita Vedānta consciousness defines existence, not vice versa, even as in our everyday experience, consciousness *per se* both precedes and follows awareness of the presence or absence of something. Swami Satprakashananda makes this point in discussing existence: 'The distinction between existence and nonexistence depends in the last analysis on our consciousness, which can by no means be denied. Its denial presupposes it.'[40] This characteristic of personal experience for the Advaita Vedāntin reflects the nature of the universe, and he/she would agree with Sir James Jeans' suggestion that the universe increasingly resembles an idea, but would reject attributing this idea to a transcendental creator who is totally distinct from its creation. The universal experience with which the Advaita Vedāntin begins, refers not to the ideas that flow through our minds, but the process of having ideas, not specific thoughts but thinking. The one unavoidable fact of consciousness is that we are conscious. And whether we affirm or deny this, in both cases we are demonstrating it and aware of it. And in that we share in awareness and consciousness with all beings, we are one with all beings.

Dualistic Sāṃkhya and Advaita Vedānta, like the object tradition, begin with the question as to the nature and origin of the intelligibility of the universe. If the universe is intelligible and orderly and human beings are intrinsic elements of the universe, then one might assume that one of the highest expressions and/or manifestations of this order would be its self-recognition in the human intellect. How is this possible?

Non-dualism versus dualism

Advaita Vedānta sees intelligibility as the very nature of the world, its ordered essence, and its ordered appearing. This non-dualistic view of the world is perhaps best understood in Śankara's criticism of Sāṃkhya. His first point is that by separating *prakṛti* from *puruṣa*, the Sāṃkhya have separated consciousness and purpose from the material world. It is then impossible to attribute to matter a sense of purpose, intelligibility, order, direction or any of the other characteristics which would indicate awareness and thought. If consciousness is distinct from its objects, and intelligibility is a quality brought by consciousness to experience, then objects will remain unintelligible, and matter itself would remain inactive and produce nothing.[41] Secondly, just as clay becomes a pot only if worked upon by a potter so the material world cannot become anything unless guided and worked upon by an intelligent principle.[42]

Next, Śankara credits the Sāṃkhya with the recognition that there is *puruṣa* or self, but rejects the Sāṃkhya idea that this self is multiple and individual, and distinct from the rest of the world. One should not confuse the individuality of sensations and thoughts with the universality of sensing and thinking which are aspects of the whole. In reference to the first, he draws an analogy with the solitary dreamer who sees many individuals in a dream, and with the earth which is the single origin of many different persons and races. The universal Self, however is one and is '... the internal Self of me, of thee, and of all other embodied beings ...'[43] The whole of consciousness is composed of its many manifestations. One might compare this perspective with a society and its members, each one of whom manifests in many ways the ideas, values, language of the whole. Śankara believes that a self or *puruṣa* which is viewed as separate from the world without sense organs or mind or intelligence, such consciousness could not possibly function as a spectator.[44]

True knowledge for the Sāṃkhya will lead to a clear dualism between *puruṣa* and *prakṛti*, whereas true knowledge for Śankara will demonstrate non-dualistic *Ātman/Brahman* because: '... true knowledge of all existing things depends on the things themselves, and hence the knowledge of *Brahman* also depends altogether on the thing, that is, *Brahman* itself'.[45]

Śankara adds to perception, inference, and verbal testimony, the three additional methods of comparison, postulation, and non-apprehension. Perception is internal or external and is direct knowledge. Inference, comparison and postulation are indirect and rely for their basis on perception. Non-apprehension is direct and entails knowing that something is not present.

Each of these methods represents a level of knowing and each corresponds to truth on its appropriate plane. On the sense plane, the sense world is real, and Śankara stresses empiricism. However, the truth of one plane does not apply to that of the next. Sense knowledge which is valid at its own level, becomes invalid on a higher level of awareness. The relationship of truth to level is often misunderstood outside the Advaita Vedānta system which has no difficulty embracing the empirical world and all of its truths, but maintains these do not define the Self, *Ātman*, or Consciousness.[46] To confuse the two entails a confusion of consciousness with knowledge levels. *The Māṇḍūkya Upaniṣad*, for example, identifies four planes of the 'imperishable Brahman': The first is its physical nature and represents awareness of the external world and its objects. Here sense knowledge is truth. The second is its 'mental nature' which includes all mental operations, reasoning, concepts, memory, dreams. Here inferential and conceptual knowledge is truth. The third is that of dreamless sleep, or deepest meditation in which all mental impressions and distinctions are quieted while consciousness *per se* is without object categories. Here no knowledge is truth. The fourth level:

> ... say the wise, is not subjective experience, nor objective experience, nor experience intermediate between these two, nor is it a negative condition which is neither consciousness nor unconsciousness. It is not the knowledge of the senses, nor is it relative knowledge, nor yet inferential knowledge. Beyond the senses, beyond the understanding, beyond all expression, is the Fourth. It is pure unitary consciousness, wherein awareness of the world and of multiplicity is completely obliterated. It is ineffable peace. It is the supreme good. It is One without a second, It is the Self. Know it alone![47]

One of the most important differences between Sāṃkhya and Advaita Vedānta is seen in their approaches to sacred texts, especially the *Upaniṣads* (*upa* + *ni* + *sad* = to sit near, that is, to sit at the feet of a teacher). While both reflect Upaniṣadic origins, Śankara denies the validity of Sāṃkhya claims upon them and insists their interpretations are fallacious because in Śankara's non-dualistic interpretation of the texts, he can find no reference in them to consciousness in non-conscious *prakṛti*.[48]

There are three sets of relationships in Advaita Vedānta that have particular relevance to any discussion of the subject dimension of philosophical space, especially when one goes from subject/object equality as in Sāṃkhya to consciousness as an absolute: The first is the *Brahman* → *Ātman* relationship which emphasizes *Brahman* and then its implications for its individual manifestation or *Ātman*. The second is the *Ātman* → *Brahman* relationship which begins with the individual *Ātman* and proceeds to *Brahman*. The third is the *avidyā/māyā* relationship which consists of knowledge levels as well as the ground of illusion which keeps individuals from recognizing their *Ātman/Brahman* nature. These three relationships reflect the three-fold challenge to Śankara and Advaita Vedānta to present *Brahman* as cosmic principle, *Ātman* as the human manifestation of cosmic principle, and to explain how it is possible to miss this synthesis of *Brahman/Ātman* in the ignorance of *avidyā* and the illusion of *māyā*, as well as how it is possible via *avidyā māyā* to grasp it.

Brahman → *Ātman* → *neti, neti* (not this, not that)

Śankara traces his non-dualistic *Brahman/Ātman* insight primarily to the *Upaniṣads*, 16 of which he held to be the authentic and inspired revelations of *Riṣis* or forest teachers and mystics. The dates like their authors are unknown, but some certainly pre-date the fourth to sixth century BCE. They are the collected thoughts of many individuals over a considerable time-span and contain certain inconsistencies with one another just as philosophical systems do everywhere. However, one of their most important themes is that of *Brahman* as absolute and ultimate non-dual principle and origin of the cosmos, and *Ātman* as the emanation of *Brahman* in the human being.

For Śankara, the revealed omniscience of the scriptures reflects the omniscience of their source as *Brahman* who is not the author but their essence and one cannot understand the non-dual nature of the cosmos as *Brahman* without reference to the scriptures.[49] However, the knowing of *Brahman* is not knowing in any standard sense: 'He among us knows him best who understands the spirit of the words: "Nor do I know that I know him not." He truly knows *Brahman* who knows him as beyond knowledge: he who thinks that he knows, knows not. The ignorant think that *Brahman* is known, but the wise know him to be beyond knowledge.'[50]

Brahman is '... the irreducible substratum after the negation of all tangible objects'.[51] One might try to think of one's own consciousness as a continuum of intending and attending, with the mind and intellect producing intentions and directing attentions. One can then extend this view to the cosmos itself as a unity of sequences and levels of intending and attending within one's individual self is an aspect.[52] This continuum would also include the human presupposition of a non-conscious, material universe. The essence of this universe is *Brahman* as presupposition and presupposing. In the beginning *Brahman*: '... thought, may I be many, may I grow forth'.[53] And as such is both material cause and the agent, both cause and effect. For Śankara, *Brahman*: 'represents the Self as well as the agent ... although in full existence previously to the action modifies itself into something special, viz. the Self of the effect'.[54] Albert Einstein in his acceptance of the pantheistic deity of Spinoza would also seem to be approaching such a continuum view: 'I believe in Spinoza's God who reveals Himself in the orderly harmony of what exists, not in a God who concerns himself with the fates and actions of Human beings.'[55] Einstein's deity, like the *Brahman* of Śankara might seem to be the cosmos itself and not an external force: 'This firm belief, a belief bound up with deep feeling, in a superior mind that reveals itself in the world of experience, represents my conception of God. In common parlance this may be described as "pantheistic".'[56]

I specifically use the term *intending–attending* continuum and not intentions and attentions because intention often implies static thought states or specific concepts, and the idea of attention slips too easily into objects of attention as the sources of attending, which is not the case. Consciousness as the possibility of intending–attending cannot be made an object of intention or attention except in language and concept.[57] And, according to the *Vedānta Sūtras*, although *Brahman* is the source of names and forms, *Brahman* cannot even be conceived or named. One can speak of the whole and its essence only as *neti neti*, not this, not that.[58] This intending and attending continuum is the possibility of knowing and its manifestations in the knower and the known. It is: '... not only the beginning of the act of knowing but also the end of it'.[59]

Ātman → Brahman → Tat twam asi

In the *Taittirīya Upaniṣad*, a philosopher, Bhrigu, asks the God, Varuṇa, to 'teach him *Brahman*'. Varuṇa replies that *Brahman* is food, breath, the eye, the ear, mind, speech. Varuṇa then recommends that Bhrigu meditate upon each of these, perform austerities, and realize that that from which all beings come, which supports their living presence, and to which they return at death is *Brahman*. At the end of Bhrigu's meditations, Varuṇa then explains that 'He who is this (*Brahman*) in man, and he who is that (*Brahman*) in the sun, are both one.' *Tat twam asi* (That art Thou).[60]

In the process, sensation is very important for the senses relate the knower to the empirical world as appearance or *māyā*. But they cannot give us self-knowledge because their knowledge is dualistic and self-knowledge is non-dual as intending/attending consciousness. According to Professor Malkani when we: 'Get down to actual knowledge ... we find that there is no dualism, no things. There is only pure consciousness. The dualism is a product of thought or imagination. It is not available in knowledge.'[61] It is this possibility of knowing the non-dual in the dual that is the source and function of superimposition by consciousness or duality upon the world. The attempt to find consciousness in the non-consciousness of the world leads to an awareness of this impossibility. This in turn leads to an awareness that what one calls non-consciousness is so only within consciousness. But this insight begins with the process of superimposition of world on self, then self on world.

One can also transcend intention and attention by the negation of negation, that is, one negates real, not-real, both real and not-real distinctions as the *māyā* of intentions and attentions, for the: '... ultimate ground, must not only negate the things but it must also negate the negation of those things. This ultimate negation cannot have an objective character. It cannot therefore be conceived. It can only be intuited.'[62] Thus, 'He truly knows *Brahman* who knows him as beyond knowledge; he who thinks that he knows, knows not.'[63]

Consciousness as a continuum of intending, interpreting, thinking, explaining, affirming, denying is also a meaning functional continuum. The variables of experience as things, thoughts, and symbols are the sources of our concepts of same and different and enable us to make distinctions, classify, and differentiate. The *Kena Upaniṣad* extends the meaning functional continuum of the individual within which all experience is related variables, beyond the individual to all of nature and to the meaningless meaning functional continuum of the cosmos itself as *Brahman.* Individual mental operations which reflect intentions and attentions can be said to be meaning functional, but as reflections of an intending/attending continuum, they are meaningless. These operations as meaning functional can be associated with intentions, attentions, dreams, questions, explanations, affirmations, denials. From this perspective, the *I* is a meaning variable. But I-ing or the meaning functional process of I-ing is meaningless.[64] For example, I can write 'I' on all sorts of application forms, imagine 'I' in all sorts of situations, identify 'I' with 100 aches and pleasures. In each case, it is a variable and the 'I' doing this is meaning functional but meaningless as it decides upon the meaning of each of these situations. No matter what the variable 'I' wears, owns, or becomes, the meaning functional 'I' remains meaningless. And in this meaninglessness it is none other than *Brahman.*The self could be said to be the 'I' of the I, just as in the *Kena Upaniṣad*:

> The Self is ear of the ear, mind of the mind, speech of speech ... breath of the breath, and eye of the eye... That which is not comprehended by the mind but by which the mind comprehends – know that to be *Brahman*. ... That which is not seen by the eye but by which the eye sees – know that to be *Brahman*. ... He truly knows Brahman who knows him as beyond knowledge; he who thinks that he knows, knows not.[65]

'I' as a term is used to demarcate meaning in intention as my thoughts from the meaning of the objects of my attention, 'I see that rock.' 'I want that book.' 'I cut myself.' 'I think therefore I am.' This demarcation does not preclude the attempt to superimpose the source of my meaning onto the objects which I assume are the source of my attention, that is to objectify in some fashion the 'I'. According to K.C. Bhattacharyya: 'The metaphysical controversy about the reality of the subject is only about the subject viewed in some sense as object. The thinnest sense in which it is objectified is "being taken as meant".'[66] This represents a linguistic and/or analytical, dichotomy.

Avidyā → māyā → vidyā

The term *avidyā* means 'ignorance' or 'nescience' (non-knowledge), and Śankara uses it to explain the superimposition of non-Self upon the Self in attributing to the Self natures, qualities and characteristics that are non-Self.[67] *Māyā* is the principle of creative illusion which is responsible for the multiple appearances of what is ultimately non-dual. However, *avidyā māyā* performs a very critical function in Advaita Vedānta for as the beginning of the illusion of dualism, it is also necessary to understanding non-dualism. Only in recognizing non-duality beyond duality does *Ātman* realize *Brahman*, much as *puruṣa* through the displays of *prakṛti* recognizes that it is not *prakṛti*. This illusion or *māyā* is necessary according to Śankara because: '... the means of right knowledge cannot operate unless there be a knowing personality, and because the existence of the latter depends on the erroneous notion that the body, the senses, and so on, are identical with, or belong to, the Self of the knowing person. For without the employment of the senses ... right knowledge cannot operate.'[68] The empirical world of our intentions and attentions is dual and multiple. The world of intending/attending consciousness is non-dual and non-multiple. Ignorance is a precondition for knowledge in that one must recognize one's ignorance in order to grasp either what one does not know or seek intuitively for that which is beyond knowing.

Experience consists of vast networks of intention/attention variables superimposed upon one another as I/it, subject/object distinctions. Śankara in the opening lines of his commentaries upon the *Vedānta Sūtras of Bādarāyana* defines superimposition as the attributing to one object or element of experience the qualities and characteristics of another.[69]

Consciousness at any level can and does superimpose itself upon the world and superimposes the world upon itself. As thinking, perceiving subjects we superimpose our intentions upon the objects of our attention. When we direct our attentions to our selves we then intend our selves as objects by superimposing back upon awareness the objects of awareness. The subject tries to know itself within the object contexts it has superimposed upon experience. It objectifies the world in some fashion and then objectifies itself from this objectified world.The world of sense objects is there for the senses and this world is to be known and explained by the senses or sense references and not the senses explained by references to a pre-existing physical and non-sensual world.[70]

This entire process is facilitated by language, especially those Indo-European languages which structure statements about the world in subject/predicate patterns, and so tend to miss the intending consciousness as the source of subject/predicate distinctions. If we superimpose upon the world of our experience the mechanistic definition of a Cartesian clockwork, then as subjects we may begin to view the superimposing-self as clockwork as well.This is the path that any concept takes as it is superimposed upon the world as intention/attention and then is superimposed back upon intending/attending as its conscious source.

Conclusion: proximity and superimposition

I have tried to present two view of conscious: One is dualistic and explains our experience and knowledge as the *proximity of puruṣa and prakṛti*. The second is non-dualistic and explains knowledge and experience as a super-imposition process of *māyā* in a monistic *Brahman/Ātman continuum* of intending and attending. I believe these assumptions and their various methods can be compatible, complementary, and ultimately essential to one another in our pursuit of understanding. When we stress the objects of experience as in natural science, then a dualistic view may prove initially more useful, but when we would understand the nature of the understanding of the scientist, of consciousness and its place in the totality of the world, then non-dualism would keep us from dividing ourselves and the world into irresolvable dichotomies. Hopefully, the application of these dualistic and non-dualistic views will become increasingly apparent as we now explore the subject and situational logics of the Jains, Nyāya, and Buddhist philosophers.

8 The Jain Axiom of Non-absolutism

Perhaps the best introduction to the philosophy and subject logic of the Jains is their story of the six blind men reporting on the nature of the elephant. Each man contacts a different portion of the elephant and pronounces upon the nature of the whole from the part with which he is familiar. For the blind man who feels the leg, an elephant is a pillar, for the one who touches the trunk, an elephant is a pipe, another touches its tail and claims it to be a rope, and so on. The Jain, while affirming the truth of the experience that each blind man has, rejects the attempt to turn this individual experience into the whole. This is what we do when we insist that any one point of view is the only point of view and therefore excludes all others.

Jain philosophy is dualistic, but this dualism, while as fundamental as that of the Sāṃkhya, provides a more critical and thorough analysis of the relationship of consciousness (*jīva*) to the non-conscious, dynamic object world (*ajīva*) which is a mixture of change and constancy, being and becoming, substance and manifestation. In this complex mixture of subjects and objects, any claim to knowledge is always relative to subject/object contact and interpretation. This does not mean that knowledge is arbitrary. But it is the subject that is critical to the knowing process for it is from the point of view of a subject that objects are known. Sensation is important in this process, but for the Jain it is the subject who knows what things are, not the sense organs.[1]

Historical overview

By the sixth century BCE, asceticism had become widespread in India. In part this was a reaction to the rising power and corresponding ritualism of the priestly *brāhmin* caste. In part, as with the Stoics in the West, asceticism was a search for human spirituality and meaning which turned away from ritual and sacrifice in an inner pursuit of enlightenment and self-understanding. This does not mean that asceticism replaces sacrifice and ritual but rather provides an alternative. Both approaches continue in India into the present.

This is the age of the *Upaniṣads* and the beginning of the various Indian philosophical schools. And it is not accidental that two of the greatest teachers of the time come not from the *brāhmin* caste, but from the ruler/warrior caste of the *kṣatriya*. The one was Vardhamāna Naya, or Mahāvīra (The Great

Hero) who, building upon a yet older tradition, founded the Jain system. His contemporary was Gotama of the Sakyas, named Siddharta, known today as the Buddha (enlightened one). Mahāvīra probably died in about 468 BCE at the age of 72, and the Buddha in about 480 BCE at age 80. Both responded to a time of chaos, invasion and brutality with ethical philosophies of self-understanding and nonviolence (*ahiṁsā*). The Indologist Dr N.N. Bhattacharyya attributes the bloodshed and violence of the period to the accumulation of extreme wealth by some and extreme poverty of others as smaller tribal groups and kingdoms were destroyed by greater states. Both Gotama and Mahāvīra were surrounded by conflict and struggle. Gotama's people, the Sakya tribe, were conquered and destroyed in his own time by a ruler from Kosala.[2] At the beginning of the Jaina *Akaranga Sūtra*, one reads: 'The (living) world is afflicted, miserable, difficult to instruct, and without discrimination. In this world full of pain, suffering by their different acts, see the benighted ones cause great pain.'[3]

However, the problems were not merely social and economic. In addition, as in Athens at the time of Plato, there was a proliferation of dogmas and positions. At least 363 such philosophical views were supposed to have existed in Mahāvīra's own time.[4] Within the contexts of the period, one can understand the search for a nonviolent, inner spiritual approach to living in an age that seemed corrupt, cruel and senseless. Mahāvīra's ethical doctrine of non-violence has its counterpart in logic in his doctrine of non-absolutism.[5] It is with this latter that we are primarily concerned here. Dasgupta notes in his *History of Indian Philosophy* that the roots of Jain logic go back at least to the fifth century BCE.[6] It achieves much of its final expression in the *Tattvārthāhigama Sūtra* of Śri Umāsvāti (1–85 AD). It is essentially from this text and its modern commentaries that I will present it as an example of subject logic.[7]

The Jains accept Mahāvīra as the last of 24 *Tīrthaṇkaras*, or conquerors, who achieved absolute release from the world within the present cosmic cycle. The Jain believes that in any one of many vast cosmic cycles, wise individuals will emerge to teach a path of enlightenment and liberation from rebirth. They do not worship these *Tīrthaṇkaras* but view them as inspirations to contemplation. As for the Gods, the Jains accept their existence, but they too occupy stages in the cycles of transmigration and as soon as their good *karma* ends, they are reborn.[8] One achieves some insight into the temporal scope of the Jaina world view when one realizes that Mahāvīra's predecessor, Parsva, died 280 years before Mahāvīra, and that Parsva's predecessor died 84,000 years before this.

In any tradition whose teachings have lasted for hundreds of years, there will be many different positions and disagreements over texts. This is true for the Jains as well. However, on the nature of the world, the knower, knowledge in general, and logic in particular, there is great consistency and agreement.

Reality as *jīva* and *ajīva*

For the Jains, reality is composed of *jīva* which are the unique irreducible atoms of individual consciousness and as such are the source of perceiving and conceiving; and *ajīva* which is the totality of the world of objects of attention. Where other traditions affirm the material world and then speak of *jīva* as the non-material, giving precedence to the material principle, the Jaina begin with the *jīva* and then address the physical as the non-conscious or *ajīva*. For the Jains, as for the Sāṃkhya, both principles are conserved and qualitatively different. And it is in their proximity to one another that we experience ourselves and the world. The Jains differ, however, from the Sāṃkhya both in their conception of *jīva* as the changing yet constant source of mental events,[9] and in their view of *ajīva* which does not exist for the sake of *jīva*. Atomic matter mixes with atomic *jīva* like oil and water or water and milk but neither loses its identity. This mixture is the basis for the dependency of knowledge upon points of view.[10]

In the analysis of the relationships of *jīva* to *ajīva*, the Jains although essentially dualists, subscribe to an epistemological pluralism which holds that reality is a many faceted, active, changing process – a mix of permanence and change, existence and non-existence, creation and destruction, and any statement or observation is relative to one of these facets at a particular time and from a particular perspective. Every statement and every judgment is essentially relative because, as the philosopher Narendra Bhattacharyya notes: '... every judgment expresses one aspect of reality and is therefore relative and subject to some condition. It is due to the fact that every object has innumerable characters.'[11] What appear to be contradictions in the object dimension with its emphasis upon the identity of things, resolve themselves in Jain thought into different points of view.

In the object tradition, knowledge is treated as it can be objectified (objectively). In the subject tradition, knowledge will be treated as it can and must be subjectified, for any object is known as it presents a facet to a knowing subject's sensation and interpretation. However, the material nature of an object is qualitatively different from the knowledge of it for: '... knowledge is immaterial and what is immaterial cannot possess the form of what is material ... The mirror can possess the form of the object because it is itself material ... What is material is perceived only through the senses; it cannot be perceived without them.'[12] This difference between sensation and knowledge is very important and is the heart of the subject dimension. Thus, sensation is the physical process of sensing physical entities as these are 'reflected in the sense organs', and knowledge is non-material and always 'from a point of view'.

It is precisely because the Jain will be objective that objectivity is relative. This does not mean that objects are not real. The Jains are realists and subscribe to the absolute given nature of the *ajīva* world. However, knowledge is dependent upon both objects and subjects as co-equal elements in the reality of a changing world. While the Jain accepts plural relativism, this relativity is never arbitrary. Another consequence of this relative realism is that the Jaina view of language does not equate the identity of the word with the identity of the object. Word and thing are two different objects and to perceive the one is not to perceive the other.[13]

Like the Sāṃkhya, the Jains are concerned with how objects and consciousness relate in the production of knowledge in a perceptual/conceptual complex of multiple viewpoints (*anekāntavāda*) in which neither *jīva* nor *ajīva* is clearly known in isolation. Pushpa Bothra in her study of Jain theory of perception explains that: 'The Jainas, who believe in the doctrine of *anekāntavāda*, do not accept either complete nondifference or complete difference between the self and knowledge.'[14] The object shares co-equal status with the subject in all knowledge because it does so in reality. According to Dr Satkari Mookerjee, neither has a privileged position in relation to the other: 'The subjective thought is as much existent as the objective datum and both have to be determined by experience to be what they are. That our consciousness and modes of consciousness are known by themselves does not confer any privilege on them in so far as the question of their validity and truth are concerned.'[15] Although knowledge is mental, because an object as non-mental can be perceived as such only via the senses, senses and inference from them are knowledge's beginning.[16] *Jīva* and *ajīva* are responsible for different experiences of human beings who are temporary syntheses of both.

The fundamental characteristic of *jīva* is consciousness.[17] And consciousness has at least three aspects that are implicit in the subject dimension of philosophical space:

1. Consciousness of consciousness. For example, knowing of an object is also knowing that one knows, for all knowledge is also self-knowledge.[18] Even if one doubts what an object might be, one knows one is doubting. Consciousness of consciousness is inseparable from the knowing of the object and yet is different from it.[19] For this reason knowing *per se* cannot be reduced to knowing self as an object.

2. Consciousness of objects. This is immediate perception. Objects are the external source of knowing, but knowledge is not object, it is relationship.[20] The subject does not invent the object. The object does not create the subject. Right belief is the belief which one gains, within a point of view, a perspective upon things as they are.[21]

3. Consciousness as questioning. The questioning of knowing subjects is the dynamic source of knowledge of relationships. The subject directs consciousness with the questions posed and arrives at answers relative to the point of view of these questions. Professor Sukhlalji in his *Commentary on the Tattvārtha Sūtra*, referred to questions as 'gateways to knowledge'.[22]

Ajīva

The world is a combination of creation, destruction, and permanence which are experienced as existence and non-existence. This accounts for our awareness that while all things seem to change they also seem to endure in some form. Anand Kashyap in his study of Jainism and social awareness maintains that in social institutions too, this mixture of permanence and change is a critical element: 'In any notion regarding the nature of social reality the idea of change as well as that of something which constitutes "non-change" and which can integrate the diversity into some concept of unity is one of the basic requirements.'[23] The existence and non-existence stressed in speaking about or describing an object and its perception are not merely a matter of usage, or convention; these are attributes of the object itself in time and space as Mookerjee explained: 'A thing is existence, is non-existence and is both existence and nonexistence, but always subject to limitations imposed by objective differences of substance, time, space and attributes ...'[24] The elements of experience are a synthesis of opposites. The continuous and the discontinuous, the same and the different, the combining and the separating are complementary and non-contradictory. The comprehension of an object is comprehension of its continuity and discontinuity with its self and with others.[25]

Reality consists of six reals or substances (*dravyas*). Two of these are the basic *jīva* and *ajīva*. *Ajīva* can be divided into five elements: matter (*pudgala*) which is the stuff of things, space (*ākāsá*), time (*kāla*), motion (*dharma*), and rest (*adharma*). *Pudgala* too is viewed as atomic and composed of infinite, similar indivisible physical particles from which the substantive nature of all else comes. But this is a dynamic process for the word *pudgala* (matter) is composed of two terms: *pud* which means to combine and *gala* which means to separate. Thus *pudgala* is the substance which combines and separates. In contemporary physical science this might be expressed as fusion and fission.[26] Every object is a combination of substance (*dravya*) and its modes or attributes (*paryāya*) like color, shape, size, and so on. One cannot separate *dravya* from *paryāya*, for neither is in isolation. The combination upon which one focuses is determined by one's point of view.[27]

Jīva, too, is a substance whose capabilities are perceiving and thinking.[28] One must not apply occidental ideas of substance here, for the modes of consciousness as a substance are desire, will, pleasure, pain. These are its attributes, however, not its nature. Liberation for the Jaina is related to getting beyond these modes. Of particular relevance to subject logics are the ways and modes in which consciousness manifests itself in experience of the world.

In any given object, there are an unlimited number of differences and so no matter how comprehensive our grasp of it, it is always a partial grasp.[29] Existence of the object itself depends upon the co-existence of these differences with one another and where there is no difference there is no unity for it is the opposites and the many that identify the whole.[30] However, the differences in an object can be the source of conflict between and among perceiving subjects, who see objects from different points of view. Contradictions then occur when a point of view is presented as the only point of view, the only real. This can lead to the intolerance and violence associated with ideology and dogmatism which are contrary to the ideal of nonviolence (*ahiṁsā*) of Mahāvīra.

Subject logic: basic terms and concepts

Subject logic is a system for reasoning and knowing. It begins with consciousness as *jīva*, and proceeds to the objects of attention as these are identified from a point of view. Such a logic cannot be absolute, for it begins with the assumption of non-absolutism, that is, with the presupposition that knowledge reflects a point of view and thus leads to a relativity of propositions and judgments.[31] Cognition of both diversity and identity are equally valid. The one cannot demonstrate the invalidity or unreality of the other. Trees are trees from a point of view and not a forest, and a forest is a forest from a point of view and not the trees. An individual human being will be observed from a different point of view in physics, chemistry, sociology, psychology, biology, religion. Each of these represents an emphasis implicit in observation and recognition. And while negation and affirmation are essential to making statements about human experience, and both are possible and necessary, these are relative possibilities and necessities, and are directly related to the degree to which knowledge is to be considered in any comprehensive sense.

The more comprehensive, the less affirmation and negation are applicable to it, because the more comprehensive it is the more it is both.[32]

Anekānta and *Anekāntavāda*

Anekānta is the theory that the world consists of infinite characteristics,[33] and the logic of the Jains is an *Anekānt Logic*.[34] *Anekāntavāda* (*an* = not, *eka* = one, *anta* = side, *vada* = statement, view) is the doctrine of relative pluralism of viewpoints. Its opposite is *ekāntavāda*, or one-sided point of view. Knowledge is relative to the permanent, changing, and substantive elements manifested in and by an object as viewed by a subject from a point of view. The Jaina developed two logics to accommodate the relativity of *anekāntavāda*. The first is a logic of points of view or *nayavāda*: *naya* = opinion or point of view, *vada* = view, thus the viewpoint of viewpoints. This logic focuses primarily upon self-awareness as awareness of one's point of view or *naya* and leads to the elimination of one's ignorance both of one's perspective and the ignorance of other possible perspectives. The second logic consists of a sequence of seven propositional steps in which the characteristics of objects are stated in subject/predicate relationships as these are known relatively. This is the logic of *syādvāda*: *sayat* = relatively = *syādvāda* = relativistic view.

In Jain subject logic, one encounters intuitive self-awareness as a co-equal aspect of the awareness of objects and events. It is this self-awareness which enables one to recognize the viewpoint from which one perceives.[35] The knowing of one's knowing is the source of the Jain logic to eliminate ignorance, or *nayavāda*. It is the logic of points of view from which we claim to know and speak about the world.[36] Knowledge is always the knowledge of a subject, but, as Satkari Mookerjee notes, it is also knowledge of a facet of infinite reals and infinite relationships: 'The central thesis of the Jaina is that there is not only diversity of reals, but each real is diversified. ... each real is possessed of an infinite number of modes at every moment.'[37]

Pramāṇa

Pramā means true knowledge, and for the Jain, true knowledge is knowledge of an object as it is.[38] *Pramāṇa* is the means to this end and is perhaps best translated as the means of knowing the multiple thatness of an object or its characteristics.[39] At the same time *pramāṇa* is always valid knowledge of self.[40] However, there can also be false non-absolute knowledge as well. This would entail mistaking one facet of an object for another, or seeing a snake instead of a rope.[41] *Pramāṇa* can be divided into direct knowing as perception (*pratyakṣa*), and indirect and mediated knowing (*parokṣa*) as inference, comparison, verbal testimony, assumption, probability, and non-existence (knowing that something is absent). Direct knowledge is immediate knowledge of objects and attributes as they are perceived by *jīva* via the senses. There are five external senses and the internal mind sense, which is an instrument for knowing objects but is not the self. The mind sense is not limited by the other senses but rather interprets, and co-ordinates their knowing.[42]

Naya

Pramāṇa is considered the means to right knowledge of an object as it is, and *naya* is knowledge of the object in relationship.[43] *Naya* always reflects the perspective from which statements are made, affirmed, and/or denied and are the point of view from which relationships are perceived.[44] Since *naya* is relationship knowledge, and since there are infinite relationships involved in the knowledge of any object, there are infinite *nayas*.[45] But when any perspective rejects the doctrine of non-absolutism and becomes the only perspective as an absolute affirmation or negation, it is then considered fallacious reasoning, or a flawed point of view called *nayābhāsa*.[46]

Dravya and paryāya

The *nayas* like the world of objects in general can be divided into substance *nayas* (*dravya*) and modal or attribute *nayas* of substances (*paryāya*).[47] *Dravya* or substance is that which is the same in changing states and conditions as with iron in tools or with organic compounds in different living organisms. Substance is that which can become something. *Paryāya* or attributes describe the qualities and characteristics which modify substances, as soft, sour, loud, red. Together they are knowledge of what something is and how it is.

I. *Nayavāda:* a logic to eliminate ignorance

The Jains evolved a logic of relationships which helps to establish the accuracy of knowledge by eliminating the knower's ignorance of the points of view that are implicit in it.[48] When we make statements, we distill experience of subjects and objects into language symbols and construct a verbal third world which is neither the experiencing subject nor the experienced object. Therefore to understand a statement is to understand this relativity of statement and proposition.[49]

The Jain theory of *nayavāda* holds that even though the points of view are infinite, it is possible to group them into two very broad categories using substance and attribute: (a) those *nayas* we associate with things and substances to be known, and (b) the *nayas* we associate with their conditions and properties.These are *dravyanaya* and *paryāyanaya* respectively. Life as an essence will be different from life (alive) as an attribute.

Though there can be many more viewpoints, seven are emphasized in the Jain logic of 'knowledge from points of view'.[50] Consistent with most Jain logicians I shall consider the first three as substance and attribute *nayas* the last three as language *nayas*. The fourth seems to be a border point between these two *nayas*.[51] In my discussion of each *naya*, I have tried to combine basic Jain positions with interpretations that would be particularly useful toward incorporating the *nayavada* into contemporary explanations and interpretations of experience:

Universal Viewpoint (Saṁgraha Naya)

This is the view of an object, event, or person from a universal point of view which gives preference to the whole over a particular individual or attribute. From this *naya*, one looks at the common element in diverse objects. Sameness takes precedence over difference. The individual is seen as a manifestation of the collective. The focus is upon the forest and not the trees.[52] From this point of view, the responsibilities of the individual to the collective might be emphasized over personal rights. One is male, German, middle class, immigrant first, and then an individual.

Fallacious Reasoning (Nayābhāsa)

A fallacy occurs with the universal view when it is considered exclusive or absolute, and the particular loses its identity or reality in the sameness of a universal essence. For example, the state exists while the individual is denied existence except as an extension of the state. Racial, religious, and gender prejudice tend to see only the group as real and view the individual as a manifestation of what one assumes is the nature of the collective. Another version of this fallacy can easily occur with the use of statistics in which a norm or the normal are defined as real or acceptable and then individuals have meaning only within this statistical norm.

Particular Viewpoint (Vyavahāra Naya)

In the particular *naya*, the emphasis is upon individuals and differences, while universals are de-emphasized. This is an empirical viewpoint and focuses upon the part and particular characteristics rather than upon the whole. To understand an object, event, or person is to take it apart. The more individual and unique the part, the more fundamental one's knowing. This *naya* may also look at an object in terms of its utility value and not its definition or greater significance beyond application. Difference is emphasized over sameness. The individual is emphasized over the state and in political systems it might mean a focus upon individual rights rather that upon the responsibilities toward the collective or group.

Fallacious Reasoning (Nayabhāsa)

The fallacy within this point of view would be that of absolutizing the particular perspective to the exclusion of the general, for example, individual rights would take absolute precedence over collective responsibilities and duties. Difference and distinctions become real, and the universal or same become imaginary or unreal.

Whole and Part Synthesis (Naigama Naya)

The *naigama naya* is a synthesis of extremes and could be called a union of substance and qualities, whole and part, and of the literal and the figurative. For example, literally I may be carrying wood for a fire, placing rice in a pot, and adding water to it – when I am asked what I am doing, I reply 'cooking'. 'Cooking' is a figurative and collective term which includes all the individual activities in which I am engaged. In this sense *naigama naya* refers to the: 'purpose (*saṅkalpa*) or the end of a certain continuous series of actions which are represented by one or a few of their number'.[53] It is a non-distinguishing viewpoint in which the general and the particular, the one and the many, are equally real. Professor Raju refers to this as the conventional *naya*.[54] We use this *naya* when we speak of collectives like science, philosophy, medicine which have both a figurative and a literal meaning, for example 'science is instrumental in ... medicine assumes ...' and so forth. In order to achieve this synthesis, one or more qualities of objects or individuals are treated as the substantive nature of these objects or individuals within a continuum which unites differences.[55]

One of the best ways to explain the *naigama naya* would be to examine the nature of figurative and literal points of view. The figurative unites what the literal separates or distinguishes. For example, in English *man* taken figuratively means all human beings and includes male, female and child. The root of the term is probably the Sanskrit *manas* or mind which implies to think. Whereas, man taken literally as a property or attribute of human being is a gender and age designator and means adult male, but not female or child. From the *naigama* point of view, man is a synthesis or union of both the literal and figurative, and within it no distinction is made. One can speak of a chairman or postman whether the individual is male, female, or child. One might also from the *naigama* point of view say that a wheel touches the ground, which means that figuratively the whole wheel as well as literally a point on the outer rim is in contact with the earth, and no distinction is made when we refer to the wheel's 'holding the road'. We also use this synthesis of the literal and the figurative when we construct computer and/or mathematical models of the world.

Fallacious Reasoning (Nayābhāsa)

Fallacious reasoning occurs within this point of view if one emphasizes absolute distinctions or absolute non-distinctions as in the case of distinctions between things and their characteristics.[56] To insist that an absolute difference can be drawn between an individual and his/her behavior, or to insist that absolutely no such distinction can be drawn are equally flawed. The fallacy would also occur if one were to assert an absolute separation between the literal and the figurative. In viewing the world as a subject/object continuum, it would be a fallacy to deny either one with the other.

Viewpoint of Present Circumstance (Ṛjūsutra Naya)

This is a *naya* with an existential orientation in that from it one emphasizes objects or individuals from a circumstance or condition possessed at the present moment in time and space. Because a woman has a child, this mother circumstance might be stressed over other characteristics and possibilities especially if these are related to past or future. The individual who is collecting garbage is a garbage collector. A person working in a laboratory or teaching a course in chemistry is a scientist. If this individual is also a mother outside of the lab, this is recognized but not primary to the present consideration of the individual as a scientist. A person who has been admitted to a hospital becomes a patient person. A person confined in a prison becomes an inmate person. In both cases the immediate patient or inmate status takes momentary precedence over being a person outside of this immediate state. One is considered primarily on the basis of that which one is at the moment. In Anglo-Saxon jurisprudence, one is viewed as innocent until proven guilty. And if found guilty, this new immediate state then defines the individual.

Fallacious Reasoning (Nayabhāsa)

The fallacy of this view would consist of absolutizing a present condition or circumstance to the exclusion of others, and/or to the exclusion of past and future conditions and circumstances. In such a case the present condition becomes the only condition. A depressed individual who views life as meaningless in the present may see the past and future as hopeless and commit suicide. If the approach to psychology one encounters at the moment is behavioristic or Freudian, then one might conclude that psychology is behaviorism or Freudianism, to the exclusion of other possibilities. One may view a student, convict, garbage collector, mother as only that which he/she is at the moment. This would be to fallaciously absolutize a characteristic.

Linguistic Meaning Viewpoint (Śabda Naya)

From this *naya* one views objects, persons, or events from a contextual point of view by emphasizing what terms mean in contexts in which they are used. In addition, this point of view recognizes that there are many synonyms whose forms are different but whose meaning is the same; or that we can use the same terms in addressing different individuals and give these terms different meanings.[57] This point of view looks at words in reference to context and meaning rather that specific symbols employed in a statement.[58]

This *naya* is most useful in translating between languages and in the creation of distilled, tool languages like symbolic and mathematical logics where contextual or formal meanings are preserved across different symbol systems or even in different languages. It is also useful in the construction of formulae in the physical and social sciences where the structure of the formula expresses the contextual essence of a set of relationships.

Fallacious Reasoning (Nayābhāsa)

In this symbolic view a fallacy results if a context is considered exclusive or absolute to the exclusion of other contextual meanings. This frequently occurs when individuals claim to have had the same experience or have collected facts but fail to realize these experiences and/or facts, even if they sound similar, were acquired in different contexts. The fallacy often expresses the assumption that a word can have only one contextual meaning, or that in taking a poll, the same question is being asked of every respondent. The knowledge gained therefrom may be used quite dogmatically.

Etymological Viewpoint (Samabhirūḍa Naya)

This too is a word-centered *naya*. It differs from *śabda naya* in that the emphasis is upon the etymological and original meanings of words or upon older special usages of a term. Here one views the world through a refinement of a semantic standpoint. One from many historical meanings of a term is emphasized.[59] With this *naya*, although every age and time has its meanings, older and/or original ones can be and are stressed and intended. For example, one might use democratic in the Greek sense which also accommodated slaves and women who could not participate in government. The framers of the American Constitution established just such a democracy. Eighteenth-century meanings of 'citizen', or 'rights', may take precedence over political and legal interpretations of the twentieth century and the US Supreme Court is always dealing with traditional intent and interpretations, even as its establishes new intents and interpretations. Other examples might be the uses of a special vocabulary historically employed in a field which would not be available to uses in other disciplines. The term catholic means universal, but it has also come to represent a particular Christian sect. If the term is used in the former sense, it might be applied to many philosophies, including Buddhist, but in the latter sense it means Roman Christianity. From this *naya* one must know the original or older meaning of a term in order to use it correctly.

Fallacious Reasoning (Nayābhāsa)

In the etymological view, if it is considered exclusive or absolute, a particular historical meaning of a term becomes that term's meaning to the exclusion of all others.[60] Older meanings become the only meanings. Only women can become hysterical, for only women possess a uterus (from the Greek, *hyster*). A word in a modern translation of a text may be rejected because it is not the older word and meaning as in the case of using maiden Mary, instead of virgin Mary in translating Christian scriptures. This switch in usage resulted in public Bible burnings of the Revised Standard Version of the New Testament in the US in the 1950s because it was felt that only the older term was acceptable, regardless of developments in scriptural scholarship that went into translating the seventeenth-century version.

Present Usage Viewpoint (Evaṁbhūta Naya)

Here the meaning of a term is restricted to present usage. From this *naya*, the meaning of a term is separated in emphasis from its past contexts and meanings. This is apt to be the case with contemporary technical vocabularies as well as slangs. For example, the Latin *personna* meant mask. In contemporary usage person, personnel, personality tend to mean essences or wearer of the masks. From this point of view, one can remove any term from traditional contexts and interpretations and give it a new meaning. Older meanings would be de-emphasized. For example the term 'gay' which until recently meant happy, now means homosexual and is often applied exclusively in this sense. There are a number of identities, functions, and activities for which the primary identity is the name or term as in contemporary combinations of time/space versus the earlier separate meanings of the terms.

Fallacious Reasoning (Nayābhāsa)

In this restrictive view, if it is considered exclusive or absolute, a term applies only to the present nature, function, or activity of an individual or object. This sort of absolute when applied to any word takes it beyond a philosophy of language, to a dogma dependent upon terminology as in the case where a particular modern jargon equates with knowledge in a field. This fallacy is one in which terminology both identifies and creates an absolute present which precludes discussion either of its nature, or of opposing viewpoints on the nature of language.

Nayavāda Logic Questions

One might summarize *nayavāda* logic in a series of what I will call gateway questions. These are the questions which are answered in the seven-step system of *syādvāda*: (1) What does one know, or want to know? What is claimed as knowledge? (2) What is the most basic viewpoint and/or purpose involved in the knowing process? What are the implicit and explicit assumptions? (3) What important points of view and assumptions were de-emphasized? (4) How might the emphasized and the de-emphasized be combined or in what sense might they be considered supplementary and/or complementary? (5) How can this emphasis be verified and expressed to someone else? What subject/predicate relationships would be presupposed, what definitions mutually accepted? (6) What cannot be expressed or measured or defined to and for another, and why?

II. *Syādvāda*: a logic for acquiring knowledge

Between the *nayavāda* system and the *syādvāda* system there is a clear relationship. The former produces the framework within which one recognizes and examines the points of view from which one knows the world. Thus *nayavāda* eliminates the lack of awareness on the part of knowers of their viewpoints and assumptions, and so removes their ignorance. The *syādvāda* provides the system and technique for this non-absolutist expression. Its great classical development is found in the *Syādvāda Mañjarī* commentary of the 13th century Jain philosopher Mallişeṇa.

Nayavāda and *syādvāda* are ultimately inseparable. *Nayavāda* is the source of *syādvāda*, and *syādvāda* is the expression of *nayavāda*. Historically the application of *syādvāda* to predication within *nayavāda* probably dates from the second or third centuries AD. And from this point on, they have been considered complementary. To speak of acquisition of knowledge without elimination of ignorance of the point of view from which such knowledge is acquired is as limiting, as is the elimination of ignorance without the following acquisition of knowledge.[61]

In *nayavāda*, we have already encountered the application of the theory of the multiplicity of reality, or realities (*anekāntavāda*) to the nature of knowledge. And we have discussed the flaws in reasoning that arise when any one standpoint becomes an absolute (*nayābhāsa*). Our next step is to translate *anekāntavāda* and *nayavāda* into their logical counterpart, *syādvāda*.

Syādvāda is a logical system within which, in a sequence of seven judgments, the relative nature of knowledge is preserved (non-absolutism), while at the same time recognition of the truth of relative aspects of knowledge is possible. *Syādvāda* permits us to link subjects and predicates in statements in sequences, while at the same time emphasizing that no particular subject/predicate combination is absolute or exists by itself. Any proposition then has seven aspects or seven stages, the truth of any one of which is restricted to that particular stage and is not applicable to any other. Each stage represents a standpoint. The term *syād* or *syāt* has a number of meanings and is usually translated with 'relatively' or 'just in this sense', or 'let it be', or 'it is thus'. Each proposition in the seven-part series (*Saptabhaṅgī*) is preceded by the term *syād* which clearly indicates its relative and non-absolutist meaning.[62] These seven stages are as follows:

1. *Syād-asti*: relatively: 'it is' or 'is so'.
2. *Syād-nāsti*: relatively: 'it is not' or 'is not so'.
3. *Syād-asti-nāsti*: relatively: 'it is and is not' or 'is and is not so'.
4. *Syād-avaktavya*: relatively: 'it is indescribable'.
5. *Syād-asti-avaktavya*: relatively: 'it is' and is 'indescribable'.
6. *Syād-nāsti-avaktavyam*: relatively: 'it is not' and is 'indescribable'.
7. *Syād-asti-nāsti-avaktavya*: relatively: 'it is and is not' and is 'indescribable'.

Each stage in the seven-step process adds a dimension to each of the preceding stages, and understanding each stage implies understanding this relationship. For example, the first *syād* affirms an object or state of affairs from a point of view. The second *syād* negates this affirmation from another point of view or another emphasis. The second does not contradict the first but rather represents a supplementary perspective. These are jointly expressed in the third stage which is a synthesis of affirmation and negation. The fourth stage incorporates the three preceding stages and adds that from a point of view the object or state of affairs is indescribable. The fourth stage introduces the element of language into the knowing process. And in the fourth stage, the subject/predicate positions are reversed. The subject cannot be predicated. Stages five, six and seven then reflect this. The fifth stage repeats the affirmation of stage one, but with the qualifying insight of the point of view expressed in four. The sixth repeats the negation of two, but with the qualification of four. With the seventh stage it is clear that one can both affirm and negate but that from a point of view the element or condition is indescribable. The Jains believe that the complete knowledge of anything would necessarily entail knowledge of everything in all relationships and vice versa.[63]

I believe that one of the most important values of the seven-step series is the challenging necessity it presents for understanding at each level the points of view from which a statement can be made. This means understanding in the first three stages the possibilities for affirming, negating, and combining affirmation/negation as well as the nature and possibility of describability implicit in affirmation and negation. The fourth stage requires an understanding of indescribability both in general and as it applies in the particular case and then its relationship to affirmation, negation, and the combination. One through three and five through seven, are separated by the position of the subject in four – and we believe it is this fourth stage which places the greatest demand upon the self-understanding of the knowing subject. In processing any observation or set of statements through the seven-part system, it is important to identify the perspective or *naya* from which the statement is made and to which its acceptance is relative. In the following example, each position identifies a point of view from which one might study any living organism:

(1) *Syād-asti*: A frog is a living organism, (This considers the frog from one's awareness as it hops across one's path. This is a frog as a whole, the *apparent* frog.)

(2) *Syād-nāsti*: A frog is not a living organism. (This considers the now reduced frog in a lab from the point of view of its particular chemical components. From this point of view, there is no compound or set of compounds that could be considered life. This is a frog of parts and pieces, the *essential* frog.)

(3) *Syād-asti-nāsti*: A frog is and is not a living organism. (This views the frog both from its atomic and molecular nature and its functioning as a hopping whole. The frog in one sense exists, in another it does not exist. It is both apparent and essential.)

(4) *Syād-avaktavyam*: A frog is indescribable. (This views the frog from the insight that no description is ever complete or becomes that which one attempts to describe, and/or is always done on the basis of certain assumptions and definitions and takes place in the lab or on the path. This entails an awareness that language is a projection upon the world of experience. From the point of view of meaning contexts, there is no particular context which is the frog.)

(5) *Syād-asti-avaktavyam*: A frog is a living organism and is indescribable. (From this point of view one describes the living frog but retains one's awareness that the description is not the frog, for it is relative, incomplete, and contextual.)

(6) *Syād-nāsti-avaktavyam*: A frog is not a living organism and is indescribable. (From this point of view, one describes the frog in terms of the parts and processes of which it is composed, but the frog is indescribable because these parts and processes are also relative and contextual.)

(7) *Syād-asti-nāsti-avaktavyam*: A frog is and is not a living organism and is indescribable. (This *syād* is particularly important for it stresses that there is no difference in the problem of a description's corresponding to a frog – whether the describing is done by a poet or a biologist or a chemist. No description is the true and only one. All are relative and operate on the basis of different perspectives, but none describes the frog as it is.)

In this seven-stage sequence, the fourth step is perhaps the most important and the most difficult for in order to fulfill it one must develop an idea and a principle for 'indescribability'.

In distinguishing between consciousness and the content of consciousness, some Chinese philosophers refer to the mind as empty. They compare it to a rice bowl whose usefulness and function, even when it is full of rice, is its emptiness. The empty mind could also be placed into the seven-step *syādvāda* system and the nature of its emptiness clarified in a sort of C'han/Zen Buddhist exercise:

(1) *Syād-asti*: The mind is empty. To study for a test one memorizes facts, but no matter how many facts one memorizes, the mind can memorize still more. Thus the mind is empty when we focus upon memorizing.
(2) *Syād-nāsti*: The mind is not empty. A mind has memories and thoughts, therefore the mind is not empty if one focuses upon memory and not memorizing.
(3) *Syād-asti-nāsti*: The mind is and is not empty. The mind is empty as thinking process in that it is neither that about which one thinks nor limited by what one thinks. The mind is not empty in that it contains thoughts. Because the mind does thinking it is both empty and not empty.
(4) *Syād-avaktavyam*: The mind is indescribable. The mind is thinking and thinking as thought is describable, but describing thinking as thought is thinking which is not that being described and is thus indescribable.
(5) *Syād-asti-avaktavyam*: The mind is empty and is indescribable. Thinking is not the thought that occurs in the mind and thus the mind is empty, but saying this is not the emptiness of the mind. Thus the mind is empty and indescribable.
(6) *Syād-nāsti-avaktavyam*: The mind is not empty and is indescribable. The mind is not empty because it contains memories, and these memories are describable, but mind as recalling and describing is indescribable and is not memory. Thus the mind is not empty and is indescribable.
(7) *Syād-asti-nāsti-avaktavyam*: The mind is empty and is not empty and is indescribable. The mind is empty because mind as thinking is not the thought that occurs in the mind, and it is not empty because the thinking mind contains this description just given. Thus the mind is empty and not empty. And it is indescribable because the thinking which produced this description is not a description.[64]

One will also use some version of this seven-part series whenever thinkers or knowers attempt to include themselves in some definition or description. That which is defining is both defining and undefinable in any absolute sense – this does not imply that one cannot define, simply that the definition is neither that which is defined nor the definer.

Each level in the sequence after the first gives us at least two very important insights: (1) a perspective upon the level before it, rendering it relative and not absolute, and thus not contradictory; (2) and this perspective produces the basis for the synthesis that occurs at the next level. Thus, in is and is not, we have the combination of the third *syād*, which in turn provides the synthesis represented in the fourth *syād*. From the fourth *syād*, we return to the first three again. Truth and certainty are possible, of course, but they are defined by the *naya* level of the *syād*. They do not define the level. This is one of the most important differences between object and subject logic. In object logic there tends to be only one level which is the real level – and this level, as well as its name, is defined by the object itself. It is critical to remember here that we are dealing with viewpoints of a subject who is making an assertion, judgment, proposition – and with objects as they are recognized and understood by observers. In an object logic, where some form of revelation either by Nature or God places things as they are into the mind, any statement about existence or any description of existing things can be checked against the revealed object or the revealed scripture.

Syādvāda could be said to have three rules for inference: (1) Propositions are made from points of view and are relative (*syād*) to same. (2) Treating any proposition from this list of seven as the only possibility and excluding or forgetting the *syad*, is a fallacy. Combining subject logic with object logic, we might say that there is no single school of psychology, or biology, or philosophy, or physics, for one can be the school only from a point of view. This second rule of inference could be summarized thus: In all statements in a logical system, the relativity of the statement must be asserted explicitly. When this does not occur, the line of reasoning is fallacious (dogmatic). (3) Any standpoint implies all others, and to understand any particular *syād*, one must be able to process a term in some sense through all *syāds*.

Summary

Although the system of *syādvāda* may seem strange at first to the individual conditioned by the object tradition, in a basic sense it corresponds to modern developments in that tradition which have changed the objectivist's way of speaking and thinking about the world within a view where there is no longer a clear subjective/objective dichotomy. For example, probability theory is a good illustration of the *syādvāda* system for it implies might be, might not be, and in terms of the concept of probability itself, indescribability.

When in modern physical and social science we incorporate subjects into observations, this should be reflected in a system of *syādvāda* which in turn reflects our awareness of the *naya* from which we make statements and acquire knowledge. Theories of proof and disproof must also reflect viewpoints, for we do not prove wholes, we prove parts and aspects. Einstein's 'We can observe only what our theories permit us to observe', can be translated into 'We can prove only what our theories permit us to prove or disprove.'

Part III

The Situational Dimension of Philosophical Space

9 Situations and Raising Dead Lions

The *Panchantantra* relates the story of four Brāhmins who, seeking fame and wealth, set out together on a journey. Three were great scholars, the fourth was a man of common sense. One day, chancing upon a carcass in a forest, the three scholars decide to demonstrate their erudition and skill by restoring it to life. The man of common sense protests that the remains look like those of a lion and to revive them would be a serious mistake. He is ridiculed by his colleagues who begin the resurrection process while the man of common sense climbs a tree to watch. The scholar who was a specialist in bones restores the skeleton, the scholar who understood skin and flesh restores the body, and the third who is a biologist and specializes in the study of life itself brings it to life, whereupon the lion devours all three. The man of common sense waits in the tree until the lion is done with lunch and leaves.[1] The moral of the story is that possessing knowledge is no guarantee that one has wisdom or understanding.

Situation comes from the Latin root *situs*, meaning location or place but in the discussion of the situational dimension of philosophical space, the term will be expanded to include mental states as well as physical places. When one incorporates consciousness into situation, one can identify two inseparable but different kinds of situation: the immediate, indeterminate, experiential situation of momentary sensing; and the reflective and determinate conceptual situation which is based on the memories, interpretations, abstractions, and ideas within which we recognize that which we sense. For example, a chest pain is felt as immediate and present, but one's definition of oneself as a 'sick man' is a conceptual situation in which one may live for years.

We tend to confuse the experiential situation with the conceptual one, sensing for the sensed. Understanding their relationship to one another is indispensable to understanding the situational dimension. In this chapter, two different systems, the Nyāya and the Buddhist, have been selected to illustrate the situational possibilities for relating conceptual and perceptual aspects of situations. Although thinkers in these two schools disagreed with one another radically on many points, they both gave a situational stress to knowledge which is expressed in their theories of inference in situational logics.

In the case of Nyāya philosophy, a situation represents a six-part synthesis of (1) the *Ātman*, soul, knower; (2) the body, which is the receptacle of the *Ātman*'s physical experience; (3) the senses which are the instruments of knowledge; (4) the objects known; (5) the circumstances and conditions of the experience; (6) the mind which processes the experience.[2] Nyāya philosophers maintain that self and the world both exist prior to their situational encounters. As a result, conceptualizing takes precedence over sensation for without conceptually recognizing what one is sensing, there is no knowledge. For the Buddhists, self does not exist prior to experience and is in fact an illusion created out of experience by memory and habit as in the case of prefacing what one says with the pronoun 'I'. Feeling hungry is quite different from stating that this 'feeling hungry' belongs to 'I'. The doctrine of no-self is called *anātman* in Sanskrit (*anatta* in Pali). For the Buddhists, there is no sensible, enduring essence which transcends the momentary 'here and now'. As a consequence, conceptualization must depend upon and follow from immediate sensing. And as far as the objects of sensation are concerned, here too there is no permanent matter which is the source of the sensed. Any moment is viewed as the effect of all previous moments and situations, to which it has only a functional relationship. This is doctrine of no-permanent matter or *anitya* in Sanskrit (*anicca* in Pali).

Although 'situational encounter' is fundamental to both Nyāya and Buddhist philosophers, there is considerable difference as to the nature of the encounter and its consequences. For the Nyāya, the revived lion is real and with its essential force restored, it devours the Brāhmins. For the Buddhist, the lion is a magic show, a mirage which like the self can seem so real that one believes one is being devoured or watching the Brāhmins being eaten.

From the Nyāya perspective, a situation provides the field for discovering permanent universals and their interrelationships. These universals are non-mental essences or realities. For the Buddhist, relationships apart from unique moments are mentally constructed conceptual objects which have their origins in the momentary sensing of objects but they are not that which is sensed nor do they possess a self-nature (*sambhava*) which is more real than being sensed. Knowledge begins with immediate sensing from which conceptualized universals may follow but such universals and essences are the products of imagination and memory and not reality. From these different positions, two different approaches to the situational dimension of philosophical space and to situational inference follow: that of the Nyāya which stresses relationships of universals in situations, and that of the Buddhist which stresses sensing, and then universals only as products of memory.

Right knowledge

The Nyāya philosopher, Vātsyāyana (fourth century AD), introduced his commentary upon the *Nyāya Sūtras of Gautama* (sixth century BC) with a discussion of right cognition – its nature and application.[3] The Buddhist logician, Dharmakīrti (sixth century AD), began his treatise on logic (*The Nyāya-Bindu*) with the proposition: 'All successful human action is preceded by right knowledge.' And he related the situation of knowledge acquisition to the situation of its application.[4] Logic for the Nyāya and the Buddhist facilitates the application of experience and knowledge from prior situations to present and future ones. In both systems, origin and application were clearly identified.

In the Nyāya, the appropriate knowledge techniques (*pramāṇas*) are perception, inference, analogy, and verbal testimony or word. Perception is the meeting of a sense organ with its object. Inference is the after-cognition or recognition of an object based upon the selection of some particular feature from the cognition. Analogy is comparison or approximation of similarities in different objects. And word is the symbol for the object, or is verbal testimony or description.[5]

The Buddhists reduced this list to *inference* and *perception.* Analogy and verbal testimony were subsumed under these two.[6] Although inference and perception are related and both were situational, they are distinctly different in what they can make known, and in their difference are mutually exclusive.[7] Perceiving is immediate experiencing but inference is trans-situational and introduces previous conditions into current experience. Based on the difference between sensing and inferring, the Buddhist logicians Dināga and Dharmakīrti identified two kinds of knowledge: that which is non-shareable (*svalakṣaṇa*) indeterminate, momentary, specific and individual; and that which is shareable (*sāmānyalakṣaṇa*) which is determinate and conceptual and is an operation of the interpreting mind.[8]

Sensing is clearly situational. Inferring is also situational in that one always reasons in a situation as in reasoning *now*. And that about which one reasons in an immediate experience is understood on the basis of experiences in other situations. Inferring means identifying similarities and dissimilarities in relationships between and among objects and events in different places and times. In logic, the relating of similarity and dissimilarity is accomplished methodologically by incorporating example and application steps into any line of reasoning.

Since the Nyāya system of logic is the older (Nyāya means logic or syllogism), and since Buddhist logic uses and then modifies the Nyāya forms in response to what Dināga and Dharmakīrti and others perceived as its limitations, we shall begin with the Nyāya system. The Nyāya, as members of the Vedic/Upaniṣadic tradition accepted the existence of a deity, Īśvara, who controlled and regulated the world. They also assumed the existence of a soul or self in the knowing subject. All of these the early Buddhists rejected. Thus, though we would term both logics situational, they reflect different views on the inclusiveness and exclusiveness of knowledge in its acquisition and its application.

NYĀYA AND THE WORLD OF ĪŚVARA

According to traditional accounts, the Nyāya school of Indian thought was founded by Gautama in the fourth century BCE, and its companion school, the Vaiśeṣika, was probably started somewhat earlier by Kaṇāda. Both are among the oldest philosophical movements in India, originating in the sixth to the third centuries BCE. Philosophically, the chaos of the age in which Gautama and Kaṇāda lived parallel in many ways the chaos of Athens, at the time of Plato and Aristotle.

Like their Socratic contemporaries, the Nyāya/Vaiśeṣika taught that beyond the infinite variety of experienced appearances, there was an ordering, controlling intelligence. This was the God Īśvara who oversees all events from the process of transmigration to the growth and decay of plants to the changes of the seasons. The world process in its totality was neither accidental nor inanimate.[9] Īśvara, though not the creator, was the efficient orderer of the way the world is.[10] Īśvara is *not a personal deity* as in the Western monotheistic sense, but rather the ultimate principle of intelligibility in the world. To understand the world process is to liberate the eternal *Ātman* from the cycles of rebirth and to this end the assumption of intelligibility was essential. It was, however, intelligibility manifested in situation, and the Nyāya philosophers viewed situational logic as divine contemplation and worship.[11]

The Nyāya and Vaiśeṣika theory of the physical world was atomistic and pluralistic. The human spirit, or *Ātman*, was the source of individual consciousness. It too was seen as pluralistic in that it was distinct in different individuals, but it was not atomic. The mind as the source of the internal sense and co-ordinator of the external senses, was atomic but was not *Ātman*. The Nyāya felt that the mind could not be *Ātman* because one can change one's mind and exercise self-control over it. It is in this sense that both knowledge in an orderly determined world and the free will of a willing *Ātman* are both possible. The function of logic was to bridge the two.

The mind understands the senses, and the *Ātman* in turn understands the mind. *Ātman* is inferred from the concept of a possessor of intelligence and the experience of cognition. There must be a possessor of intelligence for consciousness to exist.[12] The purpose of *Ātman* is that of achieving liberation from the wheel of rebirth, and thus it does not assume an immediate part in knowledge. But it is the ultimate knower who knows the world as it is in its vast variety of objects and events. The *Ātman* both transcends the world and is part of it. It is both situational and purposive beyond situations. In order to prevent attachment to any of the pain/pleasure states, one must both cognize and recognize the multiplicity of substances and characteristics that are the changing world. This is the position of a pluralist, not a dualist. Real knowledge is knowledge of the situations in which the uninvolved *Ātman* experiences the world via mind, sense, and objects of perception.

The Nyāya, as did the Jains, proposed a dualistic distinction between *Ātman* and the world of things. The Nyāya recognized universals as having an existence apart from our experience of them, but knowledge and experience of universals arises in situations.

Reality: non-situational and situational

Reality consists of nine substances: earth, air, water, fire, ether, time, space, self, mind. Associated with these nine substances are seventeen characteristics or attributes: color, taste, smell, touch, sound, number, measure, separateness, conjunction, disposition, priority, posteriority, understandings, pleasure, pain, aversion, volition. In addition to the substances and their attributes, Kaṇāda accepted five types of action: throwing upwards, downwards, contraction, expansion, and motion.[13]

These nine substances, seventeen characteristics, and five types of action are reflected in six types of human experience of the world: The first of these are of the objects and the objective: substance, quality, activity. The next three are arrived at by way of inference: generality, particularity, and inherence (belonging to, being contained in). Whether or not one accepts these listings or would substitute others, it is clear from the ideas of substance, attribute, and experience that the situational encounter is fundamental. And it is an encounter in a pluralistic world where the total number of things as combinations of the above cannot be established.[14]

This view of the world is *realist* and *empirical*, and its situational emphasis is maintained in great measure because the multiplicity of possible experiences can not be reduced to a priori universal principles and logical abstractions. Experience and inference based upon experience in situations remains central. On the other hand, one can and does experience the universal in situations according to the Nyāya and one's perception of substances are perceptions of them as they are. If there is an error, as in mistaking a rope for a snake, the error is not in cognition, but in recognition and can be clarified or eliminated by further experience. What one sees is what one sees, and if one's interpretation is in error, one must look again. It is also clear from the listing of substances, characteristics and actions that reality always presents a very complex appearance to the perceiver. These substances and attributes can influence one another, create one another, and combine with one another.[15]

Situational logic I: the Nyāya

Nyāya logic has its roots in a strict correspondence theory of perception which involves a three-step process in which the senses contact objects in situations; the mind then comes in contact with the senses, and *Ātman* then encounters the mind.[16] This latter *Ātman-to-mind* contact is important, for it is out of this that the mind can be changed, will exercised, and ethical choices made.

The situationality of knowledge also produces a situational theory of language, for symbol meaning then emerges in the situation in which it is employed. There is no natural or fixed relationship between a word or symbol and that which it symbolizes. Nor is there a correspondence between symbol and thought. Although a universal as an idea is constant, the many names for it may vary. Thus, not meaning, but the meaning of a symbol is conventional and a symbol can stand for the universal, particular and relative, according to its use in a situation.[17]

The Nyāya five-part syllogism

Our concern with Nyāya logic is with its theory and use of inference (*anumāna*) as a technique for correct knowledge. Gautama maintained that there were three kinds of inference. Two of these were *causal*, from cause to effect and from effect to cause, and the third was from the commonly or *con-jointly* seen. This latter type was inference from the perceptible to the imperceptible on the basis of constant association in experience. For example, though one may see only a horse's head and front legs, one infers that there are also hind legs and a tail. One infers from the expensive car a person drives that the person is wealthy.

The syllogism developed by the Nyāya consisted of five parts. Within these, there are at least seven situational steps. The first pair of these are identification steps, the second pair are isolation steps, the third pair are transference steps, and the final step is one which affirms the original proposition. As we examine the Nyāya five-part syllogism, we need to keep the function of each step clearly in mind. Each adds a special dimension to the total. In particular the fourth and fifth, which consist of two parts each, emphasize the situational nature of the whole:[18]

I. THESIS (*Pratijñā*): There is fire upon the mountain. The thesis identifies the relationship that is to be proved or demonstrated in connecting different situations in an inferential sequence.

II. REASON (*Hetu*): Because there is smoke upon the mountain. The reason identifies the principle of recognition which will be used in connecting situations. And as principle, it identifies whether the inference process involved is causal (cause to effect, or effect to cause), or one based upon that which is commonly/co-jointly seen, the imperceptible from the perceptible.

III. EXAMPLE (*Udāharaṇa*):
EXAMPLE: Affirmative. Where there is smoke there is fire as in the wood stove, or smoking pile of leaves, or in a cigarette (*modus ponens*).
EXAMPLE: Negative. Where there is no fire, there is no smoke as in wet wood, a lake, a puddle where there may be steam or fog but no fire (*modus tollens*).

The example step using analogies isolates in previous situations the relationship identified in steps #1 and #2. It isolates by emphasizing homogeneous or heterogeneous, affirmative or negative examples of situations where the relationship either was experienced or did not occur. It might relate objects by way of properties or properties by way of objects.[19] The examples must be clear and general enough that they facilitate both proof and understanding. The example step also identifies by implication the knowledge technique involved in knowing as in direct or indirect perception, experiment, analysis and so forth. The example step also restricts and limits the reason in correlating it with previous experience.[20]

IV. APPLICATION (*Upanaya*):
APPLICATION: Affirmative. And the smoke upon this mountain is like the smoke in the stove, leaves and cigarette.
APPLICATION: Negative. And the mountain is not like a lake, or wet wood, or a puddle where there can be no fire but where steam or fog might occur.

The application step analogically transfers the isolated relationships of both the homogeneous and the heterogeneous examples from previous situations, and applies them to the present situation. In the application step, one must now make clear that the relationships identified by the thesis and identified as the reason, isolated by both affirmative and negative examples, is indeed such a case as in the present situation. In the application step, inference transfers to the present situation the homogeneous and heterogeneous examples of past experience. Both a homogeneous and heterogeneous application should follow.[21]

V. CONCLUSION (*Nigamana*): Thus there is fire upon the mountain.

The final step of the inference appears in one sense to be a re-statement of the thesis. It is not, for it occurs here at the end of a completed inferential sequence of identifications which consists of the reason, example, and application operations. Together these reflect the total, situational reasoning process, not only as a series of isolated and transferred relationships, but also as an affirmation of the relating which has occurred and is occurring. An error or fallacy in any one of these stages renders the inference sequence fallacious.

Fallacies (*bhāsa*)

There are several hundred potential fallacies that can be identified within the five-part syllogism. And the Sūtras take two approaches to these, listing them individually and then grouping them into types.The following would seem to be the most important:

(1) Fallacies of reason (*Hetobhāsa*). Fallacious reasons are those which do not possess all the attributes of true reasons, but are sufficiently similar to the relationships asserted as to appear adequate.[22]
(2) Fallacies of Example. The fallacies of example will involve an example inappropriate in some sense in reference to the reason. Examples that are too general, too specific, or irrelevant would be unacceptable.
(3) Fallacies of Application. The fallacies of application will correspond to those of example in most cases, and they arise in applying the example to the present situation.

If one applies this five-step analysis to critical propositions in the natural and social sciences, one fairly quickly arrives at both the example origins of basic observations and theories and insight into their contemporary applicability, or lack of same. One area where this insight would be of considerable significance would be in the application of the observations of the object world to the areas of consciousness, as for example, in the treatment of mental illness, anxiety and depression where symptom and cause are often difficult to distinguish.

BUDDHIST SITUATIONALITY: DONKEYS AND TIGER SKINS

In a small village, there lived a laundryman whose only help in delivering his heavy bundles was a half-starved donkey. Unfortunately he earned so little that he could barely feed the beast. One day while gathering firewood in the forest, he came upon a dead tiger. He realized that if he were to skin it and put the skin on his donkey, it could then feed at night undisturbed in the grain fields of his neighbors who would be afraid to approach it. The scheme worked well and the donkey grew fat. However, early one morning the donkey heard a she-ass bray in the distance and automatically returned the call. The cautious farmers who had been watching the tiger from a distance realized at once that it was only an ass in a tiger's skin and killed it with clubs and stones.[23] The moral to this story might be that one doesn't become a tiger by wearing a tiger's skin, or that one cannot be other than what one is no matter how one dresses. For the no-self (*anatta*) and non-permanence (*anicca*) situational position of the Buddhists, the universals of the Nyāya were only conceptual tiger skins and products of memory and imagination with which individuals try to dress their lives with significance and meaning.

Gotama: the search for meaning

Perhaps Buddhist interpretations of the immediate, situational nature of awareness can best be illustrated with Gotama's (c.560–480 BCE) own search for enlightenment. Like all Indian philosophers, he was deeply concerned with the nature of consciousness, suffering, and the possibility of rebirth in the cycles of Samsāra as determined by Karma.

Gotama chose the path of *jñāna*, or inner wisdom, and not the path of *bhakti*, which is devotion to and worship of a deity, and so his quest for meaning was an internal and not an external one. His father, the king of a small state in Nepal, tried to keep his son isolated from the outside world, but despite the king's precautions, Gotama still encountered in the sheltered gardens of the royal compound four visions: those of an old man, a sick man, a corpse and a monk.

At 29, after these experiences, he left the palace, his wife, and son and began a seven-year search for enlightenment. During this period he deliberated with teachers from other philosophical systems, none of whom could provide what he was seeking. He practiced yoga control and meditation and even attempted an extreme form of aesceticism by starving and ignoring his physical body until one day he collapsed. Gradually, in the care of friends he recovered his strength. Aesceticism had proven itself as useless as the doctrines of the various schools, and he abandoned it too. Finally, after meditating for 49 days under a Bo tree he achieved the understanding he sought.

Gotama's enlightenment involved a middle ground between two important contemporary Indian positions: The first consisted of those philosophies which assumed the absolute existence of self. These explained consciousness as a self which accumulated *karma* in endless suffering and rebirth. Gotama, however, experienced consciousness only in the immediacy of being aware, and not as a transcendental and/or absolute spiritual framework for experience. He concluded that such a spiritual self was an illusion and that the search for such an essence was futile. He began to teach the practicing of self as immediate, situational awareness, and the understanding that *Karma* is empty.[24]

The second position with which he differed was that of the materialists who attributed an absolute existence to one or more substances and maintained that these were the real essences which produced the world of appearances. Gotama's experience of the world, like his experience of awareness, was of a multiplicity of sensations and stimuli functionally dependent and interdependent upon one another just as the immediate experience of an apple is a function of taste, texture, color, smell. These do not cause the apple, the apple does not cause these impressions. Conceptually this functional whole becomes an 'apple'. All experiences seemed functionally and sequentially dependent upon one another without a transcendental and independent self-nature or identity glueing them together or defining them: 'it remains a fact and the fixed and necessary constitution of being that all of its constituents are transitory'.[25]

Applying immediate sensing to the concepts of sensor which the other schools taught, and finding he could detect no owner of sensation, Gotama concluded there was no self, though there was desiring, obsession, anxiety, anger. For the individual who does not understand this, sensing and conceiving play illusory tricks:

> '... he conceives [himself as] the cognized, he conceives [himself] in the cognized, he conceives [himself apart] from the cognized, he conceives the cognized to be "mine." he delights in the cognized. Why is that? Because he has not fully understood it, I say.' The Buddha or Tathāgata who understands this: '... directly knows earth as earth. Having directly known earth as earth, he does not conceive [himself as] earth, he does not conceive [himself] in earth, he does not conceive [himself apart] from earth, he does not conceive earth to be "mine," he does not delight in earth ... Because the Tathāgata has fully understood it to the end ...'[26]

As Buddhaghoṣa later noted: 'Misery alone doth exist, none miserable.'[27]

Self and no-self

The application of sensing to sensor produced an analysis of person into that which would seem to be immediately sensible and knowable, and into that which is conjecture, concept, and interpretation after the fact generated by memory and imagination. Sensing is the immediacy of seeing, hearing, tasting, touching, smelling. Each of these senses will give rise to a particular kind of consciousness as visual consciousness, auditory consciousness, tactile consciousness. Thinking too produces a mind consciousness and: '... when consciousness arises dependent on the mind and mind-objects, it is reckoned as mindconsciousness. Just as fire is reckoned by the particular condition dependent on which it burns ... so too, consciousness is reckoned by the particular condition dependent on which it arises.'[28] As was suggested in the discussion of the object dimension, any one of these types of consciousness can be conceptually given primacy over the others. In the case of the tactile sense this might equate reality with space and solidity. Mind-consciousness gives rise to the 'fire' of universals, ego and self. The Buddha explains that consciousness has formations and ideas as its source and 'Formations have ignorance as their source, ignorance as their origin.'[29] But, as Nāgārjuna wrote in the second century AD: 'No agent of seeing exists either detached from or not detached from the act of seeing.'[30]

Awareness is always also awareness of awareness and thus requires no possessor of awareness. The 'I' which seems to sense conceptually is a conceptual object, not a perceptual one. If I am aware of blue, I am also immediately aware of my awareness of blue. This is cognizing and at the same time is cognizing of cognizing. According to Dināga, one does not need a self or a soul for this to occur.[31] Nor does one need a name in order for perception or an impression to take place.[32] This brings with it the interesting situational insight that often what we believe we perceive is a mind-consciousness abstraction and/or a name for other names. According to Dināga, immediate cognizing is nameless, unique, and unshareable. The interpreted perception or conception, however, can be named and shared.[33]

The Buddhist denial of self is not a denial of consciousness or awareness but rather an affirmation of being aware. What we think of as 'self' is a composite of five physical and psychic functional aggregates or *skandhas* which occur situationally: (1) *rūpa* or body: these are the aggregates of the senses and the sensed, materiality, bodyness, things; (2) *vedanā* or feelings: these are the aggregates of pleasure, pain, anger, indifference; (3) *saññā* or perceptions/conceptions: these are the aggregates of concepts, interpretations, theories, explanations; (4) *saṁskāra* or motivations and dispositions: these are the aggregates of willing, wanting, shame, anxiety; and (5) *vijñāna* or consciousness: these are the aggregates of awareness of awareness.[34]

Nāgārjuna maintained that these aggregates are like the flame of a lamp which illumines the moment.[35] Dasgupta in discussing the Buddhist *skandhas* notes: '... these states rise depending one upon the other (*paticca-samuppāda*) and when a man says that he perceives the self he only deludes himself, for he only perceives one or more of these'.[36] *The Heart Sūtra* teaches that the *skandhas* are empty individually and collectively for their very nature is emptiness.[37] They are like a bowl whose usefulness is its emptiness. Regardless of what one places in it, the emptiness never becomes that which is placed in it. However if we confuse the emptiness of the bowl for what it contains, then we may think that the bowl becomes rice or beans or water. The five aggregates are empty of self and empty of objects. Each is a way of experiencing. For example, desiring is a feeling aggregate. It is like the bowl, an empty psychic state and not an object. When a desire is 'satisfied' desiring continues because the desired object is never the desiring of it. Because 'self' as the aggregates is also empty, all attempts to find it or to discover its identity in the objects of which one is aware or which one desires, will lead to frustration and disappointment.

The idea of an independent self is linguistically reinforced when in speaking we identify the immediacy of the speaker with a first person pronoun: I, me, my, mine. However, one would find it an absurd question if asked to identify the noun for which this pronoun stands. Brentano was dealing with this 'paradox' when he observed: '... our individuality is not at all contained in a perceivable manner in our states of consciousness ... We do know, a priori, that we are individuals, but we have no intuition of the individualizing element.'[38]

The ancient Buddhist text, the *Questions of King Melinda*, is ostensibly a dialogue between King Melinda and Nāgasena, a Buddhist monk. When the King asks Nāgasena to define himself, Nāgasena's reply is that Nāgasena is a name given by one's parents, a convention, a concept, but apart from this convention there is no self or soul. The King then numbers off the mental and physical elements of a human being and asks if these individually or collectively are Nāgasena. When Nāgasena replies no to each and all of them and repeats that Nāgasena is a mere convention, the King accuses him of lying for there has to be an independent somebody that is really Nāgasena and transcends all the particular situations in which the name is used, a self independent of temporal moment and particular place.

In response, the Monk asks the King if he came in a chariot. When the King answers yes, then Nāgasena asks him what a chariot is and lists all of its parts and purposes. In each case the King answers that these individually and collectively are not the chariot, that chariot is a name, a convention, a dependent concept. It is Nāgasena's turn to accuse the King of lying for according to the King's own position there has to be an independent something that is really the chariot and transcends all the situations in which the name is used, a chariot independent of temporal moment and particular place.[39]

These two examples illustrate the Buddhist position that there is the momentary situation and there is the conceptual convention which produces a name. They are not interchangeable and the former precedes the latter.

For Gotama, no-self or *anatta* meant no rebirth of self.[40] Rebirth is a conceptual illusion just like any other which claims to transcend sensing, attending, and intending. His was an applied, pragmatic enlightenment. One of the best known illustrations of the emphasis upon practice rather than conceptual abstraction was the Buddha's analogy of the warrior wounded by an arrow. It would be both absurd and fatal for the wounded man to postpone doing something about the arrow until he had identified the archer's caste, occupation, name, weight, size, birthplace; the arrow's source, make, shaft and plume materials; the bow's type and its string's tension.[41]

The contrast between immediate experiencing and its conceptual by-products is expressed in the Buddha's numerous sermons on 'suffering (*duḥkha*) but no sufferer'. The Fourfold Noble Truths begin with this insight: There is suffering. There is a cause of suffering. There is a cure or cessation of suffering. The Eightfold Noble Path of right view, right intention, right speech, right action, right livelihood, right effort, right mindfulness, and right concentration bring about the cure or cessation. The definition of suffering is birth, death, sickness, pain, sorrow, anxiety. The cause is wanting, desiring, craving to hold on to time, place, possessions or any conceptual situation that promises to transcend the immediate. The cure is non-attachment in a world of change, and each step of the Eightfold Path delineates a way to be at every moment. These cannot be used to transcend situations or to justify and explain them after the fact. They are all ways of being in the present.

Thich Nhat Hanh, a Vietnamese Buddhist, makes this point with the example of two ways of performing the common task of 'washing dishes': the first is to wash them in order to have clean dishes, the second is to wash the dishes in order to wash the dishes.[42] Any skilled craftsman, cabinet maker, welder, weaver will understand that he/she certainly works to earn a living, but living is also her/his working. It is a way of being, in which the skilled woodworker builds a chair intuitively in an immediate partnership with the wood.

Gotama applied to the knowing of the world the same principles he had applied to knowing self. From the contact of sense organs, object and sensing consciousness arise feelings, feeling leads to perception of what one feels, this leads to 'reflection on' and 'thinking about' which lead to attachment to things and concepts. We seem to contact in our sensing various objects which are part of a continuing flow and change of experience and awareness but he discovered no permanent, independent objects or substance apart from concepts erected by memory from experience. Nor did he perceive that there were not such essences. Neither existence nor non-existence can be seen as absolutes.

The Buddha frequently urged his followers to experience in their own living the momentariness of being. Applying this principle to his own teaching he would ask: 'Would you knowing and seeing all this, say: We revere our teacher, and it is because of our reverance for him that we affirm this?' The response of his followers was a resounding: 'No Sir.'[43] And in this spirit, the Zen Master I-Hsuan over a thousand years later will admonish his followers: 'Seekers of the Way ... Kill the Buddha if you happen to meet him.'[44]

The world: perceived and conceived

Whatever Buddhist philosophers assert in different schools, they address in some form these immediate situational and experiential principles of Gotama. If there is an appeal to something real, this appeal must relate to dependent sensing in a dependent world. This will be reflected in the development later of the inference theories of Dināga and Dharmakīrti. Things are their moving, changing functions. The critical question is not what something is really, but what does it do, how does it function.[45] These assumptions also distinguish the Nyāya syllogism from the Buddhist, and they explain the Buddhist modification and later rejection of portions of the Nyāya logic. The Buddhist is concerned with functional experiencing. Buddhist situational logic treats the non-immediate and nonsituational as static concept.[46]

The Buddhist logician, Dināga, maintained there was an absolute distinction between particular sensing which is unique and non-shareable (*svalakṣaṇa*), and generalized concepts and descriptions (*sāmānyalakṣaṇa*) which are shareable and provide the basis for recognition but are not perceived. When we name and reflect upon non-shareable moments, we make them shareable within mental frames of reference so that others may vicariously have a similar experience. However, before one can vicariously experience the *sāmānyalakṣaṇa*, one must have a non-shareable *svalakṣaṇa* reference point upon which understanding can be based.

The Buddhist view of causality is similar to the modern concept of function. According to Buddhaghoṣa: 'Causation or dependent arising is the mode of causes.... The modes of causes is that according to which co-ordinate phenomena are produced mutually. Therefore it is called causation.'[47] The term *function* indicates that two events or phenomena are experienced together with regularity as in the case with the solar system where the relationships of the planets to one another and to the sun could be considered their momentary functional relationships but not causes of one another. According to Friedrich Waismann, one can then describe their orbits within concurrent, concomitant, or functional systems mathematically, without limiting the phenomenon with a concept of causality.[48]

Classical ideas of 'causality' and 'identity' as transcendent sources of events are concepts with which we may fool ourselves into ignoring the functional present which is the tasting of the apple. The Buddha rejected static knowledge of things as they really are for he claimed to know them only as they have come to be.[49] In this sense everything is dependent in its nature and origin, and each moment is new. As the Greek, Heracleitus, asserted, we cannot step into the *momentary* river twice.[50] However, we can step again and again into the same *conceptual* one. It is also Hume's position that all we sense are sequences of sensations and events from which, after the fact, we construct concepts like causality. And these concepts may even seem more real than the actual experiences which were their sources. Neither Gotama's position, nor that of Waismann implies that the world is without order, for there is a continuity of consciousness/sensing/sensed. But it is precisely our experiencing of this continuity which should make us cautious in asserting the existence of permanent natures like self or substance that transcend change. This the Buddha left untaught, and what he had not taught was as important as what he had taught and far more extensive:

> What have I left untaught? – I have not taught that the world either is or is not eternal that it is finite or infinite; that life and the body are either identical or distinct; that after death a truth-finder either passes or does not pass to a further existence, or does both or neither. And why have I left these things untaught? – Because they are unprofitable and not fundamental to the higher life; because they do not conduce to weariness with mundane things, to passionlessness, to purgation, to tranquility, to insight, to full enlightenment, and to Nirvāṇa.[51]

Language and situation

The discussion of language in the situational dimension is particularly difficult because when we use language to talk about language we are both speaking in an immediate situation and trying to transcend it by speaking about it. One possibility for both speaking about language and retaining a situational awareness of what one is doing is provided in Nāgārjuna's answer to his critics who had attacked his position as itself void if everything else is so. Nāgārjuna declared that in his use of language to discuss voidness, (*śūnyatā*) language, like an empty container: '... devoid of an intrinsic nature because of being dependently originated is engaged in the task of establishing the being devoid-of-an-intrinsic nature of the things'.[52]

The Nyāya do not accept the idea of *śūnyatā* and so Nyāya logic is referential, while the Buddhist is descriptive.[53] For both Dināga and Dharmakīrti, immediate perception *per se* is of unique particulars and so is free from mental constructs.[54] What we linguistically call the same object in different instants is a combination of name and remembered focus and not an experienceable identity possessed by an object.

Because conceptual objects are mental derivations produced by the *mind-consciousness* from the perceptual objects of the other five senses, concepts represent an affirmation of an ever more general nature which is also reflected in language. It is this which makes perceptions relatively shareable.[55] However, when one seeks to establish meaning in a situational context, one must reverse this order, that is, negate these ascending levels of abstraction or universals by reducing them as closely as possible to their perceptual origins. If one does not reverse this order, then the reference of words is only to other words and not experience. This is why the Buddha would not respond to questions whose only answers could be word references and not experience. This is expressed in the *apoha* theory of perception and language which holds that knowing an object is knowing primarily what it is not, knowing the similar by excluding the dissimilar, that is knowing a term by negating its opposite. Dhirendra Sharma writes that: '... the meaning of the word c-o-w ... is the judgment "cow = non-not-cow". The ascertainment of the cow is based on the exclusion of all the cases of 'not-cow'... We know what a thing is by cognizing what it is not; one thus, knows its distinctness by inference from all cases of not-the thing.'[56] This is not the affirmative approach to knowledge as Plato and Aristotle would have it. It is a view which keeps one aware of the not non-mental nature of universals.[57] Two entities might be said to be similar to the degree they are less unlike one another than they are to other objects and entities.[58]

Emptying the mind of hardened concepts and theories that one believes to be the only way things can be, permits one to return to the immediacy of sensation and so permits new inferences. As the English physicist, Faraday, pointed out, conceptions can become the intellectual prisons of our perceptions:

> In our conceptions and reasonings regarding the forces of nature, we perpetually make use of symbols which, when they possess a high representative value, we dignify with the name of theories. ... Such conceptions have their advantages and their disadvantages; they afford peaceful lodging to the intellect for a time, but they also circumscribe it, and by and by, when the mind has grown too large for its lodging, it often finds difficulty in breaking down the walls of what has become a prison instead of its home.[59]

The *Majjhima-Nikāya* text contains a dialogue between Gotama and a follower, Vaccha, in which Vaccha tries asking basic questions about the nature of the 'real world, enlightenment, and life after death'.[60] These are questions whose possible answers could only be conceptual and presume to transcend the actual immediacy of experience. Gotama rejects Vaccha's questions as ones which 'tend not to edification'. The Buddha in turn asks Vaccha where he would say the fire goes when it 'goes out'. Vaccha admits that this question makes no sense, and the Buddha applies this to Vaccha's attempts to ask questions about life and death that transcend the moment. The Buddha's answer to such questions is silence. For the Englightened one: '... wisdom is to be developed, consciousness is to be fully understood'.[61]

Nāgārjuna, the great philosopher of Mādhyamika Buddhism, felt that being is beyond concept and neither positive nor negative, neither something nor nothing. For these are all concepts.It is *śūnyatā*, the void.[62] His school is also known as the *śunyā-vāda*, or voidist school. It is the system of no system.[63] Though not a Buddhist, the German mathematician Herman Weyl expressed a similar insight into the nature of 'scientific explanation': 'A systematic scientific explanation ... will erect the world of symbols as a realm by itself and then, skipping all intermediate levels, attempt to describe the relation that holds between the symbols representing objective conditions on the one hand and the corresponding data of consciousness on the other.'[64] It is important to remember in reference to all concepts, what Einstein remarked of mathematics: 'As far as the propositions of mathematics refer to reality they are not certain, and in so far as they are certain, they do not refer to reality.'[65]

Situational logic II: the Buddhists

Knowledge begins in sensing but there are two kinds of knowledge: that which is directly grasped, and that which is logically constructed.[66] *Pratyakṣa* is sense experience and has its origins in the immediate moment. *Anumāna* is inference and logic and it is the reasoned and conceptual product of mind, memory and imagination. Although inference seems to transcend its origins in sensation, its validity in situations must always go back to these origins. This is one of the critical differences between the referential inference of the Nyāya and the descriptive inference of the Buddhists. The former use situational experience to discover universals which transcend experience and for which examples then become illustrations. The latter view universals only as concepts whose identity is ultimately their non-identity.

For the Buddhist logicians, the world is sensually here, but not intellectually here. That which is cognized by the senses cannot be cognized by inference. Much of the appeal of Buddhism historically rests in this separation of momentary sense impression from the conceptual and intellectual aspects that follow as the mind digests, imagines, and expresses in words which we often confuse with experience.[67] This is not to deny the usefulness of conceptions, but to avoid confusing *conceptions* with their *conceiving*.

Affirmation and negation are both implicit in conceptual objects, and so any principle of affirmation and negation is also a concept and name, and if one does not realize this, affirmation and negation can seem to carry one beyond the situationality of experience and sensing. Thus the principle of affirmation and negation is in turn negated and even its negation negated, so that one is beyond negation, whereas Nāgārjuna suggested one does not need to negate because there is nothing to negate.[68] He would use thought and term to empty thought and term.[69] This view of inference presupposes it is useful certainly, but empty. But, what is this emptiness that it can be talked about and known? Vasubandhu answered: 'The non-being of duality, and the being of this non-being, is the characteristic of emptiness. It is the non-being of duality, that is of the object apprehended and subject apprehendor. It is also the being of this non-being.'[70]

The logic of the *catuṣkoṭi*

For the logicians Dināga and Dharmakīrti, inference links direct experience with the indirect, the immediate situation with past situations, the perceivable now and the imperceivable then. This is the function of the five-part syllogism for both the Buddhists and the Nyāya. The critical difference, of course, is the understanding of the situational experience that is being processed. However, because of the mental nature of universals for the Buddhist, there can be no certainty apart from the experience upon which the syllogism rests. Thus Dināga distinguishes between use of inference for one's self and for others: 'Demonstration and refutation together with their fallacies are useful in arguing with others; and Perception and Inference together with their fallacies are useful for self-understanding: seeing these I compile this Sāstra.'(*The Nyāyapavesa Sāstra*.)[71]

Dināga (c.450–520) and Dharmakīrti (c.635 AD) believed that the five-part syllogism could be reduced to two parts. It must have seemed that the only portions necessary were the general rule or reason and then its application to the specific situation. As long as one understands both the source of the rule in experience and the limitations imposed upon it by its nature as mental universal whose meaning is its excluded possibility or class, this reduction achieves a greater economy. Even in its reduced state, as Stcherbatsky points out: 'Example and Application are the two modes of the Buddhist syllogism.'[72]

In addition to the use of the five- or two-part syllogism, the Buddhists, and especially Nāgārjuna, made much use of another situational logic form which clearly had its roots in the views of *anatta* and *anicca*. This was the four-step logic, or the *catuṣkoṭi* whose function was to relate sensing, conceiving, inferring in such a manner that the situational emptiness of the duality of being and non-being would be preserved. It is a logic which begins in simple sensing as just 'such' or 'thus', before an impression is named and interpreted. Then it proceeds to conceptualization of a sensed, then to, awareness of this conceptualization as conceptualizing, and finally to immediate situational being and sensing *beyond* both *duality* and *non-duality*. This is the realization that neither in sensing nor conceiving do we have either 'self' or 'world', and that experience is an empty container from moment to moment, which of course is the very possibility of experiencing for no experience fills awareness. The process is a synthesis of suchness (*tathatā*) and emptiness (*śūnyatā*) which as synthesis is also emptiness (*śūnya śūnyatā*) or *Nirvāṇa*.

I would call the *catuṣkoṭi* a 'logic of the middle ground' for it is both a technique for avoiding extremes, and a technique for voiding itself as an extreme. It moves from the unshareable to the shareable and then the synthesis of the two as well as their negation.

From a Buddhist situational perspective, that collection of experiences which we tend to call 'reality' is four 'realities' in the stages of the *catuṣkoṭi*:

(1) As sensation or *svalakṣaṇa* it is particular, unique, unshareable and indeterminate. This we will call reality as 'suchness' or 'thusness' (*tathatā*).[73] Everything and any thing is 'such' or 'thus', before we apply a name to it and encompass it in a concept. The suchness of experience is like the nowness of time and the hereness of space, each of which represents the immediacy of experiencing. Everything is such.

(2) As concept or *sāmānyalakṣaṇa*, reality is 'not-such', it is a mind construct created from similarities and dissimilarities that we seem to detect between and among particular cognitions. At this point perception depends, as does conception, upon recognition in a way that sensing does not. This conceptual, shareable, interpreted reality we shall call reality as relationship. It is the experience we can name. As recognizing it brings past situations into the present moment. This reality is not unshareable suchness. That is, it is 'non-suchness' or 'non-thusness'. It is a concept or idea. The unshareable *svalakṣaṇa* provides the basis for the shareable *sāmānyalakṣaṇa*, and before one can vicariously

understand another's unshareable experience, now made shareable, one must be able to associate it with one's own *svalakṣaṇa* which will provide the insight from which the other will be understood. Everything is not-such.

(3) The combination in a moment of cognizing and recognizing is reality as both 'such and not-such'. The cognizing is simply 'such', the recognizing is 'not-such'. Everything is both such and not-such.

(4) Finally, there is the intuitive awareness that reality is 'neither such nor not-such', neither cognizing nor recognizing, and that all attempts to refer to it as either 'such', 'not-such', both 'such and not-such' are empty or void. This is the view of emptiness or *śūnyatā*. Since this fourth point also involves conceptual constructions and the use of the term 'emptiness', it is critical to intuitively realize that 'emptiness' too is 'empty' or '*śūnya śūnyatā*'. Nāgārjuna expresses these four stages in the *Mūlamadhyamakakārikā* as: 'Everything is such, not such, both such and not such, and neither such and not such: this is the Buddha's admonition.'[74]

These four stages of Nāgārjuna's can be viewed as 'ways of awareness' and then outlined as follows:

(1) Sensing or sensation or cognition occurs = This is 'suchness' in a situation.
(2) Recognition, occurs = This is the interpretative 'not-suchness' in a situation.
(3) Cognition and recognition occur = This is the combination of 'suchness' and interpretative 'not-suchness' in a situation.
(4) Neither cognition nor recognition is the situation = This is the situational emptiness of 'suchness' and 'not-suchness'.

The theories of *anatta* and *anicca* place a special emphasis upon immediate situations. And the origins of the *catuṣkoṭi* are in these theories of no-self and no-substantiality, and the resultant dependent origination of all experience. Its purpose is to provide a non-conceptual understanding of the nature and limits of language and concepts so that these shareable and utterable experiences are not confused with the unshareable actuality of awareness. Its methodology is the turning of conceiving on perceiving, conceiving on conceiving, and perceiving on conceiving. A version of it appears both in the Sermons of the Buddha and in Nāgārjuna's debates with the other schools, especially the Nyāya. He makes it clear that one cannot establish any sort of non-conceptual reality for any concept of reality. Perception as perceiving cannot be turned into concepts with an existential reference.

Even more extreme is the position of the ninth-century Zen Master, Huang Po, who believed that: 'All conceptual thinking is called erroneous belief.'[75]

The *catoşkoṭi* would seem to fulfill the Buddha's four stations of mindfulness which he outlines as being ardent, composed, and mindful in four kinds of contemplation: (1) as one is a body contemplating body, both in relation to external and external body states; (2) as one feels and is feelings contemplating feelings in regard to one's self and others; (3) as one thinks and is mind contemplating mind, one's own mind and the minds of others; (4) as one is mind-states, ideas and concepts contemplating mind-states both as regards internals and externals. This carries over into situational practice of contemplation, especially by the monk or the serious follower. When one is breathing one is mindful of breathing just as a lathe operator is mindful of the cut he is making, when one is walking one thoroughly comprehends his walking; when standing, his standing; when lying down, his lying down.

Mindfulness as awareness of one's immediate situation and activity extends to every aspect of life. The mindful individual: '... in wearing his cloak, his bowl, and his robes ... in eating, drinking, chewing, and tasting ... in easing his bowels and his bladder ... in walking, standing, sitting, sleeping, waking, talking, and being silent has an accurate comprehension of what he does'.[76] In each of these cases, the comprehension of the activity in the situation is its emptiness. For one to be mindful that one is walking, walking must be empty, only then is there the immediate and unshareable, unutterable experiencing of walking.

The Buddhists have used many techniques, the Zen *Koan*, meditation on no-self, body mindful of body, feelings of feelings, mind of mind, mental state of mental states, and of course the *catuşkoṭi* four-part logic. The middle path is suchness (*tathatā*) and emptiness (*śūnyatā*) and empty emptiness (*śūny śūnyatā*). Again Nāgārjuna notes: '"Empty", "non-empty", "both" or "neither" – these should not be declared. It is expressed only for the purpose of communication.' How does one communicate not only emptiness but the insight that emptiness is empty as is its communication? For if one turns emptiness into a dogma and an absolute, a concept, it is no longer empty and becomes dangerous, for one can become attached to emptiness. One must experience empty in an immediate situation in order to comprehend it as the unshareable, the momentary cognition.

When one understands the emptiness of emptiness, one's unity with the moment is not confused with the conceptualized past or future.

Part IV

The Aspect/Perspective Dimension of Philosophical Space

10 The Way of Nature and Mind as Aspect and Perspective

INTRODUCTION

Any philosophical tradition is a combination of two elements: The first is the set of presuppositions as to the ways of the world and human awareness in it and of it. These presuppositions provide the contexts for the interpretations and explanations of experience. The second element, though related to and inseparable from the first, is not synonymous with it and consists of the philosophizing processes and methods which develop within these presuppositions and reflect their applications. The relating of these two elements is a tradition's *life force.*

In the object dimension, for example, human consciousness has often been viewed as a rational essence inserted into human beings by a deity who is either transcendent as for Plato, Aristotle, and orthodox monotheisms; or who is immanent as in the case of the Stoics and Neo-Platonists. It is this special nature and source of consciousness which accounts for the privileged postion of the objective observer. In Advaita Vedānta, where consciousness is the world, explainer and the explained are one in a cosmic synthesis of *Brahman* and *Ātman*, and *māyā* accounts for the illusion of difference. For the Sāṃkhya and the Jains, consciousness and objects of consciousness consist of two eternal and qualitatively separate essences: *puruṣa* and *prakṛti* or *jīva* and *ajīva.* Experience is a matter of the proximity of these two natures and is not their cause. For the Buddhists, consciousness is one of the five *skandhas* or aggregates of awareness that mutually and dependently occur in immediate situations. Each of these systems has created corresponding reasoning methodologies. Greek logics were categorical and propositional. The Jains developed point of view logics. The Nyāya produced the five-step situational syllogism which was supplemented by the four-stage *catuṣkoṭi* of the Buddhists.

The final dimension we are going to explore is one in which human awareness and the world of which we are aware are usually seen as aspects of a changing nature/mind continuum. In this continuum, consciousness is both in the world and of the world. Inference techniques on the one hand facilitate the making of distinctions in reference to aspects of nature and thought, and on the other hand facilitate developing perspectives upon the process of distinguishing – which, while the source of distinctions, is never a distinction. Here the approach to inference and logic will involve relating aspects of experience to perspectives upon them. I have called this the *aspect/perspective dimension* of philosophical space, and to illustrate it have selected a number of texts from various Chinese philosophers who are concerned with what Fung Yu-lan called 'working on knowledge' versus 'broadening of the mind':

> ... in the tradition of Chinese philosophy there is a distinction between working on learning and working on Tao (the Way). The purpose of the former is what I call the increase of positive knowledge, that of the latter is the elevation of the mind. Philosophy belongs in the latter category.[1]

Historical overview

The beginning of classical Chinese philosophy is in the Chou Spring and Autumn period, approximately 722–481 BCE, and the Warring States period, approximately 403–222 BCE. K'ung Ch'iu (Confucius) and Lao Tzu both lived during the Spring and Autumn period and provided the Confucian and Taoist philosophical contexts for succeeding centuries.

The period of chaos called the Warring States was a time of great transition and encompassed the fragmenting and demise of over a 100 different feudal states and of feudal China itself. It ended in 221 with the first imperial unification under the short-lived reign of the Ch'in ruler, Shi Hwang ti, the builder of much of the Great Wall and the founder of an imperial administrative structure which became the pattern for succeeding dynasties.

The time of the Warring States was one of considerable philosophical and literary activity, although only two out of the 130 or so states, Ch'i and Lu (the latter was the birthplace of Confucius) continued to support and encourage learning and public discussions. Many of the literati of the period were members of an educated aristocracy who as their states were conquered and their lands were seized wandered from city to city. The Warring States period is also called the time of the hundred schools and included the successors of Confucius: Mencius (370–270) and Hsün Tzu (298–238); the great Taoist, Chuang Tzu (c.399–300), Mo Tzu (479–438), the founder of Mohism; and the logicians Hui Shih (380–305) and Kung-sun Lung Tzu (380–?).

After the unification of China by Hwang ti in 221 BCE, many of the texts of the representatives of the hundred schools were lost or burned. The legalist philosopher Han Fei Tzu and his followers convinced the emperor that a single, unified state could have no use for great diversity and disagreement. That this destruction was neither total nor more than temporary is evidenced by the survival of the main texts of the major schools and their collection in the succeeding Han Dynasty.

The history of China can be divided in many different ways, evolving from a feudal period of warring small states, to empire and unification under great dynasties which gave their names to centuries. These elements persist into our own time in the person of the military warlord or the political commissar, and the belief in a mandate from heaven which conveys authority and power upon a central leadership, whether this leadership is imperial, capitalist, or communist. Heaven in this usage is a guiding, directing force in and of nature and not a deity. This historical span extends in legend back more than 5000 years. However, most of China's early written historical records were produced beginning with the end of the Shang and the ascendancy of the Chou about 1200 BCE.

Mahāyāna Buddhism entered China in the first century AD, during the reign of the Han. However, it was at first slowly translated and interpreted through Taoist terminologies and reached a high point of its own in a number of important schools, including C'han in the fourth to the tenth centuries AD.

A revival of Confucianism in response to the political and philosophical/religious successes of Buddhism began under the Sung in the eleventh century and produced two of the most important early modern philosophers, the Neo-Confucians, Chu Hsi (1130–1200) and Wang Yang-ming (1472–1529).

Topographical diagram of the kingdom

Chinese history refers to two dynasties prior to the Chou (1111 to 249 BCE). The older was the Hsia which lasted from the twenty-first century to the middle of the eighteenth when it was overthrown by the Shang which in turn was replaced by the Chou. It is with the Chou that the beginning of the great classical schools of Chinese philosophy are associated.

The overthrow of the last Shang King is the theme of a Ming text entitled *The Creation of the Gods* written centuries later. In it are many descriptions of the mythological battles that finally led to the fall of King Zhou who had lost the favor of heaven because of his oppression of his people. The 'Mandate of Heaven' then passed to King Wu of Chou. The armies in the conflict of Chou and Shang consisted of human heroes, animal spirits in human forms, and various deities. Their weapons were a mixture of swords, maces, axes and spears supplemented by magic, supernatural powers, potions and tricks. In the final phase of the struggle, a great Shang general, Yuan Hong, who was a transformed 'white ape spirit', is lured into and trapped in a charmed map, the 'topographical diagram of the kingdom'. Once in this map, one's thoughts take on visual shape and form. Unaware of the illusory nature of his surroundings, Yuan Hong finds and consumes a charmed golden peach which drains him of his strength and so enables his foe, Yang Jian, to roll him up inside the map and bring him to the enemy camp where he is beheaded. [2] The 'topographical diagram of the kingdom' might be seen as a metaphor for the symbolic and conceptual 'traps' that the human intellect constructs which in time capture both itself and the changing world of experience in distinctions and names. In this chapter on the aspect/perspective dimension of philosophical space, we shall explore *stopping* and *capturing* as aspects and perspectives of a nature/mind synthesis.

Aspect and perspective: philosophy

In the term *aspect*, two related but different ideas are associated: The first is implied in its root meaning of *ad* (to) and *specere* (to look), that is, 'to look at or toward'. The second meaning is implied when we use the term to indicate the position, context, or status in which a thing, event, or idea appears or from which it can be regarded. For example, a bad-tasting medicine regarded from the aspect of its taste, is bad; regarded from the aspect of its ability to cure, is good. Good and bad reflect the perspective of an observer who regards, plus those aspects regarded. The term *perspective* combines *specere* with *per* which means 'through' or 'throughout'. Thus a perspective is 'seeing through'. Neither is separable from the other in the aspective/perspective dimension, and knowledge is a synthesis of aspects of knower with aspects of the known and aspects of the knowing processes. This mixture is in turn the source of a knower's perspective on knowledge.

The aspect/perspective dimension presupposes the world is a cyclic, flowing process of aspects in which orderly change is the way of all things. As a result, objects do not possess aspects, they are aspects. This is similar to modern theories of space which try to distinguish space/time from objects in space and time.

One encounters a combination of aspect and perspective in the definition and usage of many Chinese philosophical terms which tend in their meanings to flow into one another and into their contrasts. Professor Chung-ying Cheng, for example, traces the use of the term *li* (which is usually translated as *principle*) in at least six different aspect usages, each of which implies a different perspective. These aspects range from its reference to the Ultimate Principle of being, to the nature and order of things, to reasoning and thinking processes, to mind contents as ideas, to the construction and use of things, to regulating human conduct and behavior.[3]

If one assumes that we as human beings are part of natural process, then thinking too is an aspect of nature. It is that aspect which provides a perspective within nature upon nature. The Neo-Confucian philosopher, Wang Yang-ming (1472–1529) believed that common, innate knowledge and sensitivity related all aspects of nature to one another. Because it was common, this innate aspect of knowledge enabled human beings to recognize and relate to trees, stones, wind, rain, heaven, earth, even broken tiles. It was also the source of the understanding of the curative and nutritive powers of plants, animals and minerals.[4] These assumptions have remained central to Chinese traditional medicine and therapies. Consistent with Professor Cheng's discussion of *li* is the belief that the order in nature and in the human being coincide.

But the thinking human being, as an aspect of nature, is that aspect which is at the same time a perspective on nature. In this dual character of aspect/perspective, the human being is both a creator of distinctions and a perspective upon distinguishing. Chuang Tzu explains that oxen have four feet and this is the way of Heaven, but putting a ring in the ox's nose is the way of man. The one is fate, the other is purposeful and they should not be confused.[5] Our statements and concepts are like nose rings on our physical and social experiences. However, without perspective, they become that which they represent and aspects become symbolized objects. At this point, language, rather than functioning as a tool for thinking, substitutes for it and becomes an obstacle to perspective and we may mistake the nose ring aspect for the nose aspect.

The nature of aspect and its relationship to perspective can be illustrated by moving while pointing at an 'object' like a chair. As I point, I move closer to the chair and as I do so identify that at which I am pointing. As I move, my finger points to a different aspect, arm, leg, seat, fabric, flower in the fabric pattern, grease spot on the flower. The finger represents and identifies the perspective from which these aspects are each singled out. At the same time in this experience, the finger is an aspect of the pointing as well. And knowing the aspects from moment to moment and understanding the aspective nature of the total exercise is reflected in a perspective upon experience as aspect/perspective synthesis. Of course we do not always point at aspects of experience with our fingers. Far more frequently we use various words and symbols.

It is easy to see how failure to identify perspective and aspect can lead to great confusion. We may even discover that we use words which point at nothing and do not represent a perspective because they do not direct attention to an aspect of experience beyond the experience of the word itself. In such an instance, the word seems to take on a life of its own. In Li Ju-chen's *Flowers in the Mirror*, the flower spirit, Purple Mushroom, tells the story of a Taoist, the Immortal Lu, who had mastered many magical arts. Once when a poor man asked his help, the Immortal Lu pointing at a rock turned it into gold and gave it to him. After this, whenever the man needed help, he would come to Lu who would point at a stone. One day this man, now grown very rich and powerful, again approached the priest for help. This time Lu in order to satisfy him once and for all turned a very large rock into gold. The man was quite grateful and thanking his benefactor, apologized for inconveniencing him so often. However, he let it be known that he had one last favor but was ashamed to ask it. The Immortal Lu urged him to make his request and promised to grant it. The man replied that he only wanted the wonderful pointing finger which turns stone into gold, and he sliced Lu's finger off.[6] With symbols we can point at infinite aspects of experience transforming them thereby into meaningful concepts, but when the symbol replaces the aspect of experience or the concept, then it is a symbol without perspective and is like the severed finger of the Immortal Lu.

Nature and paradox: the Tao

If observer and observed are aspects of the total process of change and transformation, then understanding the difference between the object dimension and the aspect/perspective dimension of philosophical space is central to an understanding of both. The philosophy of Plato, Aristotle, and most of the Pre-Socratics, especially Parmenides and the Eleatics, presupposed that the ultimate reals are constant and do not change. Because reality is ultimately static, it can be named and expressed in two valued views of the world as is/isn't, true/false, real/apparent. Thus one of the basic tasks of philosophy and science is to explain the possibility and nature of change which occurs in the apparent but not in the real. Here theories of identity relate to the unchanging and not to the changing, and to conception not perception.

For the Taoist in particular and Chinese philosophy in general, the ultimate 'given' is orderly change in which the task of philosophy and science is to establish 'identity in change' and not 'change in identity'. Here there is an emphasis upon aspects and the complementarity of opposites. A perspective upon distinguishing and naming are important whenever distinctions are made and names are applied. Objects are their functions and their functions are expressed in naming. Han Fei Tzu (third century BCE) in his political theory urged the emperor to make sure that actions on the part of ministers corresponded to their titles.[7] The view that the world is change and process is very close to that of Heracleitus' proposition that one cannot step into the same river twice. And modern 'chaos theory' in physical science would seem to arise in great part out of the encountering of motion and change where scientists historically have expected static or repetitive consistency. If one begins with a static view of the world, change becomes the source of paradoxes. If one begins with a changing, transforming view of the world, then the static as distinctions and names becomes the sources of paradox. For example, Chuang Tzu claimed that everything has both a 'this' and a 'that' and that these arise from one another and complement one another just as birth requires death and death requires birth. Opposites generate one another. Right requires wrong and wrong requires right. The total of this process is the endlessness of Tao.[8]

In the aspect view, paradoxes involve attempts to make sharp or permanent distinctions between and among things, thoughts and symbols. The Chinese accommodated paradox in a number of ways. One of these was the reference to silence in trying to name the Tao which cannot be named. Another was to clarify and agree upon naming conventions or the *rectification of names*.[9] A third possibility according to the contemporary philosopher, Fung Yu-lan, was trying to think what is ultimately 'unthinkable'.[10]

Nature and naturing

In the object tradition, one of the earliest and most enduring concerns has always been with the nature of reality. Thales began this tradition with his questions as to the basic nature of things. For those Chinese who see the human in nature and as nature, thinking is a synthesis of distinctions and distinguishing which the human 'as nature' introduces into nature 'as human'. The world as we know it is a process of 'naturing' and 'minding'. Whether naturing and minding are the source or consequence of the world is irrelevant here. The purpose of inference in this naturing/minding synthesis is in one respect identifying aspects of this synthesis and applying names to them. In another respect its function is to develop perspectives upon distinguishing and naming.

Nature in our knowing is a process within a process, a synthesis of being and non-being. What we encounter in experience are not static things, but aspects of this process. This influences both what we can claim to know, how we know, and the possibility for its expression in language. As the late Thome Fang suggested, man and the universe are together a harmonious, inseparable whole.[11] As a consequence of this view, much of Chinese philosophy will reflect aspects of process and non-being, not infinite classification techniques and class relationships. The Romanian philosopher, Anton Dumitriu, points out that for the European, the difficulty in understanding this approach is that it expresses an ontological concern with nature as process and not as essence.[12]

The human being participates in the *world-being continuum* in at least three related ways: we are in the world in physical space while thinking and making statements about the world in mental space; and that which we think and say, is ultimately thought and said by the world. We are author, actor and spectator aspects of nature. We are both the sources and consequences individually and collectively of our actions. A similar perspective is expressed by the American physicist, Roger Jones, who believes that because we are so concerned with difference and multiplicity in aspects of the world, we lose sight of our oneness with it and believe that we are separate individuals.[13] In the *Doctrine of the Mean*, it is explained that that aspect of human nature which is the source of sincerity so links us to the universe that when in sincerity we complete ourselves, nature too is completed, for this principle is beginning and ending of Man, Heaven, and Earth.[14]

In traditional Chinese philosophy there are no objects which fulfill some set of determinate and fixed conditions, occupying real space, possessing mass, and capable of having their identities connected by the copula, 'to be'. This view can for the occidental perhaps best be understood by reversing the conceptual order of aspect with thing, so that rather than aspects of things one views things as changing aspects. Rather than perspectives upon things, one thinks of things as our perspectives upon aspects. Understanding this distinction is critical to understanding much of Chinese philosophy and language where there is often no clear line between verb and noun, nouns can become verbs, and the meaning of the verb is basic. This is an important contrast to the object dimension where the basic form is the noun and verbs are easily turned into nouns when one discusses their operational 'essence'. This produced Aristotle's 'class logic'. In Chinese philosophy, inference is related to the cultivation of perspective leading to functioning and action, whether one is a farmer or scholar, alone or a member of a society. This difference between aspect and class was succinctly illustrated by the Neo-Mohist who wrote that in choosing the lesser of two evils, one is also selecting a 'good'.[15]

Classical Chinese physical theories of nature do speak of five basic elements: fire, metal, earth, water, wood *xings*. These are particularly important in both medicine and alchemy. However, they are not elements so much in the occidental sense of basic stuffs as they are representatives of basic processes. Professor Shu-li Ji in a paper delivered in Berkeley at the annual meeting of the Society for the Study of Comparative Civilizations in May 1989 claimed that *xing* means the activity of the element. Water is soaking and descending while fire is heating and rising. Wood is bending and flexing while metal is melting and moulding. Earth is planting and harvesting.[16] Thome Fang, translating from the *Book of Rites*, describes how each of these elements which are aspects of the whole of nature becomes an aspect and function of the human being, and how each one can be related to the right actions of the wise or prudent individual.[17]

The idea of the unity of man and nature is a theme central to Neo-Confucian philosophy as we have seen in Wang Yang-ming's idea of innate knowledge. One of its most popular and influential expressions was the *Western Transcription* of the eleventh-century philosopher, Chang Tsai which began: 'Heaven is my father and Earth is my mother, and even such a small creature as I finds an intimate place in their midst.'[18] The enlightened man realizes the unity in the universe of himself with the heavens, nature and society, according to Wang Yang-ming. And he expresses this perspective in his actions. The unenlightened individual does not realize this unity, but it is true in his/her case as well.[19]

There are at least two possible misunderstandings of the mind/nature relationship that commonly occur: The first is the assumption that the world is relative to an individual's perceptions of its aspects. This is a kind of egocentricity which leads to an illusory separation of the individual from the world. The second is the assumption that the world is somehow rendered static and stabilized in an individual's concepts of and names for it. The antidote for both of these misunderstandings is the realization that the mind is empty. This is why Hsün Tzu suggests that the individual seeking the Way but who has not yet reached it, should let *emptiness*, and *stillness* be his guides.[20] This perspective upon knowing does not imply that one cannot know, but rather that one is never the aspects of the world that one claims to know – which might lead the mind to believe that an aspect can be captured in a term. Neither mind nor nature are things, and neither mind nor nature is a place. Lao Tzu praises the individual who knows that he does not know.[21] And Confucius cautioned in the *Analects* against learning without thinking and thinking without learning.[22]

Evolution of distinctions and names

The following short paragaph from the book of Chuang Tzu outlines a series of five changes or evolutionary stages in processing mind/nature relationships. The questions posed at the end return the process again to where it began. One might call it the 'emerging and returning of mind in nature as minding in naturing':

'(1) The knowledge of the ancients was perfect. How perfect? At first, they did not yet know that there were things. This is the most perfect of knowledge; nothing can be added. (2) Next, they knew that there were things, but did not yet make distinctions between them. (3) Next they made distinctions between them, but they did not yet pass judgments upon them. (4) When judgments were passed, Tao was destroyed. (5) With the destruction of Tao, individual preferences came into being. (6) Are there really construction and destruction? Is there really no construction and no destruction?'[23]

Each of these stages presents both an aspect of human awareness and a perspective upon it. The latter is most clearly expressed in the questions of the last line.

1. *Before there are things*, Mind and Nature are one. Human awareness is one with nature. Nature as a whole is a unity of many processes: closing/opening, matter/principle (*ch'i/ li*), substance/function, contraction/expansion, creating/ destroying, coming into/going out of being. Professor Hideki Yukawa, a Nobel laureate and modern particle physicist, addresses this unity in diversity in an essay on Chuang Tzu and cautions that in the physicists' search for the basic form of matter, they may discover not one form but many, or no form at all, or perhaps even a sort of chaos.[24]

The Buddhist, Seng-chao (384–414), in discussing the processes of rest and motion, warned against rejecting either the one or the other, or trying to separate them. Rest is to be sought in motion and activity, and motion and activity are to be sought in rest.[25] Ch'eng Hao (1032–1085) spoke of *Tao* or Way as both before physical form and as physical form, past and future, present and absent, concerete things and their source.[26]

Wang Fu-chih (1619–1692) stressed the restricted and unrestricted dynamic material force as the source of all things. Although it is the source of things it is spatially restricted by none of them nor restricted by itself.[27] In Yen Yüan (1635–1704), nature in all its 'ten thousand things' is a manifesting synthesis of principle and material force regardless as to whether an aspect is balanced or unbalanced, light or dark, lofty or low, for manifestations cannot be separated from functioning processes.[28]

2. *Making distinctions is* the beginning of minding. Building upon the first proposition we can say that minding is the observing aspect of naturing in Nature. In the works of Wang Yang-ming, the oneness of nature as manifested in the human mind represents a special awareness, for in human awareness the world is 'self-aware', that is, possesses a reflexive aspect that produces 'thinking about thinking', which equates knowing and acting.[29] This is a natural awareness.

This is illustrated by Chuang Tzu's insight into himself as an aspect of the whole, trying to talk about the whole: 'The Way has never known boundaries; speech has no constancy. But because of [the recognition of a] "this", there came to be boundaries.'[30]

3. *Making judgments* is the minding of minding. When Mind not only makes distinctions, but also develops a perspective upon distinguishing as well as distinctions, it is that aspect of nature which is capable of the minding of minding and making of judgments. These enable mind to establish complementary contrasts like true/false, beautiful/ugly, subjective/objective, constructive/destructive, relevant/irrelevant. At this stage it is particularly important that one gains a perspective upon the symbolization of minding and naturing, for as Hsün Tzu noted, names are a matter of convention without intrinsic meanings apart from their usage.[31] Language enables Mind in minding to accommodate experience in analogical and metaphorical distinctions; however, as the American physicist, Roger S. Jones, suggests in reference to the terminologies of physics these are metaphorical forms which, important though they are, are never the world. The metaphors of science, however, can represent the inner unity and connectedness of things.[32]

It is in the process of making judgments that human minding realizes that 'virtue' is a common property of the human and the natural – a point also implicit in a number of modern views in biology and ecology. Tai Chen (1723–1777) wrote in his *Nature of Goodness* that the human capacity for hamony and good is also an implicit capacity and potential of the universe as a whole.[33] There are many implications of his position, but three it seems to me are most important: (1) Values reflect a way of being in the world. (2) Although values are common to the human being and to nature, in the human they can and must be developed in a 'self-reflective' way as Mencius suggested.[34] (3) And because they are a self-reflective way of being in the world, they are always dynamic and cannot be reduced to absolutes. They are expressed in analogies in an aesthetically and ethically functioning continuum which as Wang Yang-ming maintained has both moral 'knowing' and moral 'acting aspects'. If one 'knows' then one acts, and anyone who claims to know but does not act, does not know.[35]

Chinese aspect/perspective logic as a philosophizing technique can and does elevate the mind which reasons in and with it. As knowledge of the aspects of experience, it facilitates the pursuit of positive knowledge. As understanding, it provides a perspective upon the relationships of knowledge to its sources and presuppositions, the relationship of parts to the whole. This is the difference between the methods of synthesis and analysis.[36]

4. *The Tao is destroyed and individual preferences come into being* with the introduction of judgments. It is at this point that the Mind begins to separate minding from Nature. The Book of Tao in the twelfth chapter warns that taken to extremes, the eyes can be blinded by the five colors, the ears can be rendered deaf by the five tones, the sense of taste ruined by the five flavors, and activities like hunting and racing can produce madness.[37] It is this conceptual separation of mind from nature as well as the isolation of parts from wholes, that has in great measure been the source of the success of physical science and technology in the West. However, this has resulted in modern science in a tension between logics of things and logics of relationships.[38]

5. *When minding separates Mind from Nature, it begins to construct and find its being in conceptual models of nature*, thus choices between construction and destruction in nature emerge (and can become dangerously absolute). It is at this stage that we create philosophical systems, ideologies, civilizations, destinies – what the Buddhist might call the spider webs upon which we individually and collectively spin out our lives in religion, art, science and philosophy. These webs can facilitate the catching of flies, but they can also catch us as their creators in '*topograhical diagrams of our kingdoms*'.

6. *Are there really construction and destruction? Is there really no construction and no destruction?* We can now return to Chuang Tzu's questions at the end of his sketch and ask them in reference to the ultimate life and death of individuals and civilizations. On the one hand we define the world, and on the other we are aware of ourselves via these definitions and the institutions that we create with them. Paralleling this first pair of complementary aspects of minding is a pair of perspectives which are implicit in the final part of the evolutionary steps of Chuang Tzu: meanings and institutions can be constructed for social good or ill. However, in either case if we recognize that the institutions in which we live live in us, we realize their limits and relativity and return in insight and understanding to the Nature we have never left. This becomes most clear when we contemplate our mortality, our origins and ends. I believe that it is this relativity of concept and institutions that Werner Heisenberg had in mind when he suggested that our understanding of nature rests not upon some solid foundation, but like all cognition is: '... suspended over an unfathomable depth'.[39]

Perhaps the most important difference between object logic and aspect/perspective logic is that the former is a logic of distinctions, the latter is a logic of distinguishing. Chuang Tzu realized the difference when he claimed that he and the10,000 aspects of the world were one, that this 'one'and his statement about it made two, and that two plus one is three. He then suggested that if one proceeded in this direction there would be no end and so it might be best not to begin.[40] However, if one begins one must understand the process of distinguishing and realize that in a dynamic world, judgments relate to whither things are tending and not to their essences.[41] The basic concern of aspect/perspective inference is not with the distinctions of reason *per se*, but with a self-reflective reasoning about reasoning and an examining of correct conduct and motivation as well as practical living. Reasoning does not develop from the senses, nor is it distinct from the senses for these are dependent upon it.[42]

Another illustration of the application of aspect/perspective inference is to be found in the Neo-Confucian, Chu Hsi's *Reflections on Things at Hand* in which he considered the significance of the mundane aspects of life like the menial job of sweeping a floor. Even in such simple tasks like sweeping, nature and destiny are present at their most pure and profound.[43] Chuang Tzu in explaining the Tao to Master Tung-kuo, tells him that there is no place where it is not to be found. It is in the ant, the grass, even in excrement, for all aspects of nature are Tao. One who has a perspective upon the many levels and aspects of experience realizes this.[44] Indeed, the pure and profound in the world are revealed in the simple and menial.

This perspective upon the simple tasks/aspects of life is very important in Zen/C'han Buddhism as well, where even a rock can be a teacher if one concentrates one's attention upon it. Everything has Buddha-mind. This innate knowledge which the human shares with nature is also the source of empathy and sympathy not only for the human but for all of nature. Mencius and the Neo-Confucians taught that it extends from concern for the child about to fall into a well, to consideration for the ant that is trapped and in danger of losing its life.

Aspect/perspective logic

As with any inference process, the form of aspect/perspective logic is determined in great part by its purposes, and I would emphasize five of these:

(1) Aspect/perspective inference as a distinguishing logic and not a logic of distinctions, assists the reasoner to an awareness of the unlimited in the limiting that human awareness brings to nature, including nature as human society.

(2) It connects and relates perspective and aspective nature, not objects, subjects, or situations. All of these, however, will be accommodated as perspectives and aspects.

(3) The function of inference is to produce understanding, and by way of understanding lead to attitudes and purposive action and right social relationships.

(4) Aspect/perspective inference is designed to preserve process. It is not a process in the sense that process can be objectified, but in the sense that mind and nature are different aspects of a total process out of which particular processes in a changing continuum occur. This is the naturing/minding continuum.

(5) Aspect/perspective inference relates the process of thought from aspect to action in such a way that it leads to further aspect to further purposive action. It is this quality which accounts for what appears to be both its paradoxical nature and an infinite regression/progression of meaning and significance – which, beginning in words leads to no words, or beginning in no words leads to words.

We shall explore aspect/perspective logic within the context of two broad sets of relationships. The first of these contexts is that of 'Nature and naturing'. The second is that of 'Mind and minding'. In the first grouping, Nature represents the whole of all being and non-being. This is the unnamed and unnamable *Tao*, the source and container of all aspects of experience. Naturing represents the changing processes which are the content of our experiences. In Nature *naturing*, the perspectives we develop are related to various aspects of being and non-being, changing and constancy. From these we develop Nature and naturing inferences. And of course for the Confucian philosopher, society and social relationships are also aspects of Nature naturing. It is this which accounts for the *Mandate of Heaven* for a ruler.

In the second context, Mind represents the whole which is the source of all thoughts and thinking, but is none of them. Minding represents changing thoughts, ideas, interpretations, explanations, affirmations and negations. Our experience of Mind *minding* and our perspectives upon their interrelationships is the source of Mind and minding inferences. And if Mind and Nature are a unity, then these two inference systems are inseparable. Combined, they are both the world and a way of being in the world, enabling us as aspect to reflect upon the whole, and as whole to reflect upon aspects. Aspect/perspective thinking proceeds from Nature and naturing to Mind and minding and then to Nature and Mind and naturing and minding. This is a process in which the human aspect of it, in thinking about the whole, realizes its nature both as whole and part. Fung Yu-lan in his *Short History of Chinese Philosophy* explained that because: '... the universe is the totality of all that is, therefore when one think about it, one is thinking reflectively, because the thinking and the thinker must also be included in the totality'. We must first try to think the unthinkable to realize that it is unthinkable, and this aspect of its unthinkability provides us a perspective upon all the distinctions that we make in thinking and reasoning.[45]

Inferential method is determined by the fundamental Mind–Nature relationships which underlie knowledge, and by the insight that (1) Nature cannot be conceived by or in Mind, and (2) Mind cannot be perceived by or in Nature, yet they are a unity. Thus, distinguishing makes distinctions possible, but distinctions are neither distinguishing nor things. They are relationships of aspects and perspectives. Understanding this leads to logical understanding, correct attitudes, and purposive action/non-action.

Part I: Nature and naturing

There are many aspects of Nature that could be included here. However, as illustrations, three would seem to be particularly relevant for the perspectives that they produce. It is important that one remembers any aspect without corresponding perspectives is incomplete or faulty: (1) Non-Being, (2) Being, (3) The Mean. These are coupled with three ways in which Nature is expressed in naturing. These are not Nature *per se*, but its expression: (a) The One and the Many, (b) The Similar and the Different (dissimilar), (c) Order and Disorder, Harmony and Disharmony. Each of these aspects of naturing is then related to a perspective upon it which is expressed in turn in an assumption or an insight.

(1) *Non-Being*: This is the nameless source of Being. From Non-Being come Heaven and Earth and the aspects of the One and the Many of naturing. The Doctrine of the Mean explains that The Way of Heaven and Earth contains no *doubleness* and yet without doubleness produces the many in some inexplicable process.[46] The Neo-Confucian, Shao Yung (1011–1077), believed that the *Great Ultimate* when it was aroused produced spirit. From spirit came number and form and the multitude of things. But all of these resolved again into spirit.[47]

Perspective: Understanding this aspect of naturing means understanding *becoming* and *change*. The many come from the one and return to the one. For Chang Tsai, the completion of any thing, including a human being, is its beginning and end, where there is no beginning and ending there is no completion. The sage who understands this can enter into and understand all things.[48]

(2) *Being*: From Being come the aspects of similarity and difference in naturing upon which we base our concepts and distinctions. If one observes similarities, one groups together and tends to ignore dissimilarities. If one

focuses upon dissimilarities, one may concentrate upon separations and miss similarities. But according to the logician Hui Shih (fourth century BCE) great and small similarity are different from one another but at the same time all things are similar to one another and different from one another. The first state is the 'lesser similarity and difference', the second is the 'greater similarity and difference'.[49]

Perspective: Understanding the similarity and difference (dissimilarity) aspects of naturing, one understands that there is no 'sameness' and 'difference' which divides Nature into two separate beings either as subject and object, or class and contradictory. Chuang Tzu said that the 10,000 things though numerous were all one in their good order.[50] Seeing through similarity and difference enables one to intuit the unity of being in the 10,000 aspects of the world, without wearing out one's intellect trying to unify them. One of Chuang Tzu's best known stories of similarity and difference is that of the monkeys whose keeper changed their feeding schedule to give them three nuts in the morning and four at night. The monkeys were furious until the keeper offered them four in the morning and three at night and then they were overjoyed.[51] The great man and the small man are both similar to one another and to other animals. However there is also a difference or dissimilarity. Mencius urged wise men to preserve it, even as the foolish throw it away.[52]

(3) *The Mean*: From the Mean which is the equilibrium in Nature, comes the possibility of order and disorder, harmony and disharmony in naturing. There are storms and droughts. In human affairs there are revolutions. A dynasty can receive or lose the *Mandate of Heaven*. The concern of the individual is how to act or not act in such situations. Hsün Tzu believed that Heaven's ways were constant and that what human beings held to be misfortunes were their own fault. If one follows the mean that is in nature and is not divided within himself, then Heaven cannot harm one. But if one fails to prepare for disastrous eventualities, then Heaven cannot bring one good fortune. The ways of Heaven and Earth are constant, it is man's faults and foibles that are the source of disorder and disharmony. Heaven does not hold back rain because men do not want to get wet. And if heaven sends a drought, it is a problem only if men have not saved and prepared for it.[53]

Perspective: One prepares for difficult times and one is humble and reserved in good times. One maintains in one's own actions the balance that is in Nature among the seasons and the weathers. The wise individual lights his/her way with Chuang Tzu's 'torch' of 'chaos and doubt' which shows the constancy in all things.[54] For Hsün Tzu Heaven and Earth and Man together create a harmonious triad. But it is destroyed and man is in danger when he rejects his part and seeks to take on the parts of the other members of the trio.[55] If individuals take things as they appear and events as they occur then the distinctions between order and disorder will reveal themselves and the sage can respond accordingly.[56]

Part II: Mind and minding

As with Nature and naturing, there are many aspects of Mind and minding that could be included here. Three would seem to be particularly relevant in terms of the perspectives they produce. As with Nature and naturing, if the perspectives are missing, then the inference is incomplete or faulty. Mencius said that it is a great tragedy when a man loses his mind and does not know how to find it again.[57] And Confucius warned that if one lets the mind go once, one loses it.[58] The three aspects of Mind are (1) Emptiness, (2) Unity, (3) Empathy. Their corresponding aspects in minding are (a) Knowledge and Understanding, (b) Names and Distinctions, (c) Wanting and Willing. Each of these aspects is accompanied by a perspective upon it as a synthesis of Mind and minding.

(1) *Emptiness*: Emptiness in minding encompasses both knowledge and understanding. Where knowledge is positive, understanding is often negative, providing from the point of view of Mind as empty, the insight that our knowledge of the world or its aspects is neither the world nor its aspects. It is this understanding which enables us to change as individuals and societies what we have claimed to know at a certain moment in time and to work on self-completion and responsibility. But even more important is that, in understanding minding, we understand that the Mind is never the object of our knowing, but always its subject.[59] It is the emptiness of Mind that makes all knowledge possible for it is this which enables us to store up knowledge while not confusing the Mind with knowledge. Unified, it accommodates diversity, still, it is moving.[60]

Perspective: Knowing that the Mind is empty like a bowl which never becomes that which it contains, means firstly that the knower is never the object of knowledge nor his/her experience of the world. It is this which Fung Yu-lan suggested enabled him to transcend both self and experience.[61] As the unknown in all knowing, I am both free and responsible for my actions. Fung Yu-lan in his analysis of Chuang Tzu distinguished between two sorts of empty Mind. There are those 'who have no knowledge, and those who have no-knowledge'.[62] The former are ignorant, the latter are wise. The unthinkable aspect of minding provides a perspective upon both the thinkable and the position of Mind in Nature. It is one of the amazing insights that comes from the Chinese synthesis of aspect and perspective, that one can achieve a perspective upon all perspectives and that this very perspective is one of the most important aspects of the universe itself. It is, as Fung Yu-lan wrote, the beginning of all philosophy and a way of understanding in every human endeavor.[63]

(2) *Unity*: Within the unity of Mind names and distinctions arise in minding. Their meaning is in the Mind and minding, but meaning is neither Mind nor minding. It is names as matters of convention that enable us to communicate with one another, to establish systems of government and social organizations. Chuang Tzu felt that every distinction is both an act of construction and destruction. For example a table is a construction, but the tree from which it was made is destroyed.[64] To divide the world into this and that is useful and necessary, but these divisions are not absolute for everything has its 'this' and its 'that'. The 'Great Way' can neither be named nor spoken. When discriminations are expressed in names they are not adequate. In Taoism, the understanding that rests in what cannot be understood is the greatest understanding. The wise individual is the individual who understands unnamed and unspoken discriminations.[65]

Perspective: The problem with distinctions and names is that they can replace the perspectives implicit in an awareness of distinguishing and naming. When this happens we may not only mistake the aspect identified by the word or distinction for the whole, we may become obsessed by it and insist on making all other distinctions on this basis. According to Hsün Tzu, obsession with a corner of the Way is to be avoided by all men. Obsession narrows our horizons and conceals from us the innate emptiness of Mind and minding. Whenever we make distinctions we have created the potential for obsession.[66] This obsession in turn is often with names, and we lose our perspective on naming as names are confused with their meanings. Wang Yang-ming explained to one of his friends who claimed that he could not understand what he read, that his problem was that he sought meaning only in the words.[67] The Ch'an Master, Wen-yi, in explaining why he would not make distinctions said that if he were to answer the question as to what was the 'first principle' of the world, this principle would thereby become the 'second principle'.[68] Finally, distinctions and discriminations mislead us into believing that we can find self-understanding in the external.[69]

(3) *Empathy*: From wanting and willing arises the world of our desires. Each sense, said Lao Tzu, is a potential source of desire and wanting which can blind us.[70] We can bend our wills to our wants or we can bend our wants to our wills. It is the former case which enables our senses to mislead. Mencius

in comparing his preference for fish and 'bear paw' said that if he could not have both, he would choose the bear paw. He then extended this example to wanting and willing on a higher plane where if offered a choice between life and righteousness, where only one was possible, he would choose righteousness over life. His dislike of unrighteousness was greater than his dislike of death.[71] It is in the area of moral and ethical concerns that willing must take precedence over wanting.

Perspective: It is in giving precedence in minding to willing over wanting that the principle of empathy then influences behavior toward all human beings. As Mencius suggested, one must understand what one will not do before one can determine what one ought to do.[72] This is the source of the Confucian idea of man-to-manness or *jen* which is perhaps most clearly expressed in Mencius when he maintains that all men have a mind which cannot bear to see others suffer. Confucius himself described his own life-long pursuit of character and learning, and noted that at 70 he could follow his heart without violating moral principles.[73] It is this empathy which links Nature and Mind in naturing and minding.

IN SUMMARY

One might use the first two lines of the 'Tao Te Ching' to illustrate this aspect/perspective view of the world and the approach to logic that follows from it. The 'Book of Tao' begins: 'dao ke dao, fei chang dao, ming ke ming, fei chang ming', which is frequently and approximately translated as 'The Tao that can be explained or spoken is not the eternal Tao. The name that can be named is not the eternal name.' I would suggest that given the interrelationship of Nature/Mind and naturing/minding, one might loosely but correctly translate these first two lines as: 1) The Nature that can be natured is not the constant Nature. This means that the Nature which we as aspects ourselves of nature explain and explore in the historical contexts of the natural sciences like biology, chemistry, physics, astronomy, and so on, is not the constant or ultimate Nature which is a continuum of explainer–explained–explaining–explanation. 2) The Mind that can be named is not the constant Mind. This means that whatever we say about Mind in our minding processes, which include both naming and reasoning, is not the constant Mind which is the very possibility of these processes:

If we combine these aspects into a logical system, we can say that the meaning as well as the nature of any inference is a synthesis of these aspects, and to understand it, agree or disagree with it, prove or disprove it, will in turn involve us in inferences utilizing these very same aspects, though the interpretations processed through them may vary. We will begin with an aspect of experience, proceed to a perspective upon it, understand it, adopt an attitude, and proceed to act accordingly.

Aspect/perspective logic facilitates not only the elevation of the mind in the process of philosophizing, it also furthers the pursuit of knowledge in that it provides a perspective upon knowledge, its sources and assumptions. The following two examples illustrate the importance and use of such a logic. The first occurs in George Holton's discussion of the nature of light, incorporating Niels Bohr's principle of complementarity. It begins with the question 'what is light?' – although any key term in any field might be substituted here for light with the same implications:

> Our knowledge of light is contained in a number of statements that are seemingly contradictory, made on the basis of a variety of experiments under different conditions, and interpreted in the light of a complex of theories. When you ask, 'What is light?'; the answer is: the observer, his various pieces and types of equipment, his experiments, his theories and models of interpretation, and whatever it may be that fills an otherwise empty room when the lightbulb is allowed to keep on burning. All this, together is light.[74]

In the claim to knowledge and understanding of any term – light, life, mental illness, there are implicitly or explicitly aspects of Nature and Mind and naturing and minding. It would seem in Holton's example just cited, that before one can usefully employ a formal logic, an aspect logic must be employed, otherwise there can be little or no understanding of the phenomenon one seeks to explain.

The second example is taken from Knud Rasmussen's report on the Copper Eskimos, published in 1932 in Copenhagen.[75] Netsit, an Eskimo storyteller and close friend of the Danish explorer, told him the tale of two hunters, who met one day miles from their camp. One had a caribou skin, the other a wolf skin. They began to argue as to whether the wolf or the caribou had the more hairs. Each man defended his particular trophy with great vehemence. Finally each began to pull the hairs from his hide and count them. The hair on the wolf and the caribou are many. They pulled and counted day after day after day, and, since neither would relent, both starved to death.

Netsit's inference is developed in an aspect/perspective logic. Although a formal logic is essential to the counting of the hairs, it cannot guide our reason as to the wisdom or necessity of doing so. This is the place where an aspect logic with its inference sequence of aspect, perspective, understanding, attitude, action can provide great insight.

Epilogue

In 1877, the Italian astronomer, Schiaparelli discovered the great canals on Mars, and their existence was argued and studied by succeeding astronomers well into this century. The American astronomer, Percival Lowell alone saw and mapped over 400 of them. Historians wrote the histories of the great civilizations that produced them. Social scientists speculated on the social and economic structures that must have accompanied their construction. And everyone wondered what had happened to the individuals who had dug them. Might there be a message in the demise of Mar's civilization for planet Earth? There now seems to be no question that the canals like the vegetation on Mars were an illusory combination of instrument, mind, and eye. For example, the green shades of vegetation on Mars that Lowell saw in the nineteenth century were probably due to distortions of telescope lenses of the period. Lowell's perceptive remark about eyes, minds, and telescopes might preface all observations and their interpretations: '... at a telescope eyes differ surprisingly little, brains surprisingly much'.[1]

This combination of instrument, mind, and sense is always present in human observations and explanations of the world and of ourselves. Nor does the relativity of the combination disappear with the increasing refinement of instruments, the related extensions of our senses, or the comprehensiveness of our theories. Just as we feel we have identified and mastered the smallest parts of the whole, we find we cannot reverse our steps in order to arrive back at the whole without encountering relativity and chaos. The frog thoroughly known in all of its parts, juices, and processes, is a frog that no longer hops and catches flies on a lazy summer afternoon.

The way in which we observe is a matter of mind/sense relationship. In great part, the natural environment of 'homo sapiens' is a mental one, for it is in mental and philosophical space that we interpret and explain all other environments including those that we mentally consider 'non-mental'. We are *abstraction dwellers* living in a conceptual world that at the same time lives in our intellects. In it, we create the institutions, societies, ideologies, religions that in turn create us, their creators. However, in our time, as the German molecular biologist, Friedrich Cramer has suggested, '... the human brain has transformed man into a Lamarckian creature ... biological evolution has been overtaken by technological and cultural progress. That is, evolution now lies in the hands of man; ... for the first time in the history of our world we have been given the moral responsibility not only for our *history* (and its crimes) but also for *natural history* (and the crimes committed against it).'[2]

Naturing and *minding* are two fundamental processes of human experience. They are the source of our sensing/conceiving and of that which is sensed/conceived. Minding as distinguishing and defining cannot be reduced to the distinctions and definitions it develops. Attempts to do so generate awareness paradoxes like the genetics of genetic theory, objective definitions of objectivity, true definitions of truth. Causality is a concept.

But concept too is a concept, and the concept that causality is a concept is also a concept in a meaning regression. An intuitive awareness of the possibility of such *distinguishing/distinction, defining/definition* regressions has been recognized in most traditions from the Greek Skeptic to the Chinese Taoist to the Swahili wise man, to Mahāvīra's axiom of non-absolutism. I believe that these paradoxes are implicit in our consciousness and that they are the creative sources of philosophy, mathematics, scientific theories, works of art. For Henri Poincare, it is beauty which attracts and interests the scientist and gives his life and research meaning.[3] But beauty occurs in the proximity of consciousness and its objects and not in the isolation of either, nor is it caused the one by the other. And, as Leshan and Margenau in their comparison of Einstein and Van Gogh emphasize, we cannot know what the world might be without consciousness for it is consciousness which organizes what we call 'reality' for us.[4]

At the end of this journey through these four dimensions of philosophical space, I should like to return to the two relationships that were its points of departure: The first is the relationship of consciousness *in* the world to our claims to knowledge *of* the world. Second are the relationships between and among values, choices, and facts in the social, economic and political systems we create to give our lives meaning on local, national, and international levels. Sometimes we devote so much attention to the world observed and participated in, that we seem totally unaware of the philosophical nature of the observing and participating processes.

In modern science and philosophy, we have become increasingly aware of a number of the difficulties that seem inherent in observation and description. In part we are more aware of these problems today because of the greater precision that observational methodologies and techniques have made possible. And in part we are aware of them because of conflicts between various models and theories of the world, as well as conflicting approaches to knowledge of it. Three of these difficulties seem most significant:

(1) We encounter the first when we try to identify the nature and position of the observer in observation, especially as the observer senses and interprets the *nature* of the observed world of which he/she is a part. The biologist who studies life is a living organism. The sociologist is a member of a society

which defines and does sociology. Observing is focusing attention upon an aspect of experience as sense data or mental impression, and consequently, focusing isolates this aspect of experience in a several ways:

In focusing attention, we isolate a finite aspect of appearances from others in physical space. To observe the cow is to ignore the horse, or the cloud on the horizon. To see light as a particle is to ignore it as a wave. To fix position is to lose motion. The tree is not the forest. The structure of the dead cat is not the functioning of the live one. A disease is not the sick individual.

In observing we also isolate an aspect of experience conceptually as interpretation from other possible interpretations. This is an isolation accomplished via remembered past experience and it is this which permits us to view experiences as similar, dissimilar, same and different. When we observe we build upon recognition in which vastly more is excluded than is included and the past defines the present. The more accurate our observations, the less we actually observe. Modern achievements of greater and greater accuracy reflect the greater exclusion which technology makes possible. But this accuracy can lead to a confusion of values with technological methodologies and instrumental applications.

(2) The second difficulty occurs when an observer makes choices in reference to the use and development of nature itself in which the observer represents a value as the definer of values. As was suggested above in the discussion of isolation, we define aspects of experience from the perspectives that we have upon experience in which we choose what we consider relevant or irrelevant, desirable or undesirable. These choices by observers are particularly important when making decisions in reference to modifying or preserving our physical and mental environments. These perspectives are also cultural and express the values of our different traditions. A tradition may choose to tie knowledge to transcendental objects and so dichotomize its perspectives and values accordingly into objective/subjective, the source of which is then attributed to the observed objects. This is the direction physical and social science have followed in much of their history in the object dimension of philosophical space, although this is clearly changing.

Another possibility, however, might be to emphasize the conscious subject who knows objects. One then chooses to view objects from the point of view of subjects. This is the case with many Indian systems. Or one might view objects and subjects as situationally occurring and related, and thus choose to give primacy to the moments of immediate experience of perceptual objects over conceptual constructs, as do the Buddhists. Or one might think of subjects and objects as a continuum of aspects and perspectives in and by nature, as do many Chinese Taoists and Neo-Confucians.

(3) A third difficulty occurs when the observer tries to resolve the difficulties discussed above technologically. The individual who is unaware of the problems of isolation that observation creates, may appeal to some technical methodology or procedure to establish definitions of truth and objectivity, and remain unaware that this appeal itself is neither true nor objective and represents a choice of method of verification as well as a choice of definitions of *truth* and *objectivity*.

I will conclude this exploration of *philosophical space* by posing two questions: 'Where have we been?' And 'Where do we go from here?'

Where have we been?

At the beginning, I identified three sets of terms that would be used but not defined: (1) world, thing, object; (2) thought, mind, consciousness; (3) symbol, language, sign. I shall conclude with these terms still undefined, not because they cannot be, but because they are defined in so many ways. Each dimension of philosophical space uses them and explains them in different contexts. Any definition will reflect the particular dimension within which *to define* is itself defined. Consciousness, the elements of our experience, and symbols can be objectified if viewed as independent *objects*. But this is always accomplished by an observing, thinking *subject* from a point of view, in an actual *situation*, whose interpretation is dependent upon a sequence of remembered, possible situations, in which all distinctions made and names applied are a synthesis of the *aspects* of human experience and the *perspectives* that observers and their cultures have upon these.

Any statement has meaning in a context which in its totality is paradoxical in reference to itself, and is complementary to all other possible statements. The paradoxical aspect of a statement emerges when one accepts a single dimension of philosophical space or experience for the totality, and then attempts to apply the statement to itself. This would occur if we were to declare 'the absolutism of non-absolutism'; to claim to be able to non-situationally define 'situationality'; to insist that 'objectivity is objective'; to proclaim that 'thinking the unthinkable' is thinking the unthinkable.

We have also discovered that philosophical space is question space, for the dimension of the questions that we ask in producing knowledge will determine the inferences we can and will make, as well as the answers we will accept. We think on levels and in directions, and live in systems that live in us. To understand answers and inferences is to understand the questions that can and cannot be asked on levels and in directions within a thought system. Understanding this is facilitated by examining any system with the assumptions of the others.

Where do we go from here?

The answer to this question reflects values and choices and is twofold. Firstly: I believe the more dimensions we have in our thinking, the more insight we have into the choices we make, as well as responsibility for making them. These dimensions represent in different ways the position of the human intellect in nature. Ultimately our understanding of them is critical to our survival as the *minding* aspect in *naturing*. The synthesis of these four dimensions leads to our awareness that as observers we are actors, authors, and spectators of the human in nature and of nature in the human.

Paradoxes and confusion are not only implicit in our thinking, they are also the source of our intellectual independence and freedom. I think that reflective and thoughtful individuals in all traditions carry in their awareness an awareness of the limits of awareness and so are aware of both the necessity for trying to think the unthinkable and speak the unspeakable, while at the same time realizing the impossibility of doing either. This is the source of both tolerance and creative inspiration, and the very essence of *understanding* as the ground for *knowledge*. There is no observer outside of a particular philosophical space. There is no philosophical space outside of a particular observer. As Nāgārjuna said, they are such, not-such, both such and not-such, and ultimately neither such nor not-such. At the end we reaffirm what we proposed at the beginning, that we live in thought systems which live in us. And the entirety of this in and out is nature in the human and the human in nature. All human values occur in this condition.

In closing, I would suggest that we view philosophical space as the great puzzle of human experience. Each dimension represents another part of the whole and brings into focus a different aspect. Each is also a template which permits a different pattern and part of the entire to emerge. The puzzle most clearly appears in the statements we make about the world in some symbol system. Thus, it is most important that we understand the implications of philosophical space for the terms we select to express our thoughts. Perhaps our very survival depends upon this understanding. Certainly the quality of the mental and spiritual lives we live in philosophical space presupposes it.

Notes

INTRODUCTION

1. This proposition is attributed to the Chinese logician Hui Shih or one of his contemporaries of the fifth century BCE. For further information see Hu Shih, *The Development of the Logical Method in Ancient China*, (Shanghai, Oriental Book Co., 1928) p. 118.
2. Aristotle, *Metaphysics*, Bk IX, 1049b–1050a, Hippocrates G. Apostle trans., (Bloomington, Indiana University, 1966) pp. 54–5.
3. S. F. Butler, *Life and Habit*, (London, Jonathan Cape, 1924) p. 134.
4. Richard Dawkins, *The Selfish Gene*, (New York, Oxford University Press, 1976) p. 22.

CHAPTER 1

1. Ambrose Bierce, *Can Such Things Be?* (Freeport, N.Y., Books for Libraries Press, Short Stories Reprint Series, 1971) p. 286.
2. Richard Broxton Onians, *The Origins of European Thought about the Body, the Mind, the Soul, the World, Time, and Fate*, (Salem, Cambridge University, 1951) p. 76.
3. Burton Watson, trans., *Complete Works of Chuang Tzu*, (New York, Columbia University Press, 1968) pp. 300–1.
4. Jan Knappert, *Myths and Legends of the Swahili* (Nairobi, African Writers Series, Heinemann Educational, 1970) pp. 117–18.
5. Wing-tsit Chan, trans., *Reflections on Things at Hand*, (New York, Columbia University, 1967) p. 94.

CHAPTER 2

1. Swami Prabhavananda & Frederick Manchester trans., *The Upaniṣads*, (New York, Mentor Religious Classics, 1961) p. 30.
2. F. Max Mueller, trans., *The Upaniṣads, 'The Bṛhadāraṇyaka'* Part II (New York Sacred Books of the East, Reprint by Dover Publications, 1962) p. 112.
3. Edward Harrison, *Masks of the Universe*, (New York, Collier Books, 1985) p. vii.
4. Griddhrapinchchacharya Sri Umāsvāmi [Umāsvāti] Maharaj, *Tatvārthā Sūtram*, [*Tattvārthāhigama Sūtra*] 'Sutra 4' (Delhi, Barrister Champat Rai Jain Trust, 1956) p. 8.
5. Burton Watson, trans., *Hsün Tzu, Basic Writings*, (New York, Columbia University, 1963) p. 127.
6. Opening line of the first chapter of Lao Tzu, *The Tao te Ching*.
7. Watson, *Hsün Tzu*, p. 114.

8. George Devereux, *Ethnopsychoanalysis*, (Berkeley, University of California Press, 1978) p. 1.
9. B. Jowett, trans., *The Dialogues of Plato, 'Theaetetus'*, vol. iii (Oxford, Clarendon Press, 4th Edition, 1953) p. 218.
10. Nicholas of Cusa, E.G. Salter trans., *The Vision of God* (New York, E.P. Dutton 1928) pp. 47–8.
11. Sarvepalli Radhakrishnan & Charles Moore, *A Sourcebook in Indian Philosophy*, (Princeton University Press 5th Reprint 1973) p. 24.
12. E. Harrison, *Masks* p. 275.
13. Prabhavananda, *Upaniṣads* p. 51.
14. Prabhavananda, *Upaniṣads* p. 89.
15. Roger S. Jones, *Physics as Metaphor* (Minneapolis, University of Minnesota Press, 1982) p. 16.
16. John Locke, *An Essay Concerning Human Understanding*, vol. i (New York, Everyman's Library, Revised Edition, Dutton 1965) pp. 15–16.
17. Albert Einstein, *Essays in Physics* (New York, Philosophical Library, 1950) p. 68.
18. William T. Keeton, *Elements of Biological Science* (New York, W.W. Norton & Co. 1973) p. 2.
19. Karl Jaspers, Ralph Manheim trans., *Way to Wisdom, An Introduction to Philosophy* (London, Victor Gollancz Ltd 1951) p. 30.
20. Prabhavananda, *Upaniṣads* p. 43.
21. Erwin Schrödinger, Cecily Hastings trans., *My View of the World*, (Woodbridge, Conn., Cambridge University Press 1961, Ox Bow Press Reprint, 1983) p. 40.
22. Henry Clarke Warren, *Buddhism in Translations* (New York, Atheneum, 1963) p. xii.
23. Radhakrishnan, *Sourcebook*, 'Mahāyāna Viṁśaka of Nāgārjuna' p. 339.
24. Warren, *Buddhism* p. 146.
25. Fung Yu-lan, *A Short History of Chinese Philosophy* (New York Free Press/Macmillan, 1966) p. 337.

CHAPTER 3

1. Walter Benesch, Children's Logic mss.
2. Radhakrishnan & Moore, *A Sourcebook*, 'The Yoga-bhāsyya of Vyāsa' p. 476.
3. Jha, trans., *The Nyāya-Sūtras of Gauṭama* (Motilal Banarsidass, Dehli, Reprint 1984, 4 vols) vol. i, p. 111.
4. John Locke, *An Essay Concerning Human Understanding* , John W. Yolton ed. (Dutton, N.Y., Everyman's Library, 1965) vol. i, p. 78.
5. *Ibid.*, p. 249.
6. Aristotle, *Metaphysics*, Hippocrates G. Apostle trans., (Bloomington, Indiana University Press 1966) Bk XII ix 1074b 35, p. 210.
7. *Ibid.*, Bk XII vii 1072 a 15–30, p. 205.
8. Philip Wheelwright, *The Presocratics*, (New York, Odyssey Press, 1982) pp. 107–8.
9. *Ibid.*, p. 183.
10. Lucretius, *On the Nature of Things*, H.A.J. Munro, trans. (New York, Encylopedia Britannica, Great Books of the Western World,) pp. 3–4.

11. Wheelwright, *Presocratics*, p. 127.
12. R.J. Hirst, ed., *Perception and the External World*, (NewYork, Macmillan Co., 1965) p. 75.
13. Max Planck, *Where Is Science Going?* (Woodbridge, Conn., Ox Bow Press reprint 1981) p. 82.
14. Aristotle, *The Posterior Analytics*, Hugh Tredennick, trans., (Cambridge, Mass., Harvard University Press, reprint 1960) I.xxxi p. 159.
15. Aristotle, *Metaphysics*, I. ii 4–5, p. II.
16. Aristotle, *Metaphysics*, Hugh Tredennick, trans., (Cambridge, Mass., Harvard University Press, reprint, 1956) IV. vi, 3–8, pp. 197–9.
17. C.E. Law, *The Elements of Euclid*, (London, John Weale, 1853) p. 1.
18. Erwin Schrödinger, *Mind and Matter, The Tarner Lectures*, October 1956 (Cambridge, Cambridge University Press, 1959) p. 37.
19. Jones, *Physics*, p. 18.
20. Aristotle, *Metaphysics*, Apostle trans. Bk IV vii 20–30, p. 70.
21. Ernst Cassirer, *Substance and Function & Einstein's Theory of Relativity*, (New York, Dover, 1953) p. 4.
22. Aristotle, *Posterior Analytics* I.xiv, p. 93.
23. S. Sambursky, *The Physical World of the Greeks*, Mergon Dagut, trans. (New York, Collier Books, 1962) p. 199.
24. Aristotle, *Metaphysics*, Apostle trans., IX x. 1–2, p. 469.
25. Jørgen Jørgensen, *A Treatise of Formal Logic*, 3 vols (New York, Russell & Russell, 1962) vol. i, pp. 6–7.
26. Daniel E. Gershenson, and Daniel A. Greenberg, *Anaxagoras and the Birth of Physics*, (New York, Blaisdell Publishing Co.,1964).
27. A.C. Graham, *Studies in Chinese Philosophy & Philosophical Literature*, (Singapore, Institute of East Asian Philosophies, 1986) p. 377.
28. Cassirer, *Substance*, p. 7.

CHAPTER 4

1. Wheelwright, *Presocratics*, p. 239.
2. *Ibid.*, p. 250.
3. *Ibid.* p. 267.
4. Aristotle, *Parts of Animals*, IV x 686a5, A.L. Peck trans. (Cambridge, Harvard University Press reprint, 1955) p. 367.
5. Thomas Hobbes, *Leviathan*, (New York, Everyman's Library Edition, E.P. Dutton Co., 1924) p. 12.
6. 'A Talk with Einstein', *The Listener*, Sept. 1955.
7. Aristotle, *Metaphysics* Bk. XIII iv 1078b, Apostle trans., p. 218.
8. *Ibid.*, IV ii 1003a–b pp. 54–5.
9. Aristotle, *The Categories*, V 3b, Harold P. Cook, trans., (Cambridge, Harvard University, reprint, 1962) pp. 31–3. *Metaphysics*, IX i 1045b, Hugh Tredennick, trans., p. 419.
10. Aristotle, *Metaphysics* III iv 999b, Apostle trans., p. 47.
11. *Ibid.*, XII 1070a p. 199.
12. *Ibid.*, III iv 1000a, p. 47.

13. *Ibid.*, VII viii 1034a, p. 120.
14. Aristotle, *On the Soul* II i 412a, W.S. Hett trans. (Cambridge, Harvard University, reprint 1957) p. 67.
15. Aristotle, *Metaphysics* IX viii 1049b–1050a, Apostle trans., pp. 154–5.
16. *Ibid.*, Book XII vii 1072b, p. 205.
17. *Ibid.*, XII x 1075a p. 210.
18. *Ibid.*, XII viii 1073a p. 206.
19. Charles Darwin, *Origin of Species*, (New York, Harvard Classics vol. 11, 1909) pp. 328–9.
20. Aristotle, *Metaphysics*, V ii 1013a, Apostle trans., p. 74.
21. Aristotle, *On The Soul* II i 412a, p. 67.
22. Aristotle, *Parts of Animals* I i 641a, p. 69.
23. Aristotle, *On The Soul* II ii 413b 25–30, p. 77.
24. Aristotle, *The Generation of Animals*, II iii 736b; A.L. Peck trans., (Cambridge, Harvard University Press, reprint, 1953) p. 171.
25. Aristotle *On the Soul* II v 417b, p. 99.
26. *Ibid.*, III viii 431b–432a, p. 179–81.
27. *Ibid.*, II vi 418a, p. 101.
28. *Ibid.*, III ii 425b, p. 147.
29. *Ibid.*, III iii 428a p. 159.
30. *Ibid.*
31. Aristotle, *Posterior Analytics* I, xxxi 88a, p. 159.
32. *Ibid.*, II xix 100a, pp. 257–9.
33. Aristotle, *On the Soul*, II v 417b, pp. 99–101.
34. Aristotle, *Metaphysics* VII 13 1038b–1039a, Apostle trans. pp. 129–30.
35. Aristotle, *Posterior Analytics* II x 94a, p. 209.
36. Aristotle, *Metaphysics* VII xv 1039b–1040a, Apostle trans. p.132.
37. Aristotle, *On the Soul* III vi 430b, p. 175.
38. Aristotle, *Posterior Analytics* I x 76a, p. 69.
39. Aristotle, *On the Soul*, III v 430a, p. 171.
40. *Ibid.*, III vi–vii 430b–431b, pp. 175–9.
41. *Ibid.*, III iv 429a, p. 163–5.
42. *Ibid.*, III iv 429a–b, p. 165–7.
43. *Ibid.*, I iv 408b, p. 49. D.W. Hamlyn, *Aristotle's De Anima Books II and III*, (Oxford, Clarendon Press 1968) p. 142.
44. *Ibid.*, III iv 429a, pp. 163–5.
45. Aristotle, *Posterior Analytics* II xix 100b, p. 261.
46. *Ibid.*, I xii 77a, pp. 77–9.
47. Aristotle, *Categories*, XII xiv b, p. 101.
48. Aristotle, *Posterior Analytics*, II x 93 b, p. 207; Aristotle, *Topica*, E.S. Forster trans., (Cambridge, Harvard University, reprint 1960) I v 102a, pp. 281–3.
49. Aristotle, *On Interpretations*, Harold P. Cook, trans., (Cambridge, Harvard University reprint 1962) III 16b, pp. 119–21.
50. *Ibid.*, I 16a, p. 115.
51. Immanuel Kant, *Critique of Pure Reason*, Supplement II, Preface to the Second Edition, F. Max Mueller trans., (London, Macmillan Co, reprint 1920) p. 688.
52. Aristotle, *Posterior Analytics* I xxxiii 88b, p. 167.
53. Aristotle, *Topica* I i 100a–b, pp. 273–5.
54. Aristotle, *On Interpretation* III iv–v 17a, p. 121.

55. Aristotle, *Categories* V 4 b, p. 35.
56. Aristotle, *On Interpretation* IX, pp. 131–41.
57. Aristotle, *Prior Analytics* I i 24 b, pp. 201–3.
58. Aristotle, *On Interpretation* V–VI 17a, p. 123.
59. Aristotle, *Prior Analytics*, I xxx 46a, p. 359.
60. Aristotle, *Posterior Analyatics* I i 1a, p. 25.
61. *Ibid.*, I ii 71b, p. 31.

CHAPTER 5

1. *Menander, The Principal Fragments*, 'The Counterfeit Baby or The Rustic', Francis G. Allinson trans. (Cambridge, The Loeb Classical Library, Harvard University, reprint 1959) p. 443.
2. *Menander* p. 177.
3. George K. Strodach, *The Philosophy of Epicurus*, (Chicago, Northwestern University Press, 1963) p. 151.
4. Sextus Empiricus, *Outlines of Pyrrhonism*, III 12, R.G. Bury, trans., *Sextus Empiricus* vol. 1–4 (Cambridge, Loeb Classical Library, Harvard University) vol i, p. 333.
5. *Menander* p. 445.
6. Peter Green, *Alexander to Actium*, (Berkeley, University of California Press, 1990) pp. 55–6.
7. Diogenes Laertius, *Lives of Eminent Philosophers, Epicurus* 2 vols., vol. ii, Bk X, 2, vol. 2 R.D. Hicks, trans. (Cambridge, Loeb Classical Library, Harvard University reprint 1958) pp. 529–31.
8. Strodach, *Epicurus*, 124, p. 180.
9. Lucretius, *De Rerum Natura*, bk III 995, W.H.D. Rouse, trans. (Cambridge, Loeb Classical Library, Harvard University reprint 1959) pp. 239–40.
10. Lucretius, iii 136–61, pp. 181–3.
11. Lucretius, iii 193–230, p. 185–7.
12. Strodach, *Epicurus* iv 46a, p. 118.
13. Lucretius iv, 477–95, p. 283.
14. Strodach, *Epicurus*, 3–4, pp. 115–17.
15. Lucretius, iv 524, p. 285.
16. Lucretius, iv 617, p. 293.
17. Lucretius, iv 700, p. 197.
18. Lucretius, iv 43–55, p. 251.
19. Strodach, *Epicurus*, 134, p. 185.
20. Lucretius ii 251–90, pp 101–3.
21. Strodach, *Epicurus*, 132–3, p. 184.
22. Diogenes Laertius, vii 39–40, pp. 149–51.
23. Diogenes Laertius, vii 134, p. 239.
24. Josiah B. Gould, *The Philosophy of Chrysippus*, (Leiden, E.J. Brill 1970) p. 82.
25. Diogenes Laertius, vii 180, p. 289.
26. Seneca, *Moral Essays*, vol. i, John W. Basore trans., (Cambridge, Loeb Classical Library, Harvard University, reprint 1958), Bk I 8–9, p. 39.

27. Marcus Aurelius, *Meditations*, George Long trans., (Chicago, Henry Regnery Co., 1956) p. 111.
28. Epictetus, *The Discourses*, 2 vols. W.A. Oldfather trans., (Cambridge, Loeb Classical Library, Harvard University Press, reprint 1961), vol. ii p. 445.
29. Diogenes Laertius, Bk vii 137–9, vol. ii pp. 241–3.
30. Marcus Aurelius, *The Communings with Himself*, C.R. Haines trans., (Cambridge, Loeb Classical Library, Harvard University reprint 1961) p. 105.
31. For a discussion of this position, see R.C. Lewontin, *Biology as Ideology*, (New York, Harper Perennial Books, 1993); R.C. Lewontin, Steven Rose, Leon J. Kamin, *Not In Our Genes*, (New York, Pantheon Books, 1984).
32. David Hahm, *The Origins of Stoic Cosmology*, (Columbus, Ohio State University Press, 1977) p. 163.
33. Gould, *Chrysippus* p. 54.
34. Diogenes Laertius, Bk vii 50–52, vol. ii, pp. 159–161.
Josiah Gould writes of Chrysippus that his '... theory of knowledge is thoroughly empirical. The senses, functions of the soul, constitute man's messengers from the external world; and their reports are controlled by referring them, not to transcendental entities such as ideas or universals, but by determining how they compare with other reports which the soul, functioning naturally, has classified and stored away.' Gould p. 90.
35. Mates, *Stoic Logic*, (Berkeley, University of California Press, 1961) p. 41.
36. A.A. Long, ed., *Problems in Stoicism*, A.A. Long, 'Language and Thought in Stoicism' (London, Athlone Press, University of London, 1971) p. 76.
37. Gould, *Chrysippus* p. 55.
38. Gould, *Chrysippus* p. 51.
39. J.M. Rist, 'Categories and Their Uses', A.A. Long, ed., *Problems in Stoicism*, pp. 44–5.
40. J.M. Rist, 'Categories', p. 120.
41. Diogenes Laertius, Bk Vii 49, vol. 2, p. 15.
42. Samual Sambursky, *The Physical World of the Greeks*, (New York, Collier Books, 1962) pp. 203–4.
43. Sambursky, pp. 65–9 (in this section, Sambursky has an excellent discussion of the Stoics as empiricists).
44. Anton Dumitriu, *History of Logic*, 4 vols (Tunbridge Wells, Kent, Abacus Press English Ed. 1977) vol. i, p. 237.
45. I.M Bochenski, *A History of Formal Logic*, Ivo Thomas trans. and ed. (Notre Dame, Indiana, University of Notre Dame Press 1961) p. 117.
46. Gould, *Chrysippus* pp. 83–4.
47. Epictetus, *Encheiridion*, #1, Oldfather trans. vol. ii, p. 483.
48. Epictetus, *Discourses*, vol. i p. 9, and *Encheiridion* #9 vol. ii, p. 491.
49. Epictetus, *Encheiridion* #9 vol. ii, p. 491.
50. J.M. Rist, *Stoic Philosophy*, (London, Cambridge University Press, 1969) p. 15.
51. Gould, *Chrysippus* p. 169.
52. Sextus Empiricus, *Outlines* Bk i, ch. vi 12 , vol. i , p. 9.
53. Diogenes Laertius, vol. ii, Bk ix, ch. 11, 61–8, p. 475–9.
54. Diogenes Laertius, p. 475.
55. Sextus Empiricus, *Outlines* Bk i, ch. iii 7, vol. i, p. 5.
56. Sextus Empiricus, *Outlines* Bk i, ch. i 1–4, vol. i, p. 3.
57. Sextus Empiricus, *Outlines* Bk i, ch. x 19–20, vol. i p. 15.

58. Sextus Empiricus, *Outlines* Bk i, ch. iv 8–9, vol. i p. 7.
59. Sextus Empiricus, *Against the Logicians*, I27, vol. ii, p. 15.
60. Kathleen Freeman, *Ancilla to the Presocratic Philosophers*, (Cambridge, Harvard University Press, 1983) p. 24.
61. Sextus Empiricus, *Outlines*, Bk ii, ch. iv 20, vol. 1, pp. 163–5.
62. Sextus Empiricus, *Outlines* Bk ii, ch. vi 48, vol. i, p. 183.
63. Each of these groups represents a set of views to which Sextus Empiricus applied his inquiry.
64. Sextus Empiricus *Outlines* Bk ii, ch. vi, 58, vol i. p. 189.
65. Sextus Empiricus *Outlines* Bk II, ch. vi 66–9, vol. i, pp. 193–5.
66. *Menander*, p. 361.
67. Sextus Empiricus, *Outlines* Bk i, ch. x 19–20, vol. i, p. 15.
68. Sextus Empiricus, *Against the Logicians* Bk i ,78–9, vol. ii, p. 41.
69. Sextus Empiricus, *Outlines* Bk i, ch. xxii–xxiii, 196–7, vol. i, p. 115.
70. Sextus Empiricus, *Outlines* Bk ii ch. xi, 108, vol. i, p. 221.
71. Sextus Empiricus, *Outlines*, Bk ii chapt xviii 214, vol. i, p. 291.
72. Sextus Empiricus, *Against the Logicians* Bk i 84-87, vol. ii, pp. 43–5.
73. Sextus Empiricus, *Outlines* Bk ii ch. xv, 204, vol. i p. 283.
74. Sextus Empiricus, *Outlines* Bk ii ch. xvi, 207–8, vol. i, p. 285.
75. Sextus Empiricus, *Outlines* Bk ii ch. xiv 198–9, vol. i, p. 279.
76. Sextus Empiricus, *Outlines* Bk i ch. vii 14–15, vol. i, p. 11.
77. Sextus Empiricus, *Outlines* Bk i, ch. xxviii 206–8, vol. i, p. 123.
78. Sextus Empiricus, *Against the Logicians* Bk i 293, vol. ii, p. 155.
79. Sextus Empiricus, *Against the Logicians* Bk i, 364, vol. ii, pp. 191–3.
80. Sextus Empiricus, *Outlines* Bk i ch. xv, vol. i, p. 95.
81. Sextus Empiricus, *Outlines* Bk ii, ch. xxii, vol. i p. 315.
82. David Hume, *A Treatise of Human Nature, Book I, Of the Understanding*, G.C. Macnabb ed., Merican Books, (New York, World Publishing Co., 4th Printing, 1969) p. 48.

CHAPTER 6

1. Gertrud Lenzer (ed), *Auguste Comte and Positivism, The Essential Writings*, (New York, Harper Torchbooks, 1975) p. 29.
2. Auguste Comte, *Introduction to Positive Philosophy* , Frederick Ferre ed. and trans., (Indianopolis, Bobbs-Merrill, 1970) p. 3.
3. Lenzer, *Comte*, p. 28.
4. Lenzer, *Comte*, p. 463.
5. Plato, *The Dialogues of Plato*, 4 vols 'Philebus', B. Jowett trans., (Cambridge, Oxford University, 1964) vol. III, p. 382.
6. Lenzer, *Comte*, p. 475.
7. Otto Hahn, *My Life*, Ernst Kaiser & Eithne Wilkins trans., (London, MacDonald, 1970) pp. 29–30.
8. Augustine, *The City of God*, 2 vols BK VIII, ch. 6, Marcus Dods trans. (New York, Hafner Publishing Co. 1948) vol. I p. 314–15
9. Richard S. Westfall, *Science and Religion in 17th Century England*, (New Haven, Yale University Press, 1970) p. 112.

10. Isaac Newton, *Mathematical Principles of Natural Philosophy*, Andrew Motte trans., revised by Florian Cajori, BK III, (Chicago, Great Books of the Western World vol. 34, 1952) p. 369.
11. Ptolemy, *The Almagest*, Catesby Taliaferro, trans., (Chicago, Great Books of the Western World, vol. 16 Encyclopaedia Britannica, 1952 edn) p. 5.
12. Edward M. Forster, *Alexandria, A History and a Guide*, (Woodstock, N.Y., Overlook Press, 1974) pp. 74–5.
13. Williston Walker, Richard A. Norris, David W. Lotz, Robert T. Handy, *A History of the Christian Church*, (New York, Charles Scribner's Sons, fourth edition, 1985) p. 19.
14. Salvatore R. C. Lilla, *Clement of Alexandria, A Study in Christian Platonism and Gnosticism*, (London, Oxford University, 1971) p. 9.
15. Clement of Alexandria, The Stromata, from Robert L. Ferm, *Readings in the History of Christian Thought*, (New York, Holt, Rinehart, and Winson, 1964) p. 12.
16. Augustine rejects this on a chronological basis, in the 11th Chapter of the Eighth Book of the City of God.
17. Maria Boas Hall, *Robert Boyle on Natural Philosophy*, (Bloomington, Indiana University Press, 1965) p. 148.
18. Plotinus, Enneads in A.H. Armstrong, *Plotinus*, (New York, Collier Books, 1962) pp. 53–4.
19. Plato, *Timaeus*, vol. III, p. 716.
20. The Apocrypha: *Wisdom of Solomon, The Holy Bible*, (New York, Gay Brothers, 1870) pp. 40–1.
21. Plotinus, pp. 51–2.
22. Albert Einstein, *Ideas and Opinions*, (New York, Bonanza Books, 1954) p. 262.
23. Plotinus, p. 80.
24. Plotinus, I. 1. 10, p. 119.
25. Alcuin A. Weiswurm, *The Nature of Human Knowledge According to Saint Gregory of Nyssa*, a dissertation (Washington D.C., Catholic University of America Press, Philosophical Studies CXXXVI, 1952) p. 90.
26. Robert L. Ferm, *Readings in the History of Christian Thought*, (New York, Holt, Rinehart and Winston, 1964) p. 26.
27. Gottfried Wilhelm Leibniz, *Theodicy* (abridged) E. M. Huggard trans., (New York, Libary of Liberal Arts, Bobbs-Merrill Co., 1966) p. 20.
28. Max Born, *Natural Philosophy of Cause and Chance*, (Oxford, Waynflete Lectures, The Clarendon Press, 1948) p. 1.
29. Born, *Natural Philosophy* pp. 124–5.
30. Albert Einstein, *Out of My Later Years*, (New York, Philosophical Library, 1950) p. 33.
31. Leibniz, p. 10.
32. Alexander Roberts and James Donaldson, eds, *The AnteNicene Fathers*, (Grand Rapids, Wm. B. Eerdmans Publishing Co., 1978) vol. 3 p. 246.
33. Clement of Alexandria, *Exhortation to the Greeks*, G.W. Butterworth trans., (Cambridge, Mass., Loeb Classical Library, Harvard University, reprint 1960) ch. vii, p. 163.
34. Augustine, *Confessions* XI, v, 7, Edward Bouverie Pusey trans., (Chicago, Great Books of the Western World vol. 18, Encyclopaedia Britannica, 1952) pp. 90–1.

35. Gregory of Nyssa, p. 166.
36. Max Planck, *Where is Science Going?* (Woodbridge, Conn., Ox Bow Press, 1981 reprint) p. 218.
37. Thomas Aquinas, *Summa Theologica*, 2 vols, Fathers of the English Dominican Province trans., (New York, Benziger Brothers, 1947) vol. I, p. 12.
38. Isaac Newton, *Mathematical Principles...* Bk III, General Scholium, p. 371.
39. Aquinas, *Summa*, vol. I, p. ll.
40. Seyyed Hossein Nasr, *Science and Civilization in Islam*, (Cambridge, Mass., Harvard University Press, 1968) p. 24.
41. Sir James Jeans, *Physics and Philosophy*, (Cambridge, G.B., Cambridge University Press, 1948) p. 174.
42. Ernest A. Moody, *The Logic of William of Ockham*, (New York, Russell & Russell, 1965) p. 76.
43. Jeans, *Physics* p. 202.
44. John M. Robertson, ed., *The Philosophical Works of Francis Bacon*, Reprint from the texts and translations, with the notes and prefaces of Ellis and Spedding, (Freeport, N. Y., Books for Libraries Press, reprint, 1970) p. 243.
45. Robertson, *Bacon*, p. 249.
46. Robertson, *Bacon*, p. 246.
47. Galileo Galilei, *Dialogue Concerning the Two Chief World Systems – Ptolemaic & Copernician*, Stillman Drake trans., (Berkeley, University of California Press, 1953) pp. 103–5.
48. Erik Bergaust, *Wernher von Braun*, (Washington, D.C., National Space Institute, 1976) p. 113.
49. Ben Ray Redman, *The Portable Voltaire*, (New York, Viking Press, 1949, p. 170.
50. Rene Descartes, *Discourse on Method*, Arthur Wollaston trans., (London, Penguin Classics, 1960) p. 50.
51. Descartes, p. 61.
52. Newton, *Mathematical Principles...*, pp. 270–1.
53. David Hume, *A Treatise of Human Nature, Book I, Of the Understanding*, G.C. Macnabb ed., (New York, Merican Books, World Publishing Co. 4th Printing 1969) p. 48.
54. Hume, p. 110.
55. Hume, p. 46.
56. Hume, p. 283.
57. Hume, p. 54, p. 234.
58. Hume, pp. 52–3.
59. Hume, p. 232.
60. Hume, p. 233.
61. Hume, pp. 40–1.
62. Immanuel Kant, *The Prolegomena*, Carl K. Friedrich, trans. and ed. *The Philosophy of Kant*, (New York Modern Library, 1949) pp. 90–1.
63. Immanuel Kant, *Critique of Pure Reason*, F. Max Mueller trans. (London, Macmillan Co, reprint 1920) pp. 271–2.
64. Kant, *Critique*, p. 688.
65. Kant, *Critique*, pp. 715–18.
66. Friedrich Cramer, *Order and Chaos*, D.I. Loewus trans., (New York, VCH Verlagsgesellschaft, 1993) p. 192.

67. Cramer, pp. 180–1.
68. Joe Rosen, *Symmetry in Science, An Introduction to the General Theory*, (New York, Springer Verlag, 1995) pp. 172–3.
69. Heinz-Otto Peitgen, Hartmut Juergens, Dietmar Saupe, *Chaos and Fractals, New Frontiers of Science*, (New York, Springer Verlag, 1992) pp. 10–11.
70. Peitgen, Juergens, Saupe, p. 11.
71. Cramer, p. 212.
72. Karl R. Popper, *Realism and the Aim of Science*, (Totowa, New Jersey, Rowman and Littlefield, 1983) p. 6.
73. Popper, p. 96.
74. Popper, p. 163.
75. Patrick A. Heelan, S.J., *Quantum Mechanics and Objectivity, A Study of the Physical Philosophy of Werner Heisenberg*, (The Hague, Martinus Nikhoff, 1965) p. 64.
76. Bruce Gregory, *Inventing Reality, Physics as Language*, (New York, Wiley Science Editions, John Wiley and Sons Inc., 1990) pp. 69–70
77. Gregory, p. 181.
78. Gregory, p. 181.
79. Ben Ray Redman, ed., *The Portable Voltaire*, The Philosophical Dictionary, (New York, Viking Press, 2nd printing 1955) p. 170.
80. Jeans, *The Mysterious Universe* (Cambridge, Cambridge University Press 2nd ed. reprint 1948) p. 122.
81. Peter Geach and Max Black, ed. and trans., *Translations from the Philosophical Writings of Gottlob Frege*, (Oxford, Basil Blackwell, 3rd. edn, 1980) p. 62.
82. J. Breadley, *Mach's Philosophy of Science*, (London, The Athlone Press, University of London, 1971) p. 177.
83. I.M. Bochenski, *A History* p. 274.
84. Alfred North Whitehead and Bertrand Russell, *Principia Mathematica*, (Cambridge, Cambridge University Press, reprint 1962) p. v.
85. The Pythagorean, Philolaus, in Wheelwright, *Presocratics*, pp. 231–2.
86. Alfred Jules Ayer, *Language, Truth and Logic*, (New York, Dover reprint, 1952) p. 5.

CHAPTER 7

1. *The Upaniṣads*, KaṬha Upaniṣad, Swami Prabhavananda and Frederick Manchester trans., (New York, Mentor Books, 3rd printing 1961) p. 19.
2. Erwin Schrödinger, *Mind and Matter*, The Tarner Lectures, October 1956 (Cambridge, Cambridge University Press, 1959) p. 44.
3. Arthur Eddington, *The Philosophy of Physical Science*, (Ann Arbor, University of Michigan Press, Ann Arbor Paperbacks, 1958) pp. 154–8.
4. Sarasvati Chennakesavan, *The Concept of Mind in Indian Philosophy*, (Bombay, Asia Publishing House, 1960) p. 133.
5. *The Upaniṣads*, vol. 1 and 2 Kauṣītaki III: 3; Chāndogya V, 1, ii; Bṛhādaraṇyaka VI 1, 7–14; Praśna II, 1–4, F. Max Mueller trans. (New York, Sacred Books of the East, Dover Reprint 2 vols 1962).
6. *The Upaniṣads*, Kauṣītaki Upaniṣad III,, 3, Mueller trans., vol. I, pp. 294–5.

7. *The Upaniṣads*, Kauṣītaki Upaniṣad III, 5, Mueller trans., pp. 296–7, III, 8, p. 299.
8. Chennakesavan, p. ix.
9. Chennakesavan, p. x.
10. Chennakesavan, p. 7.
11. Chennakesavan, p. 132.
12. *The Upaniṣads, The Kaṭha Upaniṣad,* Mueller trans. I, 1 22–9, vol. 2, pp. 6–7.
13. Sanghavi Sukhlalji, *Advanced Studies in Indian Logic & Metaphysics*, Reprint from Indian Studies Past & Present, (Calcutta, Firma K.L. Mukhopadhyaya, 1961), p. 6.
14. A.L. Basham, *The Wonder that was India*, Ch. II, *Prehistory, The Harappa Culture and the Arayans*, (New York, Grove Press, 1959), pp. 10–43.
15. Lin Yutang ed., *The Wisdom of China and India*, (New York, The Modern Library, 1955) p. 16.
16. *The Upaniṣads*, Chāndogya Upaniṣad Viii, 7, 1–4, Mueller trans., vol. 1 p. 134–6.
17. Surendranath Dasgupta, *A History of Indian Philosophy*, 5 vols (Benares, Motilal, reprint, 1975) vol. I, p. 29.
18. For a brief and excellent discussion of ethic and life stage, see P.T. Raju, *Structural Depths of Indian Thought,* (Albany, State University of New York, 1985) p. xvi.
19. Arthur Eddington, *The Nature of the Physical World*, (New York, Macmillan, 1929) pp. 279–81.
20. Sir John Eccles and Daniel N. Robinson, *The Wonder of Being Human, Our Brain and Our Mind*, (New York, The Free Press, 1984) pp. 18, 13–14.
21. Eccles and Robinson, p. 43.
22. Gerald J. Larson, *Classical Sāṃkhya*, (Delhi, Motilal Banarsidass, 1979).
23. Larson, p. 156.
24. Larson, p. 1.
25. Larson, Kārikā XIX p. 169.
26. Larson, Kārikā XIII pp. 259–60.
27. Larson, Kārikā LXII p. 172.
28. Eccles and Robinson, p. 177.
29. Larson, p. 155.
30. Larson, Kārikā XLII pp. 268–9.
31. A.E. Gallatin, *Of Art*, (New York Wittenborn and Company, 1944) p. 12.
32. Larson, p. 10.
33. Dasgupta, vol. 1, pp. 245–6.
34. Larson, p. 190.
35. Larson, p. 199.
36. Dasgupta, p. 260.
37. Lawrence Leshan and Henry Margenâu, *Einstein's Space and Van Gogh's Sky*, (New York, Collier Books, 1982) p. 24.
38. S. Chandrasekhar, *Truth and Beauty*, (New York, Viking Penguin Inc., 1991) p. 59.
39. Radhakrishnan and Moore, *Indian Philosophy*, p. 441.
40. Swami Satprakashananda, *Methods of Knowledge, Perceptual, Nonperceptual, and Transcendental According to Advaita Vedānta*, (London, George Allen & Unwin Ltd., 1965) p. 128.

41. *The Vedānta Sūtras of Bādarāyana with the Commentary by Śankara* 2 vols, George Thibaut trans. (New York, Sacred Books of the East Series, Dover Reprint 1962) vol. 1 II, ii, 2, p. 367.
42. *Vedānta Sūtras*, II, ii, 11 vol. 1 p. 365.
43. *Vedānta Sūtras*, II, i, 2 vol. 1 p. 295.
44. *Vedānta Sūtras*, I, i, 5 vol. 1 p. 46.
45. *Vedānta Sūtras* I, i, 3 vol. 1 p. 19.
46. John Grimes, *An Advaita Vedānta Perspective on Language*, (Delhi, Sri Satguru Publications, Division of India Book Centre, 1991) p. 18.
47. *The Upaniṣads*, Māṇḍūkya Upaniṣad, Prabhavananda and Manchester trans., p. 51.
48. *Vedānta Sūtras*, I, I, 5 vol. 1, p. 47.
49. *Vedānta Sūtras*, I, I, 4 vol. 1, pp. 20–3.
50. *The Upaniṣads*, Kena Upaniṣad, Prabhavananda and Manchester trans., p. 31.
51. Swami Nikhilananda, *Self-Knowledge (Ātmabōdha)*. An English Translation of śaṅkaracharya's Ātmabodha with Notes, Comments, and Introduction (New York, Ramakrishna-Vivekananda Center, 1946) p. 164.
52. *The Upaniṣads, The Bṛhadāraṇyaka*, III,v,1 Mueller trans., vol. 2,.p 129.
53. *Vedānta Sūtras*, I, i, 5 vol. 1, p. 47; *The Upaniṣads, Chāndogya*, VI, ii, 3 Mueller trans. vol. 1, p. 93.
54. *Vedānta Sūtras*, I, iv, 26 vol. 1 p. 287.
55. Virgil G. Himshaw, Jr, *Albert Einstein, Philosopher Scientist* from 'Einstein's Social Philosophy' (New York The Library of Living Philosophers, Paul Arthur Schilpp, ed., Tudor Publishing Company) pp. 659–60.
56. Albert Einstein, *Ideas and Opinions*, (New York, Bonanza Books, 1954) p. 262.
57. S. Radhakrishnan trans. & ed., *The Brahma Sūtra, The Philosophy of Spiritual Life*, (New York, Greenwood Press, 1968) p. 30.
58. *The Upaniṣads, Bṛhadāraṇyaka Upaniṣad*, IV,vi,1 Mueller trans., vol. 2 p. 185.
59. Haramohan Mishra, *A Study in Advaita Epistemology*, (Delhi, Parimal Publications, 1990) p. 21.
60. *The Upaniṣads Taittīriya*, III, 1–8 Mueller trans. vol. 2, pp. 64–8; see also *Vedānta Sūtras*, I, i, 12 vol. 1, p. 64.
61. Ghanshamdas Rattanmal Malkani, *Philosophy of the Self or a System of Idealism Based on Advait Vedānta*, (New York, The Indian Institute of Philosophy Amalner, Reprint by Johnson Reprint Corporation, 1966) pp. 155–6.
62. Malkani, pp. 7–8.
63. *The Upaniṣads, Kena*, Prabhavananda and Manchester trans, p. 31.
64. K.C. Bhattacharyya, *Search for the Absolute in Neo-Vedānta*, George Bosworth Burch ed., (Honolulu, University of Hawaii Press, 1976) p. 160.
65. *The Upaniṣads, Kena*, Prabhavananda and Manchester trans. pp. 30–1.
66. Bhattacharyya, p. 93.
67. *Vedānta Sūtras* I ,i, 1vol. 1, p. 6.
68. *Vedānta Sūtras* I ,i, 1 vol. 1, p. 7.
69. *Vedānta Sūtras* I ,i, 1 vol. 1, pp. 4–5.
70. Satprakashananda, *Vedānta Sūtras* II, 2, 28 vol. 1, pp. 421–2.

CHAPTER 8

1. Surendranath Dasgupta, *A History of Indian Philosophy*, (Cambridge, Cambridge University, 1932) vol. 1, pp. 183–4.

2. Narendra Nath Bhattacharyya, *Jain Philosophy, Historical Outline*, (New Delhi, Munshiram Manoharlal Ltd., 1976) p. 60.
3. Herman Jacoby, trans., *Jaina Sūtras*, (Benares, The Sacred Books of the East vol. XXII, reprint, Motilal, 1964) Part 1, p. 3.
4. Bhattacharyya, p. 67.
5. Nathmal Tatia, *Studies in Jaina Philosophy*, (Varanasi, P.V. Research Institute, Jainashram, Hindu University, 1951) p. 22.
6. Dasgupta, vol. I, footnote, p. 181.
7. Umāsvāmi, [Umāsvāti] *Tatvārtha Sūtram [Tatvārthāhigama Sūtra] (A Treatise on the Essentials of Jainism)*, J.L. Jaini ed. and trans., (Delhi, republished by the Barrister Champat Rai Jain Trust, 1956).
8. Bhattacharyya, p. 93.
9. Pushpa Bothra, *The Jaina Theory of Perception*, (Delhi, Motilal Banarsidass, 1976) p. 103.
10. Bothra, p. 101.
11. Bhattacharyya, p. 111.
12. Bhattacharyya, p. 3.
13. Bothra, p. 81.
14. Bothra, p. 2.
15. Satkari Mookerjee, *The Jaina Philosophy of Non-Absolutism*, (Delhi, Motilal Banarsidass) p. 4.
16. Mookerjee, p. 1.
17. Umāsvāti, Note #1, p. 8.
18. Dasgupta, vol. I, pp. 187–8.
19. Bothra, p. 6.
20. Mohanlal D. Desai, trans. and ed., *The Naya-Karnika, a Work on Jaina Logic by Sri Vinaya Vijaya Maharaj*, (Arrah, India, Central Jaina Publishing House, 1915) p. 2.
21. Umāsvāti, p. 4.
22. Sukhlalji, *Commentary on the Tattvārthā Sūtra of Vacvaka Umāsvāti*, K.K. Dixit, trans., (Ahmedabad, India, L.D. Institute of Indology, 1974) p. 12.
23. Anand Kashyap, Jain Relgion and the Notion of Social Equality, in N.K. Singhit, *Ideal, Ideology and Practice – Studies in Jainism*, (Jaipur, Printwell Publications, 1987) p. 112.
24. Mookerjee, pp. 98–9.
25. Sukhlalji, *Advanced Studies in Indian Logic and Metaphysics*, (Calcutta) p. 22.
26. J.S. Zaveri, *Theory of Atom in the Jaina Philosophy*, (Rajastan, Agama and Sahitya Prakashan, Jaina Vishua Bharati Ladnun, 1975) p. 51.
27. Bothra, p. 18.
28. Bhattacharyya, pp. 159–60.
29. B.L. Atreya, *The Elements of Indian Logic*, (Bombay, Nalanda Publications, 1948) pp. 136–7.
30. Mohan Lal Mehta, *Jaina Philosophy*, (Banares, Vidyashram Series # 16, P.V. Researching Institute, 1971) p. 168.
31. Chandradhar Sharma, *A Critical Survey of Indian Philosophy*, (Delhi, Motilal Banarsidass, reprint 1973) p. 52; and Bhattacharyya, p. 164.
32. Desai, pp. 22–3, 32.
33. Mehta, p. 168.
34. Desai, p. 14.

35. T.G. Kalghatgi, *Jaina Logic*, (New Delhi, Shri Raj Krishen Jain Charitable Trust, 1981) p. 31.
36. Dr Umrao Sing Bist, *Jaina Theories of Reality and Knowledge*, (Delhi, Eastern Book Linkers, 1984) p. 34.
37. Mookerjee, p. 63.
38. Bothra, p. 21.
39. Sukhlalji, pp. 11–12.
40. Bist, p. 13.
41. Mookerjee, p. 155.
42. Bothra, pp. 63–4.
43. Bhattacharyya, p. 160.
44. Bhattacharyya, p. 111.
45. Mookerjee, p. 154.
46. C. Sharma, p. 50.
47. Sanghvi, p. 3.
48. Desai, pp. 2–3.
49. Desai, p. 5.
50. Atreya, pp. 138–9.
51. Atreya, p. 142.
52. Kaliprasada Sinha, *The Philosophy of Jainism*, (Calcutta, Punthi Pustak, 1990) p. 17.
53. Y.J. Padmarajiah, *A Comparative Study of the Jaina Theories of Reality and Knowledge* (Bombay, Jain Sahitya Vikas Mandal, 1963) p. 314.
54. P.T. Raju, *Structural Depths of Indian Thought* (Albany, State University of New York, 1985) p. 115.
55. Desai, p. 43.
56. Kalghatgi, pp. 58–9.
57. Nathmal Tatia, trans., '*Yuvācārya Mahāprajña*', in *New Dimensions in Jaina Logic*, (Rajasthan, India, Jaina Vishva Bhararti, 1984) pp. 58–9.
58. Sinha, p. 19.
59. Atreya, p. 141.
60. Sinha, pp. 20, 61; and Dasgupta, vol. 1, p. 181.
61. Desai, pp. 21–4.
62. Mookerjee, p. 83.
63. Padmarajiah, p. 157.
64. I am indebted to Mr Edward Barker for this particular illustration which he produced as an assignment in a course in comparative logics.

CHAPTER 9

1. Arthur W. Ryder, *Panchatantra*, (Chicago,University of Chicago Press, 1925) p. 442.
2. Ganganatha Jha, *The Nyāya-Sūtras of Gauṭama*, 4 vols (Banares, Motilal, Reprint of edition of 1912–1919, 1984) vol. 1, Lecture 3, pp. 210–11.
3. Jha, vol. 1, p. 1.
4. F. Th. Stcherbatsky, *Buddhist Logic*, 2 vols, (New York, Dover, reprint, 1962) vol. 2, p. 1.

5. Jha, vol. 1, p. 108.
6. Lata S. Bapat, *Buddhist Logic, A fresh Study of Dharmakīrti's Philosophy*, (Delhi, Bharatiya Vidya Prakashan, 1989) pp. 59–60.
7. Bapat, p. 60.
8. Mangala R. Chinchore, *Dharmakīrti's Theory of Hetu-Centricity of Anumāna*, (Delhi, Motilal Banarsidass, Delhi, 1989) pp. 12–13.
9. Ramakant A. Sinari, *The Structure of Indian Thought*, (Springfield, Ill., Charles C. Thomas Publisher, 1970) p. 34.
10. Sinari, p. 43.
11. Radhakrishnan & Moore, p. 379.
12. Jha, vol. 3, p. 1273.
13. Dasgupta, vol. 1, pp. 310–19.
14. Jha, vol. 4, p. 1524.
15. Dasgupta, vol. 1, p. 286.
16. Raju, p. 198.
17. Harold G. Coward,, *Sphoṭa Theory of Language*, (Delhi, Motilal Banarsidass, 1986) p. 59.
18. Jha, vol. 1, pp. 355–455.
19. Jha, vol. 1, p. 425.
20. Jha, vol. 1, p. 427.
21. Jha, vol. 1, p. 436.
22. Jha, vol. 1, p. 523.
23. Ryder, p. 409.
24. Chr. Lindtner, *Nāgārjuniana, Studies in the Writings and Philosophy of Nāgārjuna*, Buddhist Traditions, vol. II, (Delhi, Motilal Banarsidass, 1987) p. 53.
25. Henry Clarke Warren, Buddhism in Translations, trans from the Aṅguttara Nikāya iii 139, (New York Atheneum 1963, orig pub. by Harvard University 1896) p. xiv.
26. *The Middle Length Discourses of the Buddha*, The Majjhima Nikāya, 'Mūlapariyāya Sūtta', Bhikkhu Nanamoli and Bhikkhu Bodhi trans,. (Boston, Wisdom Publications, 1995) pp. 86–9.
27. Warren, trans. from the Mahā-Vagga, p. 146.
28. *Middle Length Discourses of the Buddha*, 'Mahātaṇhasankhaya Sūtta', p. 351.
29. *Middle Length Discourses of the Buddha*, 'Mahātaṇhasankhaya Sūtta', p. 353.
30. Mervyn Sprung, trans., *Lucid Exposition of the Middle Way, The Essential Chapters from the Prasannapadā of Candrakirti*, (London, Routledge & Kegan Paul, 1979) p. 94.
31. Amar Singh, *The Heart of Buddhist Philosophy – Dinnāga and Dharmakīrti*, (New Delhi, Munshiram Manoharlal, Publishers Pvt. Ltd, 1984) p. 63.
32. S. Chandra Vidyabhusana, S. Chandra, *A History of Indian Logic*, (Delhi, Motilal Banarsidass, 1970) p. 277.
33. Mangala R. Chinchore, pp. 12–13.
34. Bimal Krishna Matilal, & Robert D. Robert, eds, *Buddhist Logic and Epistemology*, (Dordrecht, D. Reidel Publishing Co, Studies of Classical India Series vol. 7, 1982) p. 2.
35. David J. Kalupahana, *Nāgārjuna, The Philosophy of the Middle Way*, (Albany, N.Y., State University of New York Press, 1986) p. 387.
36. Dasgupta, vol. 1, p. 94.

37. Edward Conze, trans., *Buddhist Wisdom Books Containing the Diamond Sūtra and the Heart Sūtra*, (London, George Allen and Unwin, 1958) p. 81.
38. Oskar Kraus ed., and M. Shaettle and L. Mcalister trans., *Brentano, Sensory and Noetic Consciousness*, (London, Routledge and Kegan Paul, International Library of Philosophical and Scientific Method, 1981) p. xvi.
39. *The Questions of King Milinda*, 2 vols T.W. Rhys Davids, trans., (Delhi, Sacred Books of the East Series, Reprint, Motilal Banarsidass, 1988) vol. 1, pp. 41–4.
40. Kalupahana, *Nāgārjuna* pp. 265–7.
41. *The Middle Length Discourses of the Buddha*, 'Cūḷamālunkya Sutta', p. 535.
42. Thich Nhat Hanh, *The Miracle of Mindfulness*, Mobi Ho trans., (Boston, Beacon Press, 1987) p. 4.
43. *The Middle Length Discourses of the Buddha*, Mahātaṇhasankhaya Sūtta' p. 357.
44. Wing-tsit Chan, *A Source Book in Chinese Philosophy*, (Princeton, Princeton University, fourth paperback reprint, 1973) p. 447.
45. Christine Mullikin Keyt, *Dharmakīrtis Concept of the Svalakṣaṇa*, (Dissertation at the University of Washington, Seattle 1980) pp. 92–3.
46. Stcherbatsky, vol. 1, p. 2.
47. David Kalipuhana, *Causality, The Central Philosophy of Buddhism*, (Honolulu, University of Hawaii Press, 1975) p. 54.
48. *Turning Points in Physics*, 'A series of Lectures Given at Oxford University in Trinity Term 1958 by R.J. Blin-Stoyle, D. Ter Haar, K. Mendelsohn, T. Temple, F. Waismann, D.H. Winkinson' (Amsterdam, North Holland Publishing Co. 1959) pp. 86–7.
49. Dasgupta, vol. 1, p. 84. See also Kalupahana, *Nāgārjuna*, p. 332.
50. Wheelwright, *Heracleitus* p. 71.
51. *The Middle Length Discourses of the Buddha*, 'Cūḷamālunkya Sutta' p. 536.
52. Kamaleswar Bhattacharya trans., E.H. Johnston & Arnold Kunst eds, *The Dialectical Method of Nāgārjuna Vigrahavyavartani*, (Delhi Motilal Banarsidass, 2nd edition, 1986) pp. 107–8.
53. Raghaavendra Pandeya, *Major Hetvabhāsas*, (Delhi, Eastern Book Linkers 1984) p. ix.
54. B.N. Singh, *Indian Logic*, (Varanasi, Asha Prakashan 1982) pp. 80–1.
55. Bapat, p. 63.
56. Dhirendra Sharma, *The Differentiation Theory of Meaning in Indian Logic*, (The Hague, Mouton 1969) pp. 27–8.
57. Keyt, p. 105.
58. Keyt, p. 103.
59. *Turning Points in Physics*, p. 1.
60. *The Middle Length Discourses of the Buddha*, 'Aggivacchagotta Sutta' pp. 590–4.
61. *The Middle Length Discourses of the Buddha*, 'Mahāvedalla Sutta', p. 388.
62. Sinari, pp. 57–8, see also Stcherbatsky, vol. 1, p. 5.
63. Conze, pp. 64–5.
64. Herman Weyl, *Philosophy of Mathematics and Natural Science*, (Princeton, Princeton University Press, 1949) p. 113.
65. Weyl, p. 135.
66. C. Sharma, p. 38.
67. C.S. Vyas, *Buddhist Theory of Perception with Special Reference to Pramāṇa Varttīka of Dharmakīrti*, (New Delhi, Navrang, 1991) p. 11.

68. Kamaleswar Bhattacharya, et al.: *The Dialectical Method*, p. 131.
69. Kamaleswar Bhattacharya, et al., *The Dialectical Method*, p. 90.
70. Stefan Anacker, *Seven Works of Vasubandhu, The Buddhist Psychological Doctor*, (Delhi, Motilal Banarsidass, 1984) p. 217.
71. Vidyabhusana, p. 289.
72. Stcherbatsky, vol. 1, p. 301.
73. Sinari, p. 81.
74. Kalupahana, *Nāgārjuna*, 269.
75. John Blofeld, *The Zen Teaching of Huang Po*, (New York, Grove Press, 1958) p. 74.
76. *The Long Discourses of the Buddha*, The Dīgha Nikāya, Maurice Walshe trans. (Boston, Wisdom Publications, 1995) 'Mahāsatipaṭṭhāna Sutta' pp. 335–50.

CHAPTER 10

1. Fung Yu-lan, *A Short History of Chinese Philosophy*, Derk Bodde ed. (New York, The Free Press Macmillan Co., 1948) p. 337.
2. *Creation of the Gods*, 2 vols, Gu Zhizhong trans., (Bejing, New World Press, 1992) vol. 2, p. 399.
3. Chung-ying Cheng, 'Methodology and Theory of Understanding' in *Chu Hsi and Neo-Confucianism*, Wing-tsit Chan ed. (Honolulu, University of Hawaii Press, 1986) p. 170.
4. Wang Yang-ming, *Instructions for Practical Living and Other Neo-Confucian Writings*, Wing-tsit Chan trans. (New York, Columbia University Press, 1963) p. 221.
5. *Chuang Tzu, The Complete Works*, Burton Watson , trans., (New York, Columbia University Press, 1968) p. 183.
6. Li Ju-chen, *Flowers in the Mirror*, Lin Tai-yi trans. & ed., (Berkeley, University of California Press, 1965) pp. 239–40.
7. *Han Fei Tzu, Basic Writings*, Burton Watson trans. (New York, Columbia University Press 2nd Printing 1966) pp. 256–7.
8. *Chuang Tzu*, pp. 39–40.
9. *Hsün Tzu, Basic Writings*, Burton Watson trans. (New York, Columbia University Press, 1963) p. 144.
10. Fung Yu-lan, *A Short History*, p. 337.
11. Thome H. Fang, *The Chinese View of Life*, (Taipei, Linkin Publishing Co., 1986) p. 82.
12. Anton Dumitriu, *History of Logic*, 4 vols (Kent, Abacus Press, 1977) vol. 1, p. 3.
13. Roger S. Jones, *Physics as Metaphor*, (Minneapolis, University of Minnesota Press, 1982) p. 4.
14. James Legge, *The Chinese Classics*, 5 vols, The Doctrine of the Mean, vol. 1 (Hong Kong, Hong Kong University Press reprint 1960) ch. xxv–xxvii, pp. 418–22.
15. Hu Shih, *The Development of the Logical Method in Ancient China*, (Shanghai, The Oriental Book Co. 1928) p. 85.
16. Prof. Shu-li Ji, Shanghai Academy of Social Sciences, "The Relativity of Civilization to Multi-Science", Int. Soc. for Comparative Study of Civilizations, University of California, Berkeley, June 1989.

17. Thome H. Fang, *Creativity in Man and Nature*, (Taipei, Linking Publishing Co., 2nd Printing, 1983) p. 16.
18. Wing-tsit Chan, *A Source Book in Chinese Philosophy, 'Chang Tsai,'* (Princeton, Princeton University Press, 4th Printing, 1973) p. 497.
19. Wang Yang-ming, p. 272.
20. *Hsün Tzu*, p. 128.
21. Lin Yutang, *The Wisdom of China and India*, Lao Tzu ch. 71 (New York, Modern Library, 1942) p. 620.
22. Wing-tsit Chan, *A Source Book*, *'Confucius' The Analects* 2:15, p. 24.
23. Fung Yu-lan, *Chuang Tzu*, (Beijing, Foreign Languages Press 2nd Printing 1989) p. 46–7.
24. Hideki Yukawa, 'Chuangtse, The Happy Fish', *Experimental Essays on Chuang-tzu* (Victor H. Mair ed.) (Honolulu, Asuan Studies at Hawaii #29, University of Hawaii Press, 1983) p. 57.
25. Wing-tsit Chan, *A Source Book*, Seng-chao, 'The Immutability of Things'. p. 345.
26. Wing-tsit Chan, *A Source Book*, Ch'eng Hao, 'Selected Sayings', p. 527.
27. Wing-tsit Chan, *A Source Book*, Wang Fu-chih, 'Unceasing Growth and Man's Nature and Destiny', p. 698.
28. Wing-tsit Chan, *A Source Book*, Yen Yüan, 'Learning through Experience', p. 707.
29. Wang Yang-ming, *Instruction* pp. 221–2.
30. *Chuang Tzu*, Burton Watson trans., pp. 43–4.
31. *Hsün Tzu* p. 144.
32. Jones, Roger S., *Physics as Metaphor*, (Minneapolis, University of Minnesota Press, 1982) p. 4.
33. Fung Yu-lan, *History of Chinese Philosophy* 2 vols (Princeton, Princeton University 7th Printing, 1973) vol. 1 p. 672.
34. Mencius 6A:6, Wing-tsit Chan p. 54.
35. Wang Yang-ming p. 10.
36. Thome H. Fang, *Creativity in Man and Nature*, Linking Publishing Co., Taipei 1980 p. 4.
37. Wing-tsit Chan, *A Source Book*, Lao Tzu, p. 145.
38. Ernst Cassirer, *Substance and Function*, (New York, Dow Press, 1953) p. 9.
39. Werner Heisenberg, *Philosophical Problems of Quantum Physics*, (New York, Pantheon Books, 1952) p. 117.
40. *Chuang Tzu*, p. 43.
41. Hu Shih, p. 42.
42. Wang Yang-ming, p. 150.
43. Chu Hsi and Lu Tsu-ch'ien, *Reflections on Things at Hand*, Wing-tsit Chan trans. (New York, Columbia University Press, 1967) p. 175.
44. *Chuang Tzu*, p. 241.
45. Fung Yu-lan, *A Short History* p. 337.
46. Legge, *Chinese Classics*, vol. 1, Doctrine of the Mean, xxvi 4, p. 420.
47. Wing-tsit Chan, *A Source Book*, Shao Yung, p. 491.
48. Wing-tsit Chan, *A Source Book*, Chang Tsai, p. 515.
49. Wing-tsit Chan, *A Source Book*, Hui Shih, pp. 233–4.
50. Chuang Tzu, p. 126.
51. Chuang Tzu, p. 41.
52. Legge, *Chinese Classics*, vol. 2, Mencius Bk iv, pt 2, xix, 1, p. 325.

53. Hsün Tzu, pp. 79–83.
54. Chuang Tzu, p. 42.
55. Hsün Tzu, pp. 80–1.
56. Hsün Tzu, p. 137.
57. Legge, *Chinese Classics*, vol. 2, Mencius Bk vi, pt 1, xi, 1, 1–3, p. 414.
58. Legge, *Chinese Classics*, vol. 2, Mencius Bk vi, pt 1, x, 4, p. 409.
59. Wing-tsit Chan, *A Source Book*, quoted in Chu Hsi, pp. 602–3.
60. Hsün Tzu, p. 127.
61. Wing-tsit Chan, *A Source Book*, Fung Yu-lan, p. 761.
62. Fung Yu-lan, *A Short History, p.* 117.
63. Fung Yu-lan, *A Short History,* p. 337.
64. Fung Yu-lan, *A Short History*, p. 113.
65. Chuang Tzu, pp. 44–5.
66. Hsün Tzu, pp. 121–2.
67. Wang Yang-ming, p. 32.
68. Fung Yu-lan, *A Short History*, p. 257.
69. Wing-tsit Chan, *A Source Book*, Wang Yang-ming, p. 662.
70. Wing-tsit Chan, *A Source Book*, Lao Tzu, p. 145.
71. Legge, *Chinese Classics*, vol. 2, Mencius Bk vi, pt 1, x, 1–7, pp. 411–13.
72. Legge, *Chinese Classics*, vol. 2, Mencius Bk iv, pt 2, viii, p. 321.
73. Wing-tsit Chan, *A Source Book*, Confucius, The Analects 2:4, p. 22.
74. George Holton, *Thematic Origins of Scientific Thought, Kepler to Einstein*, (Cambridge, Harvard University Press, 1975) p. 120.
75. Knud Rasmussen, *Intellectual Culture of the Copper Eskimos Report of the Fifth Thule Expedition 1921–24*, vol. IX (Copenhagen, Gyldendalske Boghandel, Nordisk Forlag, 1932) pp. 122–3.

EPILOGUE

1. Mark Washburn, *Mars At Last!*, (New York, G.P. Putnam's Sons, 1977) 66.
2. Friedrich Cramer, *Order and Chaos*, D.I. Loewus trans., (New York, VCH Verlagsgesellschaft, 1993) p. 223.
3. S. Chandrasekhar, Truth and Beauty, (New York, Viking Penguin inc., 1991) p. 59.
4. Lawrence Leshan and Henry Margenau, *Einstein's Space and Van Gogh's Sky*, (New York, Collier Books, 1982) p. 24.

Bibliography

Selected readings in comparative philosophy

Bochenski, I. M., *A History of Formal Logic*, Juo Thomas trans. (Notre Dame, University Press 1961)

Chattopadhyaya, D. P., *Induction, Probability and Skepticism*, (New York, SUNY Press, 1991)

Capra, Fritjof, *The Tao of Physics*, (Boulder, Colorado, Shambhala, 1975)

Chan, Wing-tsit, *A Source Book in Chinese Philosophy*, (Princeton, Princeton University, 1973)

Dasgupta, Surendranath, *A History of Indian Philosophy*, 5 vols (Delhi, Motilal Banarsidass, 1975)

Dumitriu, Anton, *History of Logic*, 4 vols (Kent, Abacus Press, 1977)

Encyclopedia of Philosophy, 4 vols, Paul Edwards Editor in Chief, (New York, Macmillan, reprint 1972)

Fang, Thome H, *Chinese Philosophy, Its Spirit and Its Development*, (Taipei, Linking Publishing Co., 1986)

Gregory, Bruce, *Inventing Reality, Physics as Language*, (New York, John Wiley & Sons, 1968)

Grimes, John, *A Concise Dictionary of Indian Philosophy, Sanskrit Terms Defined in English*, (New York, SUNY Press, 1989)

Harrison, Edward, *Masks of the Universe*, (New York, Macmillan, 1985)

Haywood, Jeremy W., *Shifting Worlds, Changing Minds, Where the Sciences and Buddhism Meet*, (Boston, New Science Library/Shambhala, 1987)

Jones, Roger S., *Physics as Metaphor*, (Minneapolis, University of Minnesota, 1982)

Leshan, Lawrence and Margenau, Henry, *Einstein's Space and Van Gogh's Sky*, (New York, Collier Books/Macmillan 1982)

McGreal, Ian P., *Great Thinkers of the Eastern World*, (New York, HarperCollins Publishers, 1995)

Matilal, Bimal Krishna, *Logic, Language and Reality, An Introduction to Indian Philosophical Studies*, (Delhi, Motilal Banarsidass, 1985)

Nakamura, Hajime, *A Comparative History of Ideas*, (Delhi, Motilal Banarsidass, 1992)

Needham, Joseph, *Science and Civilization in China*, 5 vols (Cambridge, Cambridge University Press, 1954)

Onians, Richard Broxton, *The Origins of European Thought*, (Salem, New Hampshire, Ayer Company, 1987)

Plott, John C, *Global History of Philosophy*, 5 vols (Delhi, Motilal Banarsidass, 1979)

Radhakrishnan, Sarvepalli and Moore, Charles A., *A Source Book in Indian Philosophy*, (Princeton, Princeton University, 1957)

Raju, P.T., *Structural Depths of Indian Thought*, (Albany, SUNY Press, 1985)

Smart, Ninian and Murthy, B. Srinivasa eds., East–West Encounters in Philosophy and Religion (Long Beach, Long Beach Publications, 1996)

Vidyabhusana, S. Chandra, *A History of Indian Logic*, (Delhi, Motilal Banarsidass, 1978)

Wheelwright, Philip, *The Presocratics*, (New York, Odyssey Press, 1982)
Wu, Yi, *Chinese Philosophical Terms*, (Maryland, University Press of America, 1986)
Yu-lan, Fung, *A History of Chinese Philosophy*, Derk Bodde trans., 2 vols (Princeton, Princeton University, 1952)
Zukav, Gary, *The Dancing Wu Li Masters*, (New York, William Morrow and Co., 1979)

Index